THE ORDEAL.

HENRY CHARLES LEA

With additional original documents in translation
by ARTHUR E. HOWLAND

Edited, with Introduction and Bibliography
by EDWARD PETERS

University of Pennsylvania Press

Philadelphia

First published 1866, as Part III, *Superstition and Force*, by
Henry Charles Lea
First *Pennsylvania Paperback* edition 1973
Introduction © 1973 by the University of Pennsylvania Press,
Inc.
Library of Congress Catalog Card No. 73-83293
ISBN: 0-8122-1061-1
Printed in the United States of America. Editorial production by
Weidner Associates, Inc., Cinnaminson, N.J. 08077.

CONTENTS.

INTRODUCTION.

HENRY CHARLES LEA, THE JUDICIAL ORDEAL, AND THE CULTURE OF EARLY EUROPE.

We have had enough of annalists to chronicle political intrigues and military achievements; but that which constitutes the inner life of a people and from which are to be drawn the lessons of the past that will guide us in the future, has hitherto been too much neglected.

—H.C. Lea to W.E.H. Lecky, 1866

In seeking to understand [the history of the Middle Ages] thoroughly he soon became impressed with two facts: first, that the legislation of an age or a country afforded the surest foundation for the comprehension of its institutions and its life; and second, that the original sources were, as far as possible, to be solely relied upon for material ... He was gradually impressed by the fact that in whatever direction he turned he was confronted by the Church. It was omnipresent and frequently omnipotent, not only in spiritual but in temporal affairs, and no one could comprehend the antagonizing forces which moulded the evolution of our civilization without understanding the sources of ecclesiastical power and the use to which it was put.

—H.C. Lea, on his own career, MS

The History of Jurisprudence is the history of civilization.

—H.C. Lea, *Superstition and Force,*
Preface to the edition of 1878.

There are few intellectual and political biographies in the history of nineteenth-century America more interesting than Henry Charles Lea's, and few more generally neglected. Lea is probably best remembered for his monumental studies in ecclesiastical and legal history, for the recognition he received from Europeans as the first American historian of the Middle Ages regarded by them as an equal, and as a scholar whose work in many fields is still fundamental, nearly a century later. Yet Lea's historical work, astonishing as it is, constitutes only part of a life that was filled with intellectual variety and adventure, enormously fatiguing and remarkably successful commercial enterprises, and time-consuming and often thankless work in the best traditions of liberal republicanism. His life spans a turbulent period in U.S. history, and as a leading citizen of one of the principal centers of commerce and culture, Lea perceived and acted upon many of the changes that occurred. A publisher of both fiction and scientific works, a correspondent and friend of both Lincoln and Lecky, a distinguished and frequently published scientific investigator in two separate fields by the age of twenty and a translator of Greek poetry by the age of twenty-five, Lea displayed a variety of interests and talents throughout his lifetime, comparable to those of only a few of his contemporaries.[1]

Lea was born in 1825 into a Philadelphia publishing family and, with his brother Matthew, was tutored privately until he turned eighteen. During his adolescence, his interest in both science and literature was reflected in a number of published papers in botany, chemistry, and conchology, as well as in the publication of his own verse and translations from Greek. His intense commitment to learning consumed all his energies, and when he began to work at his family's publishing firm in 1843, he continued his full scholarly schedule in the evenings, after a full day of work. His schedule soon overtaxed his physical endurance, and in 1847 his health collapsed, and his scholarly work was postponed indefinitely. Lea then undertook an increasingly prominent role in his publishing house, becoming one of the most astute, successful, and considerate publishers in

America. In the 1850s Lea took up the study of history, thinking it to be less fatiguing than his earlier scientific and literary
work. By 1858 he had produced several long reviews that indicated a new interest in the Middle Ages and Church history, as
well as in the history of law. In the 1860s, however, Lea added
a new role to his others: that of energetic citizen. Both Philadelphia and the Union appealed to his civic interests, and Lea
spent most of the 1860s and 1870s involved in a number of
civic reform projects and the Union cause. In 1880 Lea retired
from his publishing firm, and the remaining twenty-nine years
of his life were devoted to civic concerns in Philadelphia and
his vast historical enterprises.

Superstition and Force, Lea's first history volume, was published in 1866. Many of the views in the volume and the qual-
ity of the work itself reflect interests he had begun to develop
in the 1850s, during his recuperation. The book consists of
four sections, the first two dealing with the process of compurgation and the judicial duel, the third, reprinted here, with the
ordeal, and the fourth with judicial torture. In considering
these institutions of medieval legal procedure, Lea held
strongly to three convictions: first, that history had to be written from the original source materials; second, that legal institutions, rather than "political intrigues and military achievements," more clearly reflected the "inner life of a people"; and
third, that to understand any aspect of medieval European culture it was first necessary to understand the place of the
Church in medieval society. At a time when historical literature was still often no more than a literary undertaking, when
ecclesiastical history of any kind was largely confessional, and
when the writing of history still had a strong political, military, and diplomatic bias, these criteria, which Lea had developed purely on his own, were extremely novel. The involve-
ment of the study of history with the social sciences did not
begin in a substantial way until late in Lea's life, and the
attempts of social and economic history to get at what Lea
called "the inner life of a people" were still in their infancy
when he wrote. The vast projects of editing and publishing
original source materials and their ancillary works—dictionar-
ies, chronologies, and calendars—had begun largely in his own

lifetime, and few of the results of this body of publications were available to scholars in the United States. It was Lea's own intelligence, perceptiveness and originality which alone determined the direction of his work. His insistence upon the use of primary sources has, of course, become standard in the training of professional historians, and his interest in Church history has been echoed by many present-day scholars, for whom Lea's work is still fundamental.

Perhaps Lea's greatest contribution, however, was his profound insight into the role of legal institutions in reflecting a society's values and beliefs. Lea was not formally a legal historian; that is, he was not satisfied to study simply the internal development of legal procedures and substantive law. Like his great contemporary Frederick William Maitland, his chief interest was in the kind of life that the law reflected. By focussing upon the Church and its role in medieval legal institutions, Lea also arrived naturally at a comparative point of view that freed him from a narrow interest in what might have been the anachronistic study of national legal development.

Lea did not restrict his broad interests to medieval Europe alone, as vast as that subject was, but compared the legal institutions he studied with those of antiquity and those of non-western societies. Among his library at his death were not only several thousand valuable volumes of European materials, but studies of the religion, law, and other customs of societies in the remote past and in distant parts of the world. Lea was thus one of the first American historians to use what would later come to be termed comparative and anthropological approaches in his work. The subjects dealt with by Lea in *Superstition and Force* are still of interest to historians and social anthropologists, and Lea's treatment of many of them remains the most extensive available in English.

The Ordeal, originally part three of *Superstition and Force*, is, therefore, far more than a study of archaic European legal procedure. In the first chapter Lea considers, from his perspective as a nineteenth-century nationalist historian, the conditions according to which judicial ordeals became possible; he then briefly describes the role of the ordeal in non-western and ancient societies. The remainder of the book gives a typology of ordeals and briefly describes the growth of resistance to them and their final abolition. Other scholars have since improved upon Lea's work in details, and several major works that consider the entire phenomenon in greater detail have appeared in other languages. Yet Lea's chapters still remain the best introduction in English, and they offer the student and general reader an excellent introduction to the problems and the possibilities in the study of legal institutions in terms of cultural values, a study which may still yield much to the inquirer.

At the end of *Superstition and Force*, Lea suggested a rational, almost utilitarian excuse for his work:

> In the slow evolution of the centuries, it is only by comparing distant periods that we can mark our progress; but progress nevertheless exists, and future generations, perhaps, may be able to emancipate themselves wholly from the cruel and arbitrary domination of superstition and force.[2]

Lea's terms—"evolution," "progress," and "superstition"—clearly date both his vision of human society and the rationalist optimism he shared with so many contemporary thinkers. But some of the "future generations" of whom Lea spoke so hopefully experienced not an emancipation from superstition and force, but a new and even more dangerous subjection to them, sometimes subtle and barely detectable and at other times naked and obvious. Although the system of ordeals was, by Lea's thinking, "superstitious" and in terms of modern legal scholarship "irrational," it nevertheless reflected a human attempt to see that justice was done, not simply that injuries were corrected. By the thirteenth century, a more complex and more sophisticated interpretation of this same concept of justice ultimately abolished the ordeal and placed the burden of establishing legal proof upon human efforts and human reason. But the ordeal had been the last resort of that ideal of justice for six centuries, and although the ordeal itself disappeared, the concepts it had helped to preserve survived and placed new responsibilities upon the legal systems of Europe. Some of those responsibilities influenced the development of modern systems of justice, and others led into even greater horrors than the ordeal: torture, unregulated inquisitorial procedures, secret courts, and the placing of the powers of extraordinarily fragile and complex judicial authority into the hands of incompetents and criminals. The ordeal is not the happiest chapter in the cultural and legal history of the West, but it is certainly not the darkest, and its disappearance marked the demise of neither irrationality nor inhumanity in European history.

● ● ●

The reprinting of Lea's study and the appendix of documents translated from the original source materials illustrating Lea's text offer an excellent general introduction to the nature and the details of the judicial ordeal. The remaining sections of this introductory essay will focus upon several details that may clarify aspects of the problem that are only lightly touched upon by the text and documents: the legal culture of late Roman and early Germanic Europe; the main directions and emphases of scholarship on the ordeal since Lea wrote; finally, some remarks upon the general subject of legal procedures and cultural history and suggestions for further research.

II.

The social bonds of the Germanic peoples who occupied most of the western part of the Roman Empire and created a new Europe between the fifth and the eleventh centuries reflect the formation of a distinctively new culture and a new worldview. Older explanations of the origins of early medieval culture, particularly those that posited a sharp contrast between classical civilization and the barbaric traditions of the invaders, have generally given way to explanations that suggest a more modulated picture, one that takes into account both the extensive transformations of the world of late antiquity and the continuous and sometimes violent acculturation of the Germanic immigrants.[3] For the newcomers, generations of migration and warfare, prolonged and varied exposure to new cultures and cultural frontiers, the dividing and redividing of peoples and crises in political leadership, and the varying intensity of pressures upon tribe, kindred, and religion left few social institutions in their original state by the time the first enduring barbarian kingdoms sprang up in Roman Europe and Africa in the fifth and sixth centuries. Among the Romans, new social, economic, and religious pressures and the ubiquity of Roman imperial laws and imperial officials outwardly transformed the aristocratic elitism of the early Empire into a rigidly stratified society in which new kinds of power developed and traditional concepts of citizenship disappeared. Culturally, the lowering of educational levels, the marked shift toward both pagan and Christian religious sensibilities, the spiritualizing of the material world, and the combined revulsion and fascination felt toward the barbarians created a great cultural divide between the late Empire and the Empire of the first and second centuries A.D. By the sixth century Roman and Germanic society had begun to merge, partly through political necessity and partly through social and cultural transformation; by the end of the eighth century, in most of Europe, the process was complete.

Few social institutions reflect these changes better than the law. The classical age of Roman jurisprudence came to an end by the middle of the third century. During that age great individual jurists, members of the aristocracy and protégés of the first- and second-century emperors, had completed the change of the Roman legal system from the rigid and primitive Law of the Twelve Tables to an extensive, rational system readily and successfully applicable to the broad spectrum of legal problems that faced the new empire. After the third century, however, the façade of classical jurisprudence was weakened. The growing influence of the imperial bureaucracy, the failure of individual legal thinkers to continue the literary tradition, the consequent increasing disorder of legal literature and the growing importance of ill-prepared imperial edicts, and the influence within the legal system of new philosophical and religious values marked the end of the classical tradition and the beginning of the postclassical period. From the third century on,

Roman law was characterized by a new kind of legal literature. Private collections of imperial edicts, excerpts and abbreviations anthologized from the writings of the great classical jurists, masses of imperial edicts, and a new social configuration of the legal profession preserved only parts of the earlier tradition.[4] The great imperial codes, that of Theodosius II in 438 and that of Justinian in 534, managed, often with great genius, to preserve important imperial edicts, selections from the classical jurists, and principles of law. The *Theodosian Code*, however, which contained only edicts, remained far better known in the West than the *Corpus Iuris Civilis* of Justinian. The practice of Roman law in the West relied upon the *Theodosian Code*, several private collections, abridgements of the works of earlier jurists, such as the *Sentences of Paulus* (*Pauli Sententiae*) of the late third century, and the limited abilities of a diminished group of legal scholars and administrative officials. This "Vulgar Law" of the late Roman Empire in the West gave way, between the fifth and the eighth centuries in most of Europe, first to special collections of Roman law promulgated by the Germanic kings for their Roman subjects and later to collections and treatises on Roman law devised for those areas, generally in Italy and the northern Mediterranean, where Roman law survived as the general law of the land.[5]

The Germanic peoples, of course, brought no such extensive legal tradition with them into the Roman Empire. In the Germanic society of the pre-invasion period, as in most primitive societies, law was part of a system of "undifferentiated social control by religion, ethical custom, and kin discipline."[6] Germanic society observed what historians have called the idea of the personality of the law; that is, that an individual recognized only the law of the group into which he or she was born, and that that law applied to him everywhere, under all circumstances, just as did his social identity. The Germanic law of the pre-invasion period was thus customary, because it was in large measure part of a wider body of undifferentiated custom that embraced other areas than those which a modern jurist would consider "law." Custom, identified by the elders of a kindred, tribe, or group, was transmitted orally and, presumably, by all the other complex methods of teaching the young that a primitive society possesses. The experiences of many Germanic peoples between the third and the sixth centuries, however, may well have imposed stresses upon law and other social bonds with which traditional strategies were unable to deal effectively. The breaking-up of kindred groups, the scattering of a people over a relatively wide area of land once inside the Roman Empire, the attractions of Roman life and the complexities of transactions with Roman people, the growing authority of king and aristocracy, and the increasing differentiation within Germanic society—all of these factors must have contributed heavily to the next stage of Germanic legal history, the selective identification of some social acts as differentiated law by writing them down in legal codes.

From the late fifth century on, Germanic kings, certainly with the advice of their most powerful followers and probably with the aid of the literate Christian clergy and Roman legal advisors, began to issue codes of law for their own peoples. With the exception of the laws produced in England, these codes were written in Latin, and in their earliest versions they indicate already a strong strain of Roman secular and religious interests. At the same time, those kings, still recognizing the personality of law, also issued codes of Roman law for their Roman subjects, in which they relied heavily upon the kinds of sources discussed briefly above. By the late sixth, seventh, and eighth centuries, however, these bodies of law had generally ceased to distinguish between Romans and Germans, although there remained areas in Europe where a more distinctly Roman kind of law remained in operation, often down to the eighteenth century. The very act of writing down what had hitherto been transmitted as oral custom, and writing it, moreover, in Latin, a language that must have suggested many new legal concepts, probably helped to transform the Germanic perception of law and society, in spite of the fact that such codes were allegedly only written versions of oral custom. Moreover, the increasing influence of churchmen in Germanic-Roman society suggests the addition of a religious dimension to Germanic law, just as Christianity had influenced Roman law in the fourth, fifth, and sixth centuries.[7]

Thus, it is particularly dangerous for the student of history and society to assume that one aspect of early medieval law is "customary" and therefore "purely" Germanic, while another is "written and technical" and "purely" Roman, while yet another "deals with religious affairs" and is therefore "purely" Christian. The history of early law is not independent of the history of society and the history of culture, and it is unlikely in the extreme that legal ideas and institutions were exempt from the same processes that so significantly transformed other aspects of life in early Europe. The French legal historian Jean Gaudemet has suggested some of these points and their consequences:

> It is not at all certain that during the fifth century the judges in the Roman provinces were particularly able; the complaints of the emperors against an incompetent magistracy were undoubtedly not without some basis in fact. On the other hand, it is just as certain that the Germans were not wholly incapable of adopting elements from the juridical heritage of Rome, and it is well known that Roman law, until at least the middle of the eighth century, left profound traces upon the legislation and practices of the barbarian kingdoms... The introduction of the ordeal is thus not exclusively an indication of decadence and convenience. It also suggests a transformation of a social mentality, a confidence accorded to proofs furnished by the Divinity, a recognition of the superiority of God to human reason.[8]

Between the fifth and the eighth centuries, then, the transformation of both Roman and Germanic law reflects the social and spiritual experience of two worlds in the process of becoming one.

Law, whether analytical, differentiated, and Roman or limited, undifferentiated, and Germanic, nevertheless reflects ideas about the individual and society, about personality and motivation, and about the nature of reality held by the culture out of which it emerges. Historians of legal procedure and anthropologists have described the ritual of law in a terminology that is approximately applicable to a broad range of societies. A procedure may be accusatorial, in which a specific charge is brought against an individual by another individual and determined by a judge, whether an individual or an aggregation; or it may be inquisitorial, in which a charge is initiated by the judge without an accuser. In different societies, of course, the entire spectrum of social relationships and culture determine the conditions under which either system will operate. In early Rome, the accusatorial process was strictly limited by a rigid system of accusatorial forms, by the different legal statuses of freemen and slaves, and by the unofficial character of the legal profession. In late imperial Rome, the inquisitorial processes had become the chief instrument of imperial justice. Torture, in early Rome only applicable to slaves, was first applied to freemen in particular cases of exceptional crime, such as treason, and later to all ranks of society at the imperial order.[9] In Germanic society, the accusatorial process survived long after the invasions, and torture, unknown to the society of Germanic freemen, did not appear in European law until after the reception of Roman law in the twelfth century. The accusatorial process, wherever it is in use, often depends upon the differentiation of personal status, the limited universe of possible legal action, and the concept of delict. If "crimes" or "civil offenses" are conceived only as affronts to individuals, and not as offenses against society, then such matters as proof, satisfaction, procedure, and liability are conditioned by such factors as the status of the individual in society, personal dignity and honor, and the concept of personal offenses as a concern of society as a whole. If, on the other hand, crimes and civil offenses are conceived as affronts to society as well as to individuals, more specialized institutions usually develop, status plays a more limited role, and procedures, proofs, and punishments possess a very different character. Legal historians have suggested that the accusatorial procedure is generally an earlier stage of legal development, and that the inquisitorial process is the product of a relatively more differentiated idea of society, one which contains a concept of public crime and potentially limits the role of personal status. As historians have shown, the Germanic kingdoms of the fifth through the eleventh centuries developed concepts of public crime first in terms of treason to the king and certain religious offenses. Only very slowly did the concept which a modern lawyer would call tort become crime in a public sense. Torture belongs to the world of inquisitorial procedure and the differentiated concept of public order, and reflects the society's confidence that the powers of the public order are sufficient to establish legal fact, whether through testimony and interrogation or torture itself. The ordeal, on the other hand, belongs to the world of accusatorial procedure and a limited concept of the public order, and to a worldview that places less faith in purely human methods of inquiry than in the belief in supernatural intervention to remedy injustice. The judicial ordeal in early medieval society thus emerged from changing Roman and Germanic legal concepts and institutions, the concept of the personality of law and the range of legal offenses, and, perhaps most complex of all, from a theory of divine intervention based upon the assumption of immanent justice and the necessary limitations of judicial enquiry.

Insofar as the pre-literate, traditional structure of the Germanic peoples was untouched by both the obvious and subtle influences of nearby Roman society, those peoples may be studied comparatively with other primitive or archaic societies, and the descriptive and analytical work of anthropologists may be used as a basis to understand some elements of the Germanic legal consciousness. Anthropologists have had a great deal to say about primitive law, although some things that they have said have come under heavy criticism.[10] On the one hand, an anthropologist trained in modern legal science may run the risk either of neglecting some institutions and values because they do not conform to what he had been taught to call law or to identify and label other values and institutions as "legal," thereby suggesting a type of intellectual differentiation that the people under consideration would have trouble recognizing. On the other hand, the difficulties of establishing comparative criteria that are effective in describing the institutions of societies that exhibit enormous variety, even though they may all be technically "primitive," are numerous. Anthropologists have written much about primitive legal procedure, and the literature on such institutions as the ordeal is extensive. The early history of the Germanic peoples, however, has not yet been carefully studied in this fashion by anthropologists. Therefore, the written law in the codes and the procedures that we know accompanied this law display at best an ambiguous relationship with earlier Germanic law and procedure. At this stage of research, an anthropological approach to early European law is needed, but there is little anthropological material available today to the student who wishes to begin such work. The highly suggestive approaches by such anthropologists as Max Gluckman are as yet unfollowed by most historians of this period.[11] Anthropology, therefore, may best be used by the application of postulates about primitive law to other elements of early Germanic culture in an attempt to see if "law" in early Germanic society behaves in the same or in similar ways as it behaves in other societies. Thus, early Germanic law may be considered in terms of its role in a system of social controls that aim at maintaining moral and social order and preparing new generations for their social roles. The greatest function of anthropological investigation, however, may well be its suggestion that law cannot be considered apart from the cultural matrices in which it operates, and that legal procedure, like legal institutions generally, provides information for the sociologist and the anthropologist as well as for the legal historian.

There is little evidence that the judicial ordeal was a part of early Germanic customary law. One of the strongest arguments for its existence is by analogy to other primitive societies who have possessed it at comparable states of development. Yet analogy may take us only so far, and the judicial ordeal as it existed between the sixth and the thirteenth centuries in Europe emerges clearly in the Germanic law codes of only the late fifth and the sixth centuries. In those codes, the ordeal appears as a means of determining the justice of an accusation through the subjecting of the accused or his designated representative to physical trials that ordinarily would, without supernatural intervention, produce certain physical results. For example, the ordeal of hot iron requires that the subject carry a piece of red-hot iron a stated distance, and that the subject's hand be bound up and examined at a specified later time. If the burns are healing, the iron has proven the subject innocent. Part of the conceptual universe to which these early forms of the ordeal belong has been succinctly summarized by Gaudemet:

> This terminology [of the early Germanic law codes dealing with various ordeals] already marks an evolution of the ordeal and of its basis. The archaic concept of the solidarity of the forces of nature, which would reject the guilty party or the liar, gives way to a concept somewhat further evolved, although not yet specifically Christian (because it is found among pagans as well, and it seems, when found among Christians, more pagan than Christian), according to which God, all powerful and omniscient, knowing the truthful and the just, expresses that knowledge by signs and by the elements of material creation... Thus, the judicial duel, as does the oath, takes on a religious significance. A kind of hierarchy of proofs is established; if the oath and the judicial combat are impossible, one then has recourse to the elements themselves (water, iron, and earth). That is the ordeal.[12]

Although Germanic society was certainly not thoroughly "Christianized" until long after the sixth and seventh centuries, it was certainly not unchanged, and in terms of many aspects of social life, a kind of Christianity undoubtedly influenced that change. The superficial transference of older pagan attitudes to the new religion; simplified, incomplete, or distorted interpretations of religious doctrines; and the domination of religious life by the laity all combined to impart a distinct and particular religious cast to early European culture. In the medium of that "liturgical culture," fundamental social institutions and relationships underwent considerable change. Reception into the spiritual community through baptism, requirements for personal salvation, the demands legitimately made upon wealth by the new norms of charity, the importance of marriage, the specialized status of the clergy, and the rituals of death and the afterlife all constituted a new and expanded framework for both individual actions and social values and institutions. As that area marked out as "law" received a new definition, it also acquired a religious character. Among the lower ranks of the Roman provincial populations as well as among the barbarians, the appeal of Christianity had long since been made on the level of the immanence of spiritual forces, in saints' lives, moral stories, sermons, and histories. By the sixth century in the old Roman West, there was little difference in the perception of spiritual reality on the parts of the Roman provincial and the Germanic invader and settler. The limitations of late Roman law, the sociology of Christianity, the acculturation process among the Germans, and the new systems of litigation among both Germans and Romans all go far toward explaining both the alterations in the substance of law and in legal procedures and the wide spread of such institutions as the ordeal between the sixth and the eighth centuries.

The appearance of the ordeal, whether from earlier Germanic law or more recent Germanic experience, its wide use between the sixth and the eighth centuries, and the value placed upon it by early European societies indicate the second step in its history in the West, the sanctifying of the materials used in ordeals and the procedure according to which they were applied by liturgical prayers and acts. From the ninth century on there appear a number of manuscripts which contain prescribed rituals for the administration of ordeals, prayers, and the designation of particular places for their execution.[13] The sacring of the instruments and ordeals should be considered as part of the process which R.W. Southern has called the "identification of the church with the whole of organized society." Between the ninth and the twelfth centuries the adaptation of prayer and liturgy to the activities of lay life constituted an elaborate and, for several centuries, a successful attempt to create a totally Christian society. Not only the liturgical ceremonies surrounding ordeals, however, but also the blessing of banners and swords, the development of the ideas of a just war, the sacring of German emperors, the institutions of the Peace and the Truce of God, and finally the Crusade idea itself all reflected the active process of Christianizing society according to principles first felt in the fifth through the eighth centuries. The powerful role of laymen in the life of the Church, the elevating of monastic life to the highest societal ideal, and the free co-operation between clerical and lay authorities all tended to break down the barriers between religious values and the daily lives of the aristocracy and freemen. The liturgical elevation of social rituals, from the ordeal to the Crusade, is a significant and generally neglected aspect of that process, which itself only slowly came to an end under the combined forces of the Gregorian reformers of the late eleventh and early twelfth centuries and the new importance of logic and a rational concept of law in the intellectual world of the twelfth century. The confidence in the immanence of Divine aid was no less strong between the sixth and the twelfth centuries than was the confidence in a new social relationship between clerical and lay society and in human reason after the twelfth century. When ordeals generally disappeared from European ecclesiastical and temporal law after the late twelfth century, their departure was in part a result of the same forces that de-sacralized temporal rulers, expressed criticism of the Crusade idea, and insisted anew upon the sharp distinction between the Church and the world.

III.

Historians, including Lea himself, have concentrated their attention on some aspects of the history of the ordeal at the expense of others. The following remarks on the state of scholarship on the subject since the appearance of *Superstition and Force* in 1866 will suggest where such concentration has been located. In 1890 Frederico Patetta published *Le Ordalie*: *Studio di storià del diritto e scienza del diritto comparato* (Turin, 1890), a longer and more ambitious work than Lea's, dealing in considerably greater detail with the ordeal in non-western and ancient societies. The edition of *Superstition and Force* that appeared in 1892 (from which the present reprint is

made) included several revisions based upon Lea's reading of
Patetta. The greatest history of the ordeal is that of Hermann
Nottarp, *Gottesurteilstudien*, Bamberger Abhandlungen und
Forschungen 2 (Munich, 1956). Nottarp's work, if not the def-
initive study of the ordeal, will remain for a long time the best
single account of this complex subject.

Texts and commentaries on the procedural and liturgical
aspects of the ordeal may conveniently be found in K. Zeumer,
Formulae Merovingici et Karolini Aevi, Monumenta Germaniae Historica, Legum, Sectio V, pp. 601-722, and for England
in F. Liebermann, *Die Gesetze der Angelsachsen*, 3 vols.
(Halle, 1903-1916). The best collection of original sources
concerning attitudes toward the ordeal is that of Petrus Browe,
De Ordaliis, 2 vols., Pontificia Universitas Gregoriana, Textus
et Documenta, Series Theologica, Vol. IV (Rome, 1932) and
Vol. XI (Rome, 1933). The first small volume deals with pontifical and conciliar materials and the second contains texts of
procedure and liturgical *ordines* as well as the opinions of the-
ologians, canon lawyers, and legal and political theorists. In
English translation, the best collection of materials has long
been Arthur Howland, *Ordeals, Compurgation, Excommunication, and Interdict*, Translations and Reprints from the Original Sources of European History, Vol. IV, No. 4 (Philadelphia, n.d.). The section of Howland's pamphlet dealing with
ordeals is reprinted below in the Appendix.

Much more scholarly attention has been focussed upon the
opposition to ordeals, and the most comprehensive and accessi-
ble study is that of John W. Baldwin, "The Intellectual Preparation for the Canon of 1215 Against Ordeals," *Speculum* 36
(1961), pp. 613-636, much of which, with several additions,
also appears in Baldwin's *Masters, Princes, and Merchants:
The Social Views of Peter the Chanter and His Circle*, 2 vols.
(Princeton, 1970), Vol. I, pp. 323-332. Earlier studies that still
contain much of interest are those of S. Grelewski, *La réaction
contre les ordalies en France depuis le IXe siècle jusqu'au
Décret de Gratien* (Rennes, 1924), which focusses principally
upon Agobard of Lyons and Ivo of Chartres, and Charlotte
Leitmaier, *Die Kirche und die Gottesurteile*, Weiner
Rechtsgeschichtliche Arbeiten, Band II (Vienna, 1953).

Two works by R.W. Southern intelligently suggest the cultural background of ordeals: *The Making of the Middle Ages* (New Haven, 1953) and *Western Society and the Church in the Middle Ages* (Baltimore, 1970). Perceptive studies on this complex topic include A. Esmein, *Les ordalies dans l'église gallicane au IXe siècle: Hincmar de Reims et ses contemporains* (Paris, 1898); P. Rousset, "La croyance en la justice immanente a l'époque féodale," *Le Moyen Age* 54 (1948), pp. 225-248 (an ambitious and interesting study, unfortunately marred by some ill-considered pseudo-anthropological observations in its concluding pages); Paul Fournier, "Quelques observations sur l'histoire des ordalies au moyen age," *Mélanges Gustave Glotz,* Vol. I (Paris, 1932), pp. 367-376. There is excellent material on the procedural aspects of the ordeal in Yvonne Bongert, *Recherches sur les cours laiques du Xe au XIIIe siècle* (Paris, 1949), pp. 211-252. In addition to the notes given here, most of the works cited contain extensive bibliographical materials for further research.

Some of the most useful materials dealing with the anthropological approach to legal history are the works of E. Adamson Hoebel, *The Law of Primitive Man* (Reprinted New York, 1970); P. J. Bohannon, *Justice and Judgment among the Tiv* (London, 1957); William Seagle, *The History of Law* (New York, 1946). The most useful work in this field for medieval historians, however, is that of Max Gluckman, *Politics, Law and Ritual in Tribal Society* (New York, 1968), a book that is stimulating, wide-ranging, and enormously suggestive for historians of post-tribal Europe.

No student of legal history and the sociology of law can safely neglect the important four volumes devoted by the *Société Jean Bodin* to the topic *La Preuve.* Indispensable in this series is *La Preuve: Deuxième Partie, Moyen Age et Temps Modernes,* Receuils de la Société Jean Bodin pour l'histoire comparative des institutions, Vol. XVII (Brussels, 1965). This volume contains a number of important recent studies, particularly that of Jean Gaudemet, "Les ordalies au moyen age: Doctrine, legislation, et pratique canoniques," pp. 99-134, and the essays by F. L. Ganshof, Jean-Philippe Lévy, Marguerite Boulet-Sautel, R. C. van Caenegem, and Jean Gilissen.

IV.

In its earliest appearances, the ordeal was generally a last resort, employed whenever irresolvable doubt or a defect of testimony or witnesses threatened to bring a case to a hopeless impasse:

> But if he who must take oath wishes to take it with raised hand (*de manu*), and if those who are ordered to hear the oath—those three whom we always command to be delegated by the judges for hearing an oath—before they enter the church declare they do not wish to receive the oath, then he who was about to take oath is not permitted to do so after this statement, but they (the judges) are hereby directed by us to commit the matter to the judgement of God (i.e., to ordeal). [14]

This passage from the *Burgundian Code* of the late fifth century suggests some of the background of the process of judicial ordeals as it developed between the fifth and the ninth centuries. The status of freemen in Germanic society imparted to the personal oath a great weight in the resolution of judicial conflicts. So profound was this faith in the sworn word of a free man (and in the quantitative oaths of a designated number of free men for specific occasions), that it usually constituted the primary level of resolution. The oath and compurgation, whenever possible, constituted the usual methods of resolving litigation in barbarian courts. From Roman and Germanic law, the word, supported or unsupported, of certain classes of individuals—ultimately the clergy alone—came to designate one standard form of litigous resolution, the *purgatio canonica*, the sworn word alone. Yet *purgatio*, with its full range of allusion from penitence to judicial satisfaction, began to depend more and more, probably from as early as the fifth century, upon a wider range of proofs. *Purgatio canonica*, as it emerged after the ninth century, was reserved for certain cases in canon law and cases involving the clergy. The oath, for so long the fundamental manner of judicial resolution, appears to have weakened in public opinion after the fifth century, and the texts reflect a concern for the dangers of perjury, and some even consider the taking of the oath as a form of ordeal, because men presumed that even a minute error in the form of the oath would indicate the injustice of the side on whose behalf the oath was taken. Thus, as the universal acceptance of the unsupported or supported oath diminished, men turned to other forms of certainty, and from the eighth to the twelfth centuries, the ordeal came to fulfill that need. Next to the *purgatio canonica,* there developed the *purgatio vulgaris,* the ordeal. Oath, judicial duel, and ordeal are all referred to as the *judicium Dei,* the judgment of God, and from the ninth century on, the two kinds of purgation—by oath or by ordeal—became an increasingly acceptable form of judicial resolution.

The history of legal procedure, as that of all other forms of social ritual, may suggest, if carefully considered, indications of particular areas of social stress and shifts of traditional attitudes. The ordeal itself indicates a decreasing reliance upon kin and friends and an increasing reluctance to accept traditional kin solidarity on the part of a society in the process of shaping new and wider social bonds. The ninth century was far from providing a public order of sufficient magnitude to assume any powers remotely resembling those of a modern state, nor did ninth century rulers ever conceive such a possibility. The ordeal appears to have increased in popularity between the eighth and the twelfth centuries, and a study of that increase in the light of contemporary social bonds would be very useful. Equally useful would be a study of the particular kinds of cases in which ordeal was most frequently used and the kind of verdict in which most ordeals resulted. In short, how commonplace was the process of ordeal, and what did its participants expect when they undertook it? There is considerable evidence that suggests that the preparation of ordeals influenced the outcome of the process, and a well-known document from early thirteenth-century Hungary indicates that guilt and innocence seemed to appear about evenly. Finally, to what extent may the ordeal have been one stage in a ritual process that might be expected to end before the actual ordeal itself? The liturgical surroundings of the later ordeals offered a widely accepted terminating point for litigation, and they may in addition have constituted acceptable occasions for settling disputes before the actual imposition of the ordeal itself. These problems all belong to the sociological role of the ordeal, and many of them deserve further examination.

Another area of consideration may tentatively be called the economics of ordeals. Between the eighth and the thirteenth centuries, the places in which ordeals were administered (usually churches), the instruments of ordeals, and the requisite clerical presence constituted part of that vast body of privileges that indicated both economic and political power. Particularly in terms of the resistance to the abolition of ordeals, there may well be fruitful material for further research along economic and political lines. Was resistance to the abolition of ordeals part of the general resistance to the homogenizing of ecclesiastical practices that was part of the papal reform movement of the late eleventh and twelfth centuries? Did the right to administer ordeals procure economic advantages for some churches in much the same way as did well-known shrines and relics or particular privileges?

A third area of suggested further study concerns the ending of ordeals as legal procedure and the particular ways in which the ordeal survived in European culture. As scholars have shown in the case of the judicial duel, what was once a general practice in all forms of litigation ultimately became a legal privilege of the aristocracy, and, as the private duel, survived well into modern European history. The ordeal, first abolished in ecclesiastical courts, then deprived of its clerical personnel, survived in other ways. In literature, the ordeal acquired considerable popularity in romances, especially the Arthurian cycle, and it survived in law in cases of witchcraft. Both these areas present problems. Both represent novel demonstrations of social concerns that invoke archaic procedures, one on the level of literature, the other on that of an exceptional criminal process that quickly became exempt from many of the procedural developments of the twelfth and thirteenth century reforms. The preservation of archaic social rituals, either in different media (as in literary representations) or in particularly specialized courts (as in those ecclesiastical and secular courts that tried cases of witchcraft through the mid-seventeenth century), present questions of cultural history that the historian should not avoid. In this case, those works by sixteenth- and seventeenth-century jurists defending the ordeal, torture, and the judicial duel deserve more attention from historians of early modern Europe than they have customarily received.

These suggestions do not exhaust the problems that face the student of the relations between law and society, particularly as these occur in the variegated religious culture of medieval Europe and touch not only ecclesiastical politics and high theology but the areas of penitence, liturgy, common beliefs and legal procedures, those neglected bridges between high and low culture. In the mid-nineteenth century Lea explored some of this rich and difficult territory, and his studies of the ordeal and torture, sacerdotal celibacy and auricular confession, excommunication, the Inquisition, and witchcraft reflect not only his own personal insight but also the early stages of a new kind of history, one that sought to get, as Lea himself said, at the "inner life" of a society. That task, of course, has not turned out to be as simple as Lea perhaps thought, and the disputes among historians and social scientists still fill far too many pages of scholarly journals and popular reviews. Lea's own rationalist approach to social history led him to label the chief characteristics of the age he studied most as superstition and force, but in spite of this pejorative characterization of his model, Lea laid out lines of investigation that are still well worth following, and made substantial contributions to what Gabriel Le Bras once called "the great seven-storey library which should be devoted to studies of the structure and whole life of every religion at every moment of its history."

PHILADELPHIA, 1973   EDWARD PETERS

NOTES.

1. The standard biography of Lea is E. Sculley Bradley, *Henry Charles Lea: A Biography* (Philadelphia, 1931), which contains bibliographical references to other accounts of Lea's career. A recent appreciation may be found in the "Historical Introduction" by Walter Ullmann in H.C. Lea, *The Inquisition of the Middle Ages: Its Organization and Operation* (New York, 1969).

2. *Superstition and Force* (Philadelphia, 1892), p. 590.

3. Among many recent studies, see particularly A. Momigliano, ed., *The Conflict between Paganism and Christianity in the Fourth Century* (Oxford, 1963); Lynn White, ed., *The Transformations of the Roman World: Gibbon's Problem after Two Centuries* (Berkeley and Los Angeles, 1966); Peter Brown, *The World of Late Antiquity* (New York, 1971).

4. A good brief introduction, with a useful bibliography, is Hans Julius Wolff, *Roman Law: An Historical Introduction* (Norman, Okla., 1951).

5. See Paul Vinogradoff, *Roman Law in Medieval Europe*, 3rd edition (Oxford, 1961); Ernst Levy, *West Roman Vulgar Law: The Law of Property* (Philadelphia, 1951); Ernst Levy, "Reflections on the First 'Reception' of Roman Law in Germanic States," *American Historical Review* 48 (1942), pp. 20-29; Ernst Levy, "Vulgarization of Roman Law in the Early Middle Ages," *Medievalia et Humanistica* 1 (1953), pp. 14-40.

6. Roscoe Pound, *Jurisprudence* (St. Paul, Minn., 1959), p. 369.

7. There are useful approaches considered in Katherine Fischer Drew, "Barbarian Kings as Lawgivers and Judges," in R. S. Hoyt, ed., *Life and Thought in the Early Middle Ages* (Minneapolis, 1967), pp. 7-29.

8. Jean Gaudemet, "Les ordalies au moyen age: Doctrine, legislation, et pratique canoniques," *Receuils de la Société Jean Bodin*, Vol. XVII, *La Preuve: Deuxième Partie, Moyen age et temps modernes* (Brussels, 1965), pp. 99-134 at 104-105.

9. See Henry C. Lea, *Torture* (Philadelphia, 1973) for further discussion.

10. See pp. xxii and xxiii for suggested readings.

11. See, however, J. M. Wallace-Hadrill, "The Bloodfeud of the Franks," in his *The Long-Haired Kings and Other Studies in Frankish History* (New York, 1962), pp. 121-147, an extremely suggestive approach to a related problem.

12. Gaudemet, art. cit., pp. 103-104.

13. For a bibliography of original materials, see pp. xii and xxiii.

14. Katherine Fischer Drew, trans., *The Burgundian Code* (Philadelphia, 1972), pp. 29-30 (VIII, 2).

15. G. Le Bras, "The Sociology of the Church in the Early Middle Ages," in Sylvia Thrupp, ed., *Early Medieval Society* (New York, 1967), pp. 47-57 at 57.

THE ORDEAL.

CHAPTER I.

UNIVERSAL INVOCATION OF THE JUDGMENT OF GOD.

ALTHOUGH the wager of battle and the other ordeals have much in common, there is sufficient distinction between them to render convenient their separate consideration, even at the risk of a little occasional repetition. The development and career of these forms of the judgment of God were not in all respects similar, nor was their employment in all cases the same. The mere fact that the duel was necessarily a bilateral ordeal, to which both sides had to submit, in itself establishes a limit as to the cases fitted for its employment, nor were all races of mankind adapted by character for its use. Moreover, in its origin it was simply a device for regulating under conditions of comparative fairness the primitive law of force, and the conception of the intervention of a Divine Power, whereby victory would enure to the right, probably was a belief subsequently engrafted on it. In the other ordeals this is the fundamental idea on which they were based, and we may perhaps assume that they represent a later development in human progress, in which brute strength has declined somewhat from its earliest savage supremacy, and a reliance upon the interposition of a superhuman agency, whether the spirit of a fetish or an omnipotent and just Godhead, single or multiform, has grown sufficiently strong to be a controlling principle in the guidance of daily life.

Yet this, too, is only a step in the evolution of human thought, before it can grasp the conception of an Omnipotence that shall work out its destined ends, and yet allow its mortal creatures free scope to mould their own fragmentary portions of the great whole—a Power so infinitely great that its goodness, mercy, and justice are compatible with the existence of evil in the world which it has formed, so that man has full liberty to obey the dictates of his baser passions, without being released from responsibility, and, at the same time, without disturbing the preordained results of Divine wisdom and beneficence. Accordingly, we find in the religious history of almost all races that a belief in a Divine Being is accompanied with the expectation that special manifestations of power will be made on all occasions, and that the interposition of Providence may be had for the asking, whenever man, in the pride of his littleness, condescends to waive his own judgment, and undertakes to test the inscrutable ways of his Creator by the touchstone of his own limited reason. Thus miracles come to be expected as matters of every-day occurrence, and the laws of nature are to be suspended whenever man chooses to tempt his God with the promise of right and the threat of injustice to be committed in His name.

To this tendency of the human mind is attributable the almost universal adoption of the so-called Judgment of God, by which men, oppressed with doubt, have essayed in all ages to relieve themselves from responsibility by calling in the assistance of Heaven. Nor, in so doing, have they seemed to appreciate the self-exaltation implied in the act itself, but in all humility have cast themselves and their sorrows at the feet of the Great Judge, making a merit of abnegating the reason which, however limited, has been bestowed to be used and not rejected. In the Carlovingian Capitularies there occurs a passage, dictated doubtless by the spirit of genuine trust in God, which well expresses the pious sentiments presiding over acts of the grossest practical impiety. "Let doubtful cases be determined by the judgment of God. The judges may decide that which they clearly know, but that which they cannot know shall be reserved for Divine judgment. Whom God hath kept for his own judgment may not be condemned by human means. 'Therefore judge nothing before the time, until the Lord come, who both will bring to light the hidden things of darkness, and will make manifest the counsels of the hearts'"[1] (1 *Cor.* iv. 5). That Heaven would interpose to save the guiltless was taught in too many ways to admit of doubt. An innocent man, we are told, was accused of a murder and pursued till he took refuge in the cell of St. Macarius, who at once proposed to determine the question of his guilt by an appeal to God. Adjourning to the grave of the slain the saint addressed a prayer to Christ and then called upon the dead man to declare whether the accused had killed him. A voice from the tomb responded in the negative and the fugitive was released; but when the saint was asked to pursue the investigation and ascertain the name of the murderer, he replied that this was none of his duty, for the sinner might already have repented.[2]

The superstition which we here find dignified with the forms of Christian faith manifests itself among so many races and under such diverse stages of civilization that it may be regarded as an inevitable incident in human evolution, only to be outgrown at the latest periods of development. In this, however, as in so many other particulars, China furnishes virtually an exception. Her arrested thought exhibits itself, in the King or sacred books collected by Confucius five hundred years before the Christian era, in nearly the same form as is found in the orthodox opinion of to-day. In this, religious belief is but a system of cold morality, which avoids the virtues as well as the errors of more imaginative faiths.

---

[1] Capit. Lib. vii. cap. 259.
[2] Vita Patrum Lib. iii. c. 41 (Migne's Patrologia, T. LXXIII. p. 764).

In the most revered and authoritative of the Chinese Scriptures, the Shu-King, or Holy Book, we find a theo-philosophy based on a Supreme Power, *Tai-Ki*, or Heaven, which is pure reason, or the embodiment of the laws and forces of nature acting under the pressure of blind destiny. It is true that some forms of divination were practised, and even enjoined, but no fuller expression of belief in direct interposition from above is to be found than that contained in the saying attributed to Muh-Wang (about 1000 B. C.) in his instructions to his judges in criminal cases: "Say not that Heaven is unjust; it is man who brings these evils on himself. If it were not that Heaven inflicts these severe punishments the world would be ungoverned."[1] It is, therefore, in strict compliance with this philosophy that in the modern jurisprudence of China there is no allusion to any evidence save that of facts duly substantiated by witnesses, and even oaths are neither required nor admitted in judicial proceedings.[2]

These teachings, however, are too refined and sublimated for ordinary human nature, and along-side of official Confucianism, Taoism and Buddhism flourish with a wealth of legends and marvels that may fairly rival the most exuberant fancies of Teutonic or Latin mediævalism. In the popular mind, therefore, the divine interposition may perpetually be expected to vindicate innocence and to punish crime, and moral teaching to a great extent consists of histories illustrating this belief in all its phases and in every possible contingency of common-place life. Thus it is related that in A. D. 1626 the learned Doctor Wang-i had two servants, one stupid and the other cunning. The latter stole from his master a sum of money, and caused the blame to fall upon his comrade, who was unable to justify himself. By way of securing him, he was tied to a flagstaff, and his accuser was set to watch him through the night. At midnight the flagstaff

---

[1] Shu-King, Pt. IV. ch. 4, 27 § 21 (after Goubil's translation).

[2] Staunton, Penal Code of China, p. 364.

broke in twain with a loud noise, the upper portion falling upon the guilty man and killing him, while the innocent was left unhurt; and next morning, when the effects of the dead man were examined, the stolen money was found among them, thus completely establishing the innocence of his intended victim.[1] Popular beliefs such as these naturally find their expression in irregular judicial proceedings, in spite of the strict materialism of the written law, and, at least in some parts of China, a curious form of the ordeal of chance is employed in default of testimony. If an injured husband surprises his wife *flagrante delicto* he is at liberty to slay the adulterous pair on the spot; but he must then cut off their heads and carry them to the nearest magistrate, before whom it is incumbent on him to prove his innocence and demonstrate the truth of his story. As external evidence is not often to be had in such cases, the usual mode of trial is to place the heads in a large tub of water, which is violently stirred. The heads, in revolving, naturally come together in the centre, when, if they meet back to back, the victims are pronounced guiltless, and the husband is punished as a murderer; but if they meet face to face, the truth of his statement is accepted as demonstrated, he is gently bastinadoed to teach him that wives should be more closely watched, and is presented with a small sum of money wherewith to purchase another spouse.[2]

The cognate civilization of Japan yields even more readily to the temptation of seeking from the Deity a solution of doubt. Anciently there were in general use the judgments of God, so well known in mediæval Europe, of the wager of battle and the ordeal of boiling water, and the latter is still customarily employed among the Ainos, or aborigines. Even yet two antagonists may be seen to plunge their hands in

[1] Livre des Récompenses et des Peines, trad. par Stan. Julien, Paris, 1835, p. 220.

[2] W. T. Stronach in "Journal of the North China Branch of the Royal Asiatic Society," New Series, No. 2, Dec. 1865, p. 176.

scalding water, the one who suffers the most being convicted, while the innocent is expected to escape with injuries so slight that they will readily heal.[1]

Turning to the still savage races of the old world we everywhere find these superstitions in full force. Africa furnishes an ample store of them, varying from the crudest simplicity to the most deadly devices. Among the Kalabarese the *afia-edet-ibom* is administered with the curved fang of a snake, which is dexterously inserted under the lid and around the ball of the eye of the accused; if innocent, he is expected to eject it by rolling the eye, while, if unable to do so, it is removed with a leopard's tooth, and he is condemned. Even ruder, and more under the control of the operator, is the *afia-ibnot-idiok*, in which a white and a black line are drawn on the skull of a chimpanzee : this is held up before the defendant, when an apparent attraction of the white line towards him demonstrates his innocence, or an inclination of the black line in his direction pronounces his guilt. More formidable than these is the ordeal-nut, containing a deadly poison which causes frothing at the mouth, convulsions, paralysis, and speedy death. In capital cases, or even when sickness is attributed to hostile machinations, the *abiadiong*, or sorcerer, decides who shall undergo the trial ; and as the active principle of the nut can be extracted by preliminary boiling, judicious liberality on the part of the individual selected is supposed to render the ordeal comparatively harmless.[2]

Throughout a wide region of Western Africa, one of the most popular forms of ordeal is that of the red water, or "sassy-bark." In the neighborhood of Sierra-Leone, as described by Dr. Winterbottom, it is administered by requiring the accused to fast for twelve hours, and then to swallow a small quantity of rice. After this the infusion of the bark is taken in large quantities, as much as a gallon being sometimes

1 Griffis's "Mikado's Empire," New York, 1876, p. 92.

2 Hutchinson's Impressions of Western Africa, London, 1858.

employed ; if it produces emesia, so as to eject all of the rice, the proof of innocence is complete, but if it fails in this, or if it acts as a purgative, the accused is pronounced guilty. It has narcotic properties, also, a manifestation of which is likewise decisive against the sufferer. Among some of the tribes this is determined by placing on the ground small sticks about eighteen inches apart, or by forming an archway of limbs of trees bent to the ground, and requiring the patient to pick his way among them, a feat rendered difficult by the vertiginous effects of the poison. Although death not infrequently results from the ordeal itself, yet the faith reposed in these trials is so absolute that, according to Dr. Livingston, they are demanded with eagerness by those accused of witchcraft, confident in their own innocence and believing that the guilty alone can suffer. When the red water is administered for its emetic effects, the popular explanation is that the fetish enters with the draught, examines the heart of the accused, and, on finding him innocent, returns with the rice as evidence.[1] A system directly the reverse of all this is found in Ashantee, where sickness in the ordeal is a sign of innocence, and the *lex talionis* is strictly observed. When evidence is insufficient to support a charge, the accuser is made to take an oath as to the truth of his accusation, and the defendant is then required to chew a piece of *odum* wood and drink a pitcher of water. If no ill effects ensue, he is deemed guilty, and is put to death; while if he becomes sick, he is acquitted and the accuser suffers in his stead.[2]

[1] Examination of the Toxicological Effects of Sassy-Bark, by Mitchell and Hammond (Proc. Biological Dep. Acad. Nat. Sci. Phila., 1859).—T. Lauder Brunton's Gulstonian Lectures, 1877 (Brit. Med. Journ., March 26, 1877).

This would seem to support the theory of Dr. Patetta (Ordalie, p. 13) that the original form of the poison ordeals was the drinking of water in which a fetish had been washed, the spirit of which was thus conveyed into the person of the accused. On the other hand, there is the fact that in some of the poison ordeals sickness was a proof of innocence.

[2] London Athenæum, May 29, 1875, p. 713.

Further to the east in the African continent, the Niam-Niam
and the neighboring tribes illustrate the endless variety of form
of which the ordeal is susceptible. These savages resort to
various kinds of divination which are equally employed as a
guidance for the future in all important undertakings, and as
means to discover the guilt or the innocence of those accused
of crime. The principal of these is the *borru*, in which two
polished pieces of damma wood are rubbed together, after
being moistened with a few drops of water. If they glide
easily on each other the sign is favorable; if they adhere
together it is unfavorable. Life and death are also brought
in play, but vicarious victims are made the subject of experiment. Thus a cock is taken and its head is repeatedly immersed
in water until the creature is rigid and insensible; if it recovers,
the indication is favorable, if it dies, adverse. Or an oil extracted from the bengye wood is administered to a hen, and
the same conclusions are drawn from its survival or death.[1]

The Somali of Ethiopia employ the ordeals of red-hot iron
and boiling water or oil in virtually the same form as we shall
see them used in India and Europe, examining the hand of
the accused after twenty-four hours to determine his guilt from
its condition.[2]

In Madagascar the poison ordeal is customarily administered, with a decoction of the deadly nut of the Tangena
(*Tanghinia venenifera*). One of the modes of its application
is evidently based on the same theory as the ordeal of red
water and rice, to which it bears a notable resemblance. A
fowl is boiled, and three pieces of its skin are placed in the
broth. Then a cupful of the decoction of the Tangena nut
if given to the accused, followed by the same quantity of the
broth, with the pieces of skin. Unless the poison speedily
causes vomiting, it soon kills the patient, which is a satisfactory proof of his guilt. If vomiting ensues, it is kept up by
repeated doses of the broth and warm water, and if the bits

[1] Schweinfurth's Heart of Africa, New York, 1874, Vol. II. pp. 32-36.
[2] Patetta, Le Ordalie, p. 70.

of skin are ejected the accused is declared innocent; but if
they are retained he is deemed convicted and is summarily
despatched with another bowl of the poison.   In the perse-
cutions of 1836 and 1849 directed against the Malagasy
Christians, many of the converts were tried with the Tangena
nut, and numbers of them perished.[1]   The ordeals of red-hot
iron and boiling water are also used.[2]

Springing from the same belief is the process used in Tahiti
for discovering the criminal in cases of theft.   The priest,
when applied to, digs a hole in the clay floor of his hut, fills
it with water, and stands over it with a young plantain in his
hand, while invoking his god.   The deity thereupon conducts
the spirit of the thief over the water, and his reflection is recognized by the priest.[3]

The races of the Indian archipelago are fully equipped with
resources of the same kind for settling doubtful cases.   Among
the Dyaks of Borneo questions for which no other solution is
apparent are settled by giving to each litigant a lump of salt,
which they drop simultaneously into water, and he whose lump
dissolves soonest is adjudged the loser; or each takes a living
shell and places it on a plate, when lime-juice is squeezed over
them, and the one whose shell first moves under this gentle
stimulant is declared the winner.[4]

In the Philippines there are various peculiar ordeals in use.
A needle is sometimes thrust into the scalp of two antagonists,
and he from whom the blood flows most profusely is adjudged
the loser; or two chickens are roasted to death and then
opened, and the owner of the one which is found to have the
largest liver is defeated.[5]

---

[1] Philadelphia Evening Bulletin, March 7, 187: .—Ellis's Three Visits
to Madagascar, chap. I. VI.

[2] Patetta, Le Ordalie, p. 61.

[3] Ellis's Polynesian Researches, Vol. I. ch. 14.

[4] Königswarter, op. cit. p. 202.—E. B. Tylor, in Macmillan's Magazine,
July, 1876.

[5] Patetta, Le Ordalie, p. 61.

The black Australioid Khonds of the hill-districts of Orissa confirm the universality of these practices by customs peculiar to themselves which may be assumed as handed down by tradition from prehistoric times.   Not only do they constantly employ the ordeals of boiling water and oil and red-hot iron, which they may have borrowed from their Hindu neighbors, but they administer judicial oaths with imprecations that are decidedly of the character of ordeals.   Thus an oath is taken on a tiger's skin with an invocation of destruction from that animal upon the perjured; or upon a lizard's skin whose scaliness is invited upon him who may forswear himself; or over an ant-hill with an imprecation that he who swears falsely may be reduced to powder.   A more characteristic ordeal is that used in litigation concerning land, when a portion of earth from the disputed possession is swallowed by each claimant in the belief that it will destroy him whose pretensions are false.   On very solemn occasions a sheep is killed in the name of Tari Pennu, the dreadful earth-goddess : rice is then moistened with its blood, and this is administered, in the full conviction that she will slay the rash litigant who insults her power by perjury.[1]

The hill-tribes of Rajmahal, who represent another of the pre-Aryan Indian races, furnish us with further developments of the same principle, in details bearing a marked analogy to those practised by the most diverse families of mankind. Thus the process by which the guilt of Achan was discovered (*Joshua* vii. 16–18), and that by which, as we shall see hereafter, Master Anselm proposed to identify the thief of the sacred vessels of Laon, are not unlike the ceremony used when a district is ravaged by tigers or by pestilence, which is regarded as a retribution for sin committed by some inhabitant, whose identification thus becomes all-important for the salvation of the rest.   In the process known as *Satane* a person sits on the ground with a branch of the bale tree planted opposite to him; rice is handed to him to eat in the name of

<hr />

[1] Macpherson's Memorials of Service in India, London, 1865, p. 83.— See also p. 364 for modes of divination somewhat akin to these.

each village of the district, and when the one is named in which the culprit lives, he is expected to throw up the rice. Having thus determined the village, the same plan is adopted with respect to each family in it, and when the family is identified, the individual is discovered in the same manner. Another form, named *Cherreen*, is not unlike the ordeal of the Bible and key, not as yet obsolete among Christians.   A stone is suspended by a string, and the names of the villages, families, and individuals are repeated, when it indicates the guilty by its vibrations.   Thieves are also discovered and convicted by these processes, and by another mode known as *Gobereen*, which is a modification of the hot-water ordeal.   A mixture of cow-dung, oil, and water is made to boil briskly in a pot.   A ring is thrown in, and each suspected person, after invoking the Supreme Deity, is required to find and bring out the ring with his hand—the belief being that the innocent will not be burned, while the guilty will not be able to put his hand into the pot, as the mixture will rise up to meet it.[1]

Among the ancient Aztecs the oath assumed the proportions of an ordeal; the accused in taking it touched with his finger first the ground and then his tongue, and a perjury thus committed was expected to be followed with speedy misfortune. So among the Ostiaks and Samoiedes a disculpatory oath with imprecations taken on the head of a bear is held to have the same virtue.[2]

Reverting to the older races, we find no trace of formal ordeals in the fragmentary remains out of which Egyptologists thus far have succeeded in reconstructing the antique civilization of the Nile valley, but this is not attributable to an intellectual development which had cast them aside as worthless. The intimate dependence of man on the gods, and the daily interposition of the latter in human affairs, were taught by the prophets of the temples and reverently accepted by the people.

[1] Lieut. Shaw, in Asiatic Researches, IV. 67, 84.
[2] Patetta, Le Ordalie, pp. 57, 67.

It was merely a question as to the manner in which the judgment of God was to be obtained, and this apparently took the form of reference to the oracles which abounded in every Egyptian nome. In this we are not left to mere conjecture, for a story related by Herodotus shows that such an interpellation of the divine power was habitual in prosecutions when evidence of guilt was deficient. Aames II., before he gained the crown, was noted for his reckless and dissolute life, and was frequently accused of theft and carried to the nearest oracle, when he was convicted or acquitted according to the response. On ascending the throne, he paid great respect to the shrines where he had been condemned, and neglected altogether those where he had been absolved, saying that the former gave true and the latter lying responses.[1]

The Semitic races, while not giving to the ordeal the development which it has received among the Aryans, still afford sufficient manifestation of its existence among them. Chaldean and Assyrian institutions have not as yet been sufficiently explored for us to state with positiveness whether or not the judgment of God was a recognized resource of the puzzled dispenser of justice; but the probabilities are strongly in favor of some processes of the kind being discovered when we are more fully acquainted with their judicial system. The constant invocation of the gods, which forms so marked a feature of the cuneiform inscriptions, indicates a belief in the divine guidance of human affairs which could hardly fail to find expression in direct appeals for light in the administration of justice. The nearest approach however to the principle of the ordeal which has thus far been deciphered is found in the imprecations commonly expressed in contracts, donations, and deeds, by which the gods are invoked to shed all the curses that can assail humanity on the heads of those who shall evade the execution of their plighted faith, or seek to present false

[1] Herod. II. 174.

claims. Akin to this, moreover, was the penalty frequently expressed in contracts whereby their violation was to be punished by heavy fines, the greater part of which was payable into the treasury of some temple.[1]

Among the Hebrews, as a rule, the interposition of Yahveh was expected directly, without the formulas which human ingenuity has invented to invite and ascertain the decisions of the divine will. Still, the combat of David and Goliath has been cited as a model and justification of the judicial duel; and there are some practices described in Scripture which are strictly ordeals, and which were duly put forth by the local clergy throughout Europe when struggling to defend the system against the prohibitions of the papacy. When the man who blasphemed the Lord (*Levit.* xxiv. 11–16) was kept in ward "that the mind of the Lord might be showed them," and the Lord ordered Moses to have him stoned by the whole congregation, we are not told the exact means adopted to ascertain the will of Yahveh, but the appeal was identical in principle with that which prompted the mediæval judgment of God. The use of the lot, moreover, which was so constantly employed in the most important and sacred matters, was not a mere appeal to chance, but was a sacred ceremony performed "before the Lord at the door of the tabernacle of the congregation" to learn what was the decision of Yahveh.[2]. The lot was also used, if not as a regular judicial expedient, at all events in unusual cases as a mode of discovering criminals, and its results were held to be the undoubted revelation of Omniscience. It is more than probable that the Urim and Thummin were lots, and that they were not infrequently used,

---

[1] Oppert et Ménant, Documents Jurid. de l'Assyrie, Paris, 1877, pp. 93, 106, 122, 136, 191, 197, 209, 238, 242, 246, 250, 253.

It is interesting to compare with these primitive formulas the terrible imprecations which became customary in mediæval charters against those who should seek to impair their observance.

[2] Numb. xxvi. 55–6; xxxiii. 54.—Joshua xviii. 8–11; xix. 1, 10, 17, 24, 51.—I. Chron. xviii. 5–18, 31.—Nehem. x. 34; xi. 1.

as in the cases of Achan and Jonathan.[1] And the popular belief in the efficacy of the lot is manifested in the account of Jonah's adventure (*Jonah* i. 7) when the sailors are described as casting lots to discover the sinner whose presence brought the tempest upon them. The most formal and absolute example of the ordeal, however, was the Bitter Water by which conjugal infidelity was convicted and punished (*Numb.* v. 11–31). This curious and elaborate ceremony, which bears so marked an analogy to the poison ordeals, was abandoned by order of R. Johanan ben Saccai about the time of the Christian era, and is too well known to require more than a passing allusion to the wealth of Haggadistic legend and the interminable controversies and speculations to which it has given rise. I may add, however, that Aben Ezra and other Jewish commentators hold that when Moses burnt the golden calf and made the Israelites drink the water in which its ashes were cast (*Exod.* xxxii. 20), he administered an ordeal, like that of the Bitter Water, which in some way revealed those who had been guilty of idolatry, so that the Levites could slay them; and Selden explains this by reference to a tradition, according to which the gold of the calf reddened the beards of those who had worshipped it, and thus rendered them conspicuous.[2]

The teachings of Mahomet were too directly derived from the later Judaism for him to admit into his jurisprudence any formal system depending on miracles to establish justice between man and man whenever Allah might be invoked to manifest his power. Like the Jews, however, he taught that

---

[1] Josh. vii. 14-26.—I. Sam. xiv. 37-45. Cf. Michaelis, Laws of Moses, art. 304.—Ewald's Antiq. of Israel, Solly's Translation, pp. 294-6.—Kuenen's Religion of Israel, May's Translation, I. 98.

[2] Mishna, Sota ix. 9; Wagenseilii Comment. op. cit. vi. 4 (Ed. Surenhus. III. 257, 291). The curious who desire further information on the subject can find it in Wagenseil's edition of the Tract Sota, with the Gemara of the Ain Jacob and his own copious and learned notes, Altdorf, 1674.

the constant supervision of the divine power is spontaneously
exerted, and he carried this so far as to inculcate the belief
that a judge pure from self-seeking would be inspired constantly from above. "He who asks to be made judge will
not be assisted; and he who is made judge by compulsion,
God sends down to him an angel, who causes his actions and
sentences to be just." To one who hesitated to accept the
office, the Prophet said, "God will direct your heart, and
show you judicial ways, and fix your tongue in truth and
justice." On the other hand, when a judge is unjust, "he
separates from himself the assistance and favor of God, and
the devil is always with him." It was hard on litigants when
the tribunal might be presided over by either Allah or Eblis,
but they had no recourse, except in the oath, which was the
corner-stone of Mahomet's judicial system. In the absence of
evidence, the oath of the defendant was final, and this incite-
ment to perjury could only be repressed by investing the oath
with the qualities of the ordeal. Accordingly he lost no
opportunity of insisting upon the punishment, here and hereafter, of those who perjured themselves before the judgment-
seat. Sometimes this failed to deter an eager pleader, and
then he consoled the defeated party with the assurance that
his successful adversary would suffer in the end, as when the
chief of the Cindah tribe urged that a Jew, against whom he
brought suit for land unjustly held, would swear falsely, and
the Prophet rejoined, "Swearing is lawful, but he who takes
a false oath will have no luck in futurity." Tradition relates,
however, that frequently he succeeded thus in frightening
those who were ready to forswear themselves, as when a man
of Hadramut claimed land occupied by a Cindah, and, being
without evidence, the defendant was ready to take the oath,
when Mahomet interposed, "No one takes the property of
another by oath but will meet God with his tongue cut off,"
and the Cindah feared God and said, "The land is his." In
another case, when two men were quarrelling over an inherit-
ance, and neither had a witness, he warned them, "In whcse

favor soever I may order a thing which is not his right, then
I lay apart for him nothing less than a piece of hell-fire,"
whereupon each litigant exclaimed, "O messenger of God,
I give up my right to him." Sometimes, however, even
Mahomet had recourse to a more direct invocation of the
supreme power, as in a case wherein two men disputed as to
the ownership of an animal, and neither had witnesses, when
he directed them to cast lots upon oath.[1]

These cases do not bear out the tradition that, when the
Prophet was perplexed beyond his ability, he had the resource
of appealing to the angel Gabriel for enlightenment. There
is one legend respecting him, however, which manifests the
popular belief that in doubtful cases God may be relied on to
interpose for the vindication of innocence. A youth brought
before Mahomet on an accusation of murder, protested that
the act was committed in self-defence. The Prophet ordered
the corpse to be entombed, and postponed the trial until the
next day. The brethren of the slain, still insisting on ven-
geance, were then told that they might inflict upon the
murderer precisely the same wounds as those which they
should find on the body. On opening the sepulchre for the
purpose of ascertaining the exact measure of the punishment
conceded, they returned affrighted to the judgment-seat, and
reported that they had found nothing but the smoke and stench
of Gehenna; whereupon Mahomet pronounced that Eblis had
carried off the corpse of the guilty, and that the accused was
innocent.[2] The prevalence of superstitions kindred to this, in
spite of the principles laid down in the law, is shown by the
custom which exists among some tribes of Arabs, of employing the ordeal of red-hot iron in the shape of a gigantic spoon,
to which, when duly heated, the accused applies his tongue,
his guilt or innocence being manifested by his suffering, or

---

[1] Mishcat ul-Masabih, .Matthews's Translation, Calcutta, 1810, vol. II.
pp. 221–31.

[2] Loniceri Chron. Turcic. Lib. II. cap. xvii.

escaping injury.[1] A species of vulgar divination, common among the Turks, moreover, belongs to the same category of thought, as it is used in the detection of thieves by observing the marks on wax slowly melted, while certain magic formulas are recited over it.[2]

It is among the Aryan races that we are to look for the fullest and most enduring evidences of the beliefs which developed into the ordeal, and gave it currency from the rudest stages of nomadic existence to periods of polished and enlightened civilization. In the perfect dualism of Mazdeism, the Yazatas, or angels of the good creation, were always prompt to help the pure and innocent against the machinations of Ahriman and his Daevas, their power to do so depending only upon the righteousness of him who needed assistance.[3] The man unjustly accused, or seeking to obtain or defend his right, could therefore safely trust that any trial to which he might be subjected would be harmless, however much the ordinary course of nature would have to be turned aside in order to save him. Thus Zoroaster could readily explain and maintain the ancestral practices, the common use of which by both the Zend and the Hindu branches of the Aryan family points to their origin at a period anterior to the separation between the kindred tribes. In the fragments of the Avesta, which embody what remains to us of the prehistoric law of the ancient Persians, we find a reference to the ordeal of boiling water, showing it to be an accepted legal process, with a definite penalty affixed for him who failed to exculpate himself in it :—

"Creator ! he who knowingly approaches the hot, golden, boiling water, as if speaking truth, but lying to Mithra ;
"What is the punishment for it ?

---

[1] Königswarter, op. cit. p. 203.
[2] Collin de Plancy, Dictionnaire Infernal, s. v. *Cèromancie*.
[3] The Dinkard, translated by Peshotun Dustoor Behramjee Sunjana, vol. II, p. 65, Bombay, 1876.

"Then answered Ahura-Mazda: Let them strike seven hundred blows with the horse-goad, seven hundred with the craosho-charana!"[1]

The fire ordeal is also seen in the legend which relates how Sudabeh, the favorite wife of Kai Kaoos, became enamored of his son Siawush, and on his rejecting her advances accused him to his father of endeavoring to seduce her. Kai Kaoos sent out a hundred caravans of dromedaries to gather wood, of which two immense piles were built separated by a passage barely admitting a horseman. These were soaked with naphtha and fired in a hundred places, when Siawush mounted on a charger, after an invocation to God, rode through the flames and emerged without even a discoloration of his garments. Sudabeh was sentenced to death, but pardoned on the intercession of Siawush.[2] Another reminiscence of the same ordeal may be traced among the crowd of fantastic legends with which the career of Zoroaster is embroidered. It is related that when an infant he was seized by the magicians, who foresaw their future destruction at his hands, and was thrown upon a huge pile composed of wood, naphtha, and sulphur, which was forthwith kindled; but, through the interposition of Hormazd, "the devouring flame became as water, in the midst of which slumbered the pearl of Zardusht."[3]

In Pehlvi the judicial ordeal was known as *var nirang*, and thirty-three doubtful conjunctures are enumerated as requiring its employment. The ordinary form was the pouring of molten metal on the body of the patient, though sometimes the heated substance was applied to the tongue or the feet.[4] Of

---

[1] Vendidad, Farg. IV. 156-8. If Prof. Oppert is correct in his rendering of the Medic Behistun inscription, the Zend version of the Avesta is not the original, but a translation made by order of Darius Hystaspes from the ancient Bactrian, which would greatly increase the antiquity attributable to this record of primæval Aryan thought. See " Records of the Past," VII. 109.

[2] Firdusi, Shah-Nameh, XII. 4 (Mohl's Translation, II. 188). Kai Kaoos was the grandfather and immediate predecessor of Cyrus.

[3] The Dabistan, Shea and Troyer's translation, I. 219.

[4] Quoted from the Dinkard by Dr. Haug in Arda-Viraf, p. 145.

the former, a celebrated instance, curiously anticipating the
story told, as we shall see hereafter, of Bishop Poppo when he
converted the Danes, is related as a leading incident in the
reformation of the Mazdiasni religion when the Persian mon-
archy was reconstructed by the Sassanids. Eighty thousand
heretics remained obstinate until Sapor I. was so urgent with
his Magi to procure their conversion that the Dustoor Adurabad offered to prove the truth of orthodoxy by suffering
eighteen pounds of melted copper to be poured over his naked
shoulders if the dissenters would agree to yield their convictions in case he escaped unhurt. The bargain was agreed to,
and carried out with the happiest results. Not a hair of the
Dustoor's body was singed by the rivulets of fiery metal, and
the recusants were gathered into the fold.[1]

Among the Hindu Aryans so thoroughly was the divine
interposition expected in the affairs of daily life that, according to the Manava Dharma Sastra, if a witness, within a week
after giving testimony, should suffer from sickness, or undergo
loss by fire, or the death of a relation, it was held to be a
manifestation of the divine wrath, drawn down upon him in
punishment for perjured testimony.[2] There was, therefore, no
inducement to abandon the resource of the ordeal, of which
traces may be found as far back as the Vedic period, in the
forms both of fire and red-hot iron.[3] In the Ramayana, when
Rama, the incarnate Vishnu, distrusts the purity of his beloved
Sita, whom he has rescued from the Rakshasha Ravana, she
vindicates herself by mounting a blazing pyre, from which she

---

[1] Hyde Hist. vet. Persar. Relig. p. 280 (Ed. 1760). See also, Dabistan,
I. 305–6.

[2] Bk. VII. st. 108.

[3] Atharva Veda II. 12 (Grill, Hundert Lieder des Atharva Veda, Tü-
bingen, 1879, p. 16).—Khandogya-Upanishad. VI. 16 (Max Müller's Translation, p. 108). In this latter passage there is a philosophical explanation
attempted why a man who covers himself with truth is not burnt by the hot
iron.

is rescued unhurt by the fire-god, Agni, himself.[1] Manu declares, in the most absolute fashion—

"Let the judge cause him who is under trial to take fire in his hand, or to plunge in water, or to touch separately the heads of his children and of his wife.

"Whom the flame burneth not, whom the water rejects not from its depths, whom misfortune overtakes not speedily, his oath shall be received as undoubted.

"When the Rishi Vatsa was accused by his young half-brother, who stigmatized him as the son of a Sudra, he swore that it was false, and, passing through fire, proved the truth of his oath ; the fire, which attests the guilt and the innocence of all men, harmed not a hair of his head, for he spake the truth."

And the practical application of the rule is seen in the injunction on both plaintiff and defendant to undergo the ordeal, even in certain civil cases.[2]

In the more developed code of Vishnu we find the ordeal system exceedingly complicated, pervading every branch of jurisprudence and only limited by the amount at stake or the character or caste of the defendant.[3] Yet Hindu antiquity is so remote and there have been so many schools of teachers that the custom apparently did not prevail in all times and places. One of the most ancient books of law is the Dharmasastra of Gautama, who says nothing of ordeals and relies for proof wholly on the evidence of witnesses, adding the very relaxed rule that "No guilt is incurred in giving false evidence in case the life of a man depends thereon."[4]

This, however, is exceptional, and the ordeal maintained its existence from the most ancient periods to modern times.

[1] Monier Williams, Indian Wisdom, 2d ed. p. 360.
[2] Man. Dharm. Sast. VIII. 114–16, 190.
[3] Institutes of Vishnu, IX.
[4] Institutes of Gautama, XIII. 1, 3, 23 (Bühler's Translation).
So the Vasishtha Dharmasastra is equally ignorant of ordeals and even more immoral in its teaching—"Men may speak an untruth when their lives are in danger or the loss of their whole property is imminent"—Vasishtha XVI. 10, 35 (Bühler's Translation).

Under the name of *purrikeh*, or *parikyah*, it is prescribed in the native Hindu law in all cases, civil and criminal, which cannot be determined by written or oral evidence, or by oath, and is sometimes incumbent upon the plaintiff and sometimes upon the defendant. In its various forms it bears so marked a resemblance to the judgments of God current in mediæval Europe that the further consideration of its use in India may be more conveniently deferred till we come to discuss its varieties in detail, except to add that in Hindu, as in Christian courts, it has always been a religious as well as a judicial ceremony, conducted in the presence of Brahmans, and with the use of invocations to the higher powers.[1]

Buddhism naturally followed the legal institutions which it found established, and accepted the ordeal, though it could scarce form a logical incident in the great system of transmigration whereby the good and evil of the universe distributed itself automatically, without supervision from the thirty-two heavens. We have seen the influence which Buddhism exercised on Chinese materialism, and Tibetan Shamanism could hardly expect to escape it. Thus in Tibet we find the hot water ordeal assume a form which is literally evenhanded, and which, if generally enforced, must exert a happily repressive influence over litigation. Both plaintiff and defendant thrust their arms into a caldron of boiling water containing a black and a white stone, the verdict being in favor of him who brings up the white.[2]

The Hellenic tribes had already, in prehistoric times, reached a point of mental development superior to the grosser

---

[1] See Halhed's Gentoo Code, chap. iii. §§ 5, 6, 9, 10; chap. xviii. (E. I. Company, London, 1776).—Ayeen Akbery, or Institutes of Akbar (Gladwin's Translation, London, 1800), vol. II. pp. 496, sqq. Also a paper by Ali Ibrahim Khan, chief magistrate of Benares, communicated by Warren Hastings to the Asiatic Society in 1784 (Asiatic Researches, I. 389).

[2] Duclos, Mém. sur les Épreuves.

forms of the ordeal as a recognized instrument of judicial investigation. These were replaced, as we have seen in Egypt, by habitual resort to oracles, but that some recollection of the ancestral practices was handed down to later ages is shown by the allusions in the Antigone of Sophocles, when the guards protest to Creon their innocence as to the burial of Polynices, and offer to prove it by the ordeal:—

> " Ready with hands to bear the red-hot iron,
> To pass through fire, and by the gods to swear
> That we nor did the deed, nor do we know
> Who counselled it, or who performed it" (264-267).

And a remnant of the primæval customs was preserved in the solemnities under which litigation was sometimes determined by one of the parties taking an oath on the heads of his children, or with curses on himself and his family, or passing through fire.[1] The poison ordeal, also, was not wholly obsolete. The Gæum or temple of the broad-breasted Earth, Gæa Eurysternus, at Ægæ in Achaia, was served by a priestess who, though not necessarily a virgin, was yet required to preserve strict celibacy when once invested with her sacred functions. If any doubts arose as to her virtue, it was tested with a draught of bull's blood, which speedily wrought her punishment if she was guilty. The same temple also furnished an illustration of ascertaining the divine will by means of the lot, for when a vacancy occurred in the priestship, and there were several applicants, the choice between them was determined by a reference to chance.[2]

Even these traces of the ancient customs of the race disappear among the Latins, though they preserved in full force the habits of thought from which the ordeal took its rise. This is seen in the most solemn form of imprecation known to the Romans as lending irrevocable force to promissory oaths— the "Jovem lapidem jurare,"—whether we take the ceremony

---

[1] Smith's Dict. of Antiq. s. v. *Martyria.*
[2] Pausan. VII. xxv. 8.

mentioned by Festus, of casting a stone from the hand while adjuring Jupiter to reject in like manner the swearer if he should prove forsworn, or the form described by Livy as preceding the combat between the Horatii and Curiatii, in which a victim was knocked on the head with a stone under a somewhat similar invocation.[1] Even without this ceremony, imprecatory oaths were used which were based on the belief that the gods would take men at their word and punish them, for forswearing themselves, with the evils which they thus invoked. Thus, after the battle of Cannæ, P. Cornelius Scipio forced the nobles who were plotting to leave Italy to abandon their design and take an oath in which they adjured Jupiter to visit them and all belonging to them with the worst of deaths if they proved false.[2] In the legends of Rome, moreover, sporadic instances may be found of special miraculous interposition to decide the question of innocence or guilt, when the gods properly appealed to would intervene to save their worshippers. These manifestations were principally vouchsafed in favor of the Vestals, as when the pupil of Æmilia was accused of having allowed the sacred fire to be extinguished, and was preserved by its spontaneous ignition on her placing the skirt of her garment upon the altar; or when Tucca, falsely arraigned for unchastity, vindicated her purity by carrying water in a sieve; or when Claudia Quinta, under a similar charge, made good her defence by dragging, with a slender cord, a ship against the rapid current of the Tiber after it had run aground and resisted all efforts to move it—and this with an invocation to the goddess to absolve or condemn her, as she was innocent or guilty, which gives to the affair a marked resemblance to an established form of judicial ordeal.[3] Occasional instances such as these had, however, no

---

[1] Festus s. v. *Lapidem.*—Liv. I. 24; XXI. 45.—Polyb. III. xxv. 6–9.—Aul. Gell. I. 21.

[2] Liv. XXII. 53. Cf. Fest. s. v. *Præjurationes.* See an example of a similar oath taken by a whole army, Liv. ii. 45.

[3] Val. Maxim. I. i. 7; VIII. i. 5.—Ovid. Fastor. IV. 305 sqq.

influence on the forms and principles of Roman jurisprudence, which was based on reason and not on superstition. With the exception of the use of torture, as we shall see hereafter, the accused was not required to exculpate himself. He was presumed to be innocent, and the burden of proof lay not on him but on the prosecutor. The maxim of the civil law—"Accusatore non probante, reus absolvitur"—is entirely incompatible with the whole theory upon which the system of ordeals is based.[1]

The barbarian Aryans who occupied Europe brought with them the ancestral beliefs in a form more easily recognizable than the remnants which survived through Hellenic and Italiote civilization. The Feini, or Irish Celts, boasted that their ancient Brehons, or judges, were warned by supernatural manifestations as to the equity of the judgments which they rendered. Sometimes these took the shape of blotches on their cheeks when they pronounced false judgments. Sen Mac Aige was subject to these marks, but with him they disappeared when he decided righteously, while Sencha Mac Aillila was less fortunate, for he was visited with three permanent blotches for each mistake. Fachtna received the surname of Tulbrethach because, whenever he delivered a false judgment, "if in the time of fruit, all the fruit in the territory in which it happened fell off in one night ; if in time of milk, the cows refused their calves ; but if he passed a true judgment, the fruit was perfect on the trees." Morann never pronounced a judgment without wearing around his neck a chain, which tightened upon him

---

[1] A scholiast on Horace, dating probably from the fifth century of our era, describes an ordeal equivalent to the *judicium offæ*. When slaves, he says, were suspected of theft they were taken before a priest who administered to each a piece of bread over which certain conjurations had been uttered and he who was unable to swallow it was adjudged guilty (Patetta, Le Ordalie, p. 140). Not only the date of this deprives it of value as evidence of Roman custom, but also the fact that Romans might well employ such means of influencing the imagination of Barbarian or ignorant slaves.

if the judgment was false, but expanded down upon him if it were true. These quaint legends have their interest as manifesting the importance attached by the ancient Irish to the impartial administration of absolute justice, and the belief entertained that a supernatural power was ever on the watch over the tribunals, but these manifestations were too late to arrest injustice, as they did not occur until after it was committed. The Feini therefore did not abandon the ancient resource of the ordeal, as is shown by a provision in the Senchus Mor, which grants a delay of ten days to a man obliged to undergo the test of boiling water.[1] The Celts of the Rhinelands also had a local custom of determining the legitimacy of children by an ordeal of the purest chance, which became a common-place of Roman rhetoric, and is thus described in the Anthology :—

Θαρσαλέοι Κελτοὶ ποταμῷ ζηλήμονι Ρήνῳ κ. τ. λ.

Upon the waters of the jealous Rhine
　The savage Celts their children cast, nor own
Themselves as fathers till the power divine
　Of the chaste river shall the truth make known.
Scarce breathed its first faint cry, the husband tears
　Away the new-born babe, and to the wave
Commits it on his shield, nor for it cares
　Till the wife-judging stream the infant save,
And prove himself the sire.   All trembling lies
　The mother, racked with anguish, knowing well
The truth, but forced to risk her cherished prize
　On the inconstant waters' reckless swell.[2]

---

[1] Senchus Mor. I. 25, 195.　Comp. Gloss, p. 199.

[2] Anthol. IX. 125.—Cf. Julian. Imp. Epist. XVI.—Claud. in Rufinum II. 110.—Pliny describes (Nat. Hist. VII. ii.) a somewhat similar custom ascribed to the Pselli, an African tribe who exhaled an odor which put serpents to sleep. Each new-born child was exposed to a poisonous snake, when if it were legitimate the reptile would not touch it, while if adulterine it was bitten. Another version of the same story is given by Ælian (De Nat. Animal. I. lvii.).

The Teutonic tribes, anterior to their conversion, likewise exhibit the ordeal as a recognized resource in judicial proceedings. The Norræna branch, as we have seen, cultivated the *holm-gang*, or duel, with ardor, and they likewise employed the hot-water ordeal, besides a milder form peculiar to themselves entitled the *skirsla*, in which one of the parties to a suit could prove the truth of his oath by passing under a strip of turf raised so that it formed an arch with each end resting on the ground, the belief being that if he had forsworn himself the turf would fall on him as he passed beneath it.[1] The Germanic tribes, in their earliest jurisprudence, afford similar evidence of adherence to the customs of their eastern brethren. The most ancient extant recension of the Salic law may safely be assumed as coeval with the conversion of Clovis, as it is free from all allusions to Christian rules, such as appear in the later versions, and in this the trial by boiling water finds its place as a judicial process in regular use.[2] Among the Bavarians, the decree of Duke Tassilo in 772 condemns as a relic of pagan rites a custom named *stapfsaken*, used in cases of disputed debt, which is evidently a kind of ordeal from the formula employed, "Let us stretch forth our right hands to the just judgment of God!"[3]

The Slavs equally bear witness to the ancestral practice of the ordeal as a judicial process. The *prauda jeliezo*, or hot-iron ordeal, was in use among them in early times.[4] In Bohemia, the laws of Brzetislas, promulgated in 1039, make no allusion to any other form of evidence in contested cases, while in Russia it was the final resort in all prosecutions for murder, theft, and false accusation.[5]

---

[1] Keyser's Religion of the Northmen, Pennock's Translation, p. 259. The extreme simplicity of the *skirsla* finds its counterpart in modern times in the ordeal of the staff, as used in the Ardennes and described hereafter.

[2] First Test of Pardessus, Tit. liii. lvi.

[3] Decret. Tassilon. Tit. ii. § 7.

[4] Grimm, ap. Pictet, Origines Indo-Européennes, III. 117.

[5] Annal. Saxo ann. 1039.—Ruskaia Prawda, art. 28 (Esneaux, Hist. de Russie, I. 181).

As the Barbarians established themselves on the ruins of the Roman Empire and embraced Christianity they, with one exception, cultivated the institution of the ordeal with increased ardor. This exception is found in the Gothic nations, and is ascribable, as we have seen when treating of the judicial combat, to the influence of the Roman customs and laws which they adopted. For nearly two centuries after their settlement, there is no allusion in their body of laws to any form of ordeal. It was not until 693, long after the destruction of their supremacy in the south of France, and but little prior to their overthrow in Spain by the Saracens, that King Egiza, with the sanction of a Council of Toledo, issued an edict commanding the employment of the *æneum* or ordeal of boiling water.[1]

Various causes were at work among the other tribes to stimulate the favor with which the ordeal was regarded. As respects the wager of battle I have already traced its career as a peculiarly European form of the Judgment of God, which was fostered by the advantage which it gave, in the times of nascent feudalism, to the bold and reckless. With regard to the other forms, one reason for their increased prevalence is doubtless to be found in the universal principle of the Barbarians, in their successive settlements, to allow all races to retain their own jurisprudence, however much individuals might be intermingled, socially and politically. The confusion to which this gave birth is well set forth by St. Agobard, when he remarks that frequently five men shall be found in close companionship, each one owning obedience to a different law. He also states that under the Burgundian rules of procedure, no one was allowed to bear witness against a man of different race.[2] Under these circumstances, in a large proportion of cases there could be no legal evidence attainable, and recourse was had of necessity to the Judgment of God. Even when this rule was not in force, a man who appealed to Heaven against the testimony of a witness of dif-

[1] L. Wisigoth. VI. i. 3.   [2] Lib. adv. Leg. Gundobadi iv. vi.

ferent origin would be apt to find the court disposed to grant
his request.   If the judge, moreover, was a compatriot of one
of the pleaders, the other would naturally distrust his impartiality, and would prefer to have the case decided by the
Omniscient whose direct interposition he was taught to regard
as undoubted.   That the assumed fairness of the ordeal was
highly prized under such circumstances we have evidence in
the provisions of a treaty between the Welsh and the Saxons,
about the year 1000, according to which all questions between
individuals of the two races were to be settled in this manner,
in the absence of a special agreement between the parties.[1]

The most efficient cause of the increased use of the ordeal
was, however, to be found in the Church.   With her customary
tact, in converting the Barbarians, she adopted such of their
customs as she could adapt to Christian belief and practice ;
and she accepted the ordeal as an undoubted appeal to God,
whose response was regarded as unquestionable, warrant being
easily found for this in the Jewish practices already described.
The pagan ceremonies were moulded into Christian rites, and
the most solemn forms of religion were thrown around the rude
expedients invented thousands of years before by the Bactrian
nomads.   Elaborate rituals were constructed, including celebration of mass and impressive prayers, adjurations and exorcisms of the person to undergo the trial and of the materials
used in it, and the most implicit faith was inculcated in the
interposition of God to defend the right and to punish guilt.[2]
The administration of the ordeal being thus reserved for
priestly hands, the Church acquired a vastly increased influence
as the minister of justice, to say nothing of the revenues thence
arising, and the facility with which ecclesiastics could thus
defend themselves when legally assailed by their turbulent
flocks.   We are not without evidence of the manner in which

---

[1] Senatus Consult. de Monticolis Waliæ c. ii.

[2] A great variety of these *Ordines* will be found in the collections of
Baluze, Martène, Pez, Muratori, Spelman, and others.   From these we de-
rive most of our knowledge as to the details of the various processes.

the church thus favored the use of this Christianized paganism, and introduced it along with Christianity among people to whom it was previously unknown.   Thus among the Turanian Majjars, the laws of King Stephen, promulgated in 1216, soon after his conversion, contain no allusion to the ordeal, but in those of Ladislas and Coloman, issued towards the end of the century, it is found, in its various forms, thoroughly established as a means of legal proof.[1] So, when in the twelfth century Bishop Geroldus converted the Slavs of Mecklenburg, they were at once forbidden to settle questions by oaths taken on trees, fountains, and stones, as before, but were required to bring their criminals before the priest to be tried by the hot iron or ploughshares.[2]   Under the Crusaders, the ordeal was carried back towards the home of its birth, even contaminating the Byzantine civilization, and various instances of its use are related by the historians of the Lower Empire to a period as late as the middle of the fourteenth century.

The ingenuity of the church and the superstition of the people increased somewhat the varieties of the ordeal which we have seen employed in the East.   Besides the judicial combat, the modes by which the will of Heaven was ascertained may be classed as the ordeal of boiling water, of red-hot iron, of fire, of cold water, of the balance, of the cross, of the *corsnœd* or swallowing bread or cheese, of the Eucharist, of the lot, bier-right, oaths on relics, and poison ordeals.   In some of these, it will be seen, a miraculous interposition was required for an acquittal, in others for a condemnation ; some depended altogether on volition, others on the purest chance ; while others, again, derived their efficacy from the influence exerted over the mind of the patient.

---

[1] Batthyani Leg. Eccles. Hung T. I. pp. 439, 454.

[2] Anon. Chron. Slavic. cap. xxv. (S. R. German. Septent. Lindenbrog. p. 215).

CHAPTER II.

THE ORDEAL OF BOILING WATER.

THE ordeal of boiling water (*æneum, judicium aquæ fer-ventis, cacabus, caldaria*) is the one usually referred to in the most ancient texts of laws. It was a favorite both with the secular and ecclesiastical authorities, and the manner in which the pagan usages of the ancient Aryans were adopted and rendered orthodox by the Church is well illustrated by the commendation bestowed on it by Hincmar, Archbishop of Reims, in the ninth century. It combines, he says, the elements of water and of fire; the one representing the deluge —the judgment inflicted on the wicked of old; the other authorized by the fiery doom of the future—the day of judgment, in both of which we see the righteous escape and the wicked suffer.[1] There were several minor variations in its administration, but none of them departed to any notable extent from the original form as invented in the East. A caldron of water was brought to the boiling-point, and the accused was obliged with his naked hand to find a small stone or ring thrown into it; sometimes the latter portion was omitted, and the hand was simply inserted, in trivial cases to the wrist, in crimes of magnitude to the elbow; the former being termed the single, the latter the triple ordeal;[2] or, again, the stone was employed, suspended by a string, and the severity of the trial was regulated by the length of the line, a palm's breadth being counted as single, and the distance to the elbow as triple.[3] A good example of the process, in all its

---

[1] Hincmar. de Divort. Lothar. Interrog. VI.

[2] Dooms of King Æthelstan, iv. cap. 7.

[3] Adjuratio ferri vel aquæ ferventis (Baluz. II. 655).

details, is furnished us by Gregory of Tours, who relates that an Arian priest and a Catholic deacon, disputing about their respective tenets, and being unable to convince each other, the latter proposed to refer the subject to the decision of the *æneum*, and the offer was accepted. Next morning the deacon's enthusiasm cooled, and he mingled his matins with precautions of a less spiritual nature, by bathing his arm in oil, and anointing it with protective unguents. The populace assembled to witness the exhibition, the fire was lighted, the caldron boiled furiously, and a little ring thrown into it was whirled around like a straw in a tornado, when the deacon politely invited his adversary to make the trial first. This was declined, on the ground that precedence belonged to the challenger, and with no little misgiving the deacon proceeded to roll up his sleeve, when the Arian, observing the precautions that had been taken, exclaimed that he had been using magic arts, and that the trial would amount to nothing. At this critical juncture, when the honor of the orthodox faith was trembling in the balance, a stranger stepped forward—a Catholic priest named Jacintus, from Ravenna—and offered to undergo the experiment. Plunging his arm into the bubbling caldron, he was two hours in capturing the ring, which eluded his grasp in its fantastic gyrations; but finally, holding it up in triumph to the admiring spectators, he declared that the water felt cold at the bottom, with an agreeable warmth at the top. Fired by the example, the unhappy Arian boldly thrust in his arm; but the falseness of his cause belied the confidence of its rash supporter, and in a moment the flesh was boiled off the bones up to the elbow.[1]

This was a volunteer experiment. As a means of judicial investigation, the Church, in adopting it with the other ordeals, followed the policy of surrounding it with all the solemnity which her most venerated rites could impart, thus imitating, no doubt unconsciously, the customs of the Hindus, who,

[1] De Gloria Martyrum Lib. I. cap. 81.—Injecta manu, protinus usque ad ipsa ossium internodia caro liquefacta defluxit.

from the earliest times, have made the ordeal a religious ceremony, to be conducted by Brahmans, with invocations to the
divine powers, and to be performed by the patient at sunrise,
immediately after the prescribed ablutions, and while yet fasting.[1] With the same object, in the European ordeal, fasting
and prayer were enjoined for three days previous, and the
ceremony commenced with special prayers and adjurations,
introduced for the purpose into the litany, and recited by the
officiating priests; mass was celebrated, and the accused was
required to partake of the sacrament under the fearful adjuration, "This body and blood of our Lord Jesus Christ be to
thee this day a manifestation!" This was followed by an exorcism of the water, of which numerous formulas are on record,
varying in detail, but all manifesting the robust faith with
which man assumed to control the action of his Creator. A
single specimen will suffice.

"O creature of water, I adjure thee by the living God, by
the holy God who in the beginning separated thee from the
dry land; I adjure thee by the living God who led thee from
the fountain of Paradise, and in four rivers commanded thee
to encompass the world; I adjure thee by Him who in Cana
of Galilee by His will changed thee to wine, who trod on thee
with His holy feet, who gave thee the name Siloa; I adjure
thee by the God who in thee cleansed Naaman, the Syrian, of
his leprosy;—saying, O holy water, O blessed water, water
which washest the dust and sins of the world, I adjure thee by
the living God that thou shalt show thyself pure, nor retain
any false image, but shalt be exorcised water, to make manifest
and reveal and bring to naught all falsehood, and to make manifest and bring to light all truth; so that he who shall place
his hand in thee, if his cause be just and true, shall receive no
hurt; but if he be perjured, let his hand be burned with fire,
that all men may know the power of our Lord Jesus Christ,
who will come, with the Holy Ghost, to judge with fire the
quick and the dead, and the world! Amen!"[2]

After the hand had been plunged in the seething caldron,
it was carefully enveloped in a cloth, sealed with the signet of

[1] Institutes of Vishnu, IX. 33 (Jolly's Translation).
[2] Formulæ Exorcismorum, Baluz. II. 639 sqq.

the judge, and three days afterwards it was unwrapped, when the guilt or innocence of the party was announced by the condition of the member.[1] By way of extra precaution, in some rituals it is ordered that during this interval holy water and blessed salt be mingled in all the food and drink of the patient —presumably to avert diabolic interference with the result.[2]

The judicial use of this ordeal is shown in a charter of the monastery of Sobrada in Galicia, when, about 987, the Bishop of Lugo claimed of it for his church the manor of Villarplano. After a vain effort to decide the question by evidence, the representatives of the monastery took a solemn oath as to its rights and offered to confirm it by the *pœna caldaria.* In the church of San Juliano some fifty or sixty notables from both sides assembled; a monk named Salamiro was conducted to the boiling caldron by a person representing each claimant, and there he drew forth ten stones from the bubbling water. His arm was sealed up and three or four days later was exhibited uninjured to the assembly. The proof was conclusive and the Bishop of Lugo abandoned his claim.[3]

The justification of this mode of procedure by its most able defender, Hincmar of Reims, is similar in spirit to the above form of adjuration. King Lothair, great-grandson of Charlemagne, desiring to get rid of his wife, Teutberga, accused her of the foulest incest, and forced her to a confession, which she afterwards recanted, proving her innocence by undergoing the ordeal of hot water by proxy. Lothair, nevertheless, married his concubine Waldrada, and for ten years the whole of Europe was occupied with the degrading details of the quarrel, council after council assembling to consider the subject, and the thunders of Rome being freely employed. Hincmar, the most conspicuous ecclesiastic of his day, stood boldly forth in defence of the unhappy queen, and in his

---

[1] Doom concerning hot iron and water (Laws of Æthelstan, Thorpe, I. 226); Baluze, II. 644.

[2] Martene de Antiq. Eccles. Ritibus, Lib. III. c. vii. Ordo. 19.

[3] Florez, España Sagrada, XIX. 377–8.

treatise "De Divortio Lotharii et Teutbergæ," although no one at the time seriously thought of impugning the authority of ordeals in general, it suited his purpose to insist upon their claims to infallibility. His line of argument shows how thoroughly the pagan custom had become Christianized, and how easily the churchman could find reasons for attributing to God the interposition which his ancestors had ascribed to Mithra, or to Agni, or to Thor. "Because in boiling water the guilty are scalded and the innocent are unhurt, because Lot escaped unharmed from the fire of Sodom, and the future fire which will precede the terrible Judge will be harmless to the Saints, and will burn the wicked as in the Babylonian furnace of old."[1]

In the Life of St. Ethelwold is recorded a miracle, which, though not judicial, yet, from its description by a contemporary, affords an insight into the credulous faith which rendered lawgivers ready to intrust the most important interests to decisions of this nature. The holy saint, while Abbot of Abingdon, to test the obedience of Elfstan the cook of the monastery, ordered him to extract with his hand a piece of meat from the bottom of a caldron in which the conventual dinner was boiling. Without hesitation the monk plunged his hand into the seething mass and unhurt presented the desired morsel to his wondering superior. Faith such as this could not go unrewarded, and Elfstan, from his humble station, rose to the episcopal seat of Winchester.[2]

This form of trial was in use among all the races in whose legislation the *purgatio vulgaris* found place. It is the only mode alluded to in the Salic Law, from the primitive text to the amended code of Charlemagne.[3] The same may be said

---

[1] "Quia in aqua ignita coquuntur culpabiles et innoxii liberantur incocti, quia de igne Sodomitico Lot justus evasit inustus, et futurus ignis qui præibit terribilem judicem, Sanctis erit innocuus et scelestos aduret, ut olim Babylonica fornax, quæ pueros omnino non contigit."—Interrog. vi.

[2] Vit. S. Æthelwoldi c. x. (Chron. Abingd. II. 259. M. R. Series).

[3] First text of Pardessus, Tit. liii. lvi.; MS. Guelferbyt. Tit. xiv. xvi.; L. Emend. Tit. lv. lix.

of the Wisigoths, as we have already seen; while the codes of the Frisians, the Anglo-Saxons, and the Lombards, all refer cases to its decision.[1] In Iceland, it was employed from the earliest times;[2] in the primitive jurisprudence of Russia its use was enjoined in cases of minor importance,[3] and it continued in vogue throughout Europe until the general discredit attached to this mode of judgment led to the gradual abandonment of the ordeal as a legal process. It is among the forms enumerated in the sweeping condemnation of the whole system, in 1215, by Innocent III. in the Fourth Council of Lateran; but even subsequently we find it prescribed in certain cases by the municipal laws in force throughout the whole of Northern and Southern Germany,[4] and as late as 1282 it is specified in a charter of Gaston of Béarn, conferring on a church the privilege of holding ordeals.[5] At a later date, indeed, it was sometimes administered in a different and more serious form, the accused being expected to swallow the boiling water. I have met with no instances recorded of this, but repeated allusions to it by Rickius show that it could not have been unusual.[6] Another variant is seen in the case of a monk who had brought the body of St. Helena to his convent and was forced to prove its genuineness by complete immersion in boiling water—a trial which he endured successfully.[7]

The modern Hindoo variety of this ordeal consists in casting a piece of gold or a metal ring into a vessel of boiling *ghee*, or sesame oil, of a specified size and depth. Sacrifices are offered to the gods, a mantra, or Vedic prayer, is uttered over the oil, which is heated until it burns a fresh peepul leaf,

---

[1] L. Frision. Tlt. iii.; L. Æthelredi iv. § 6; L. Lombard. Lib. I. Tit. xxxiii. § 1.

[2] Grágás, Sect. VI. cap. 55.

[3] Ruskaia Prawda, Art. 28.

[4] Jur. Provin. Saxon. Lib. I. art. 39; Jur. Provin. Alamann. cap. xxxvii. §§ 15, 16.

[5] Du Cange.   [6] Defens. Probæ Aquæ Frigid. §§ 167, 169, etc.

[7] J. H. Böhmer, Jus. Eccles. Protestantium T. V. p. 597.

and if the person on trial can extract the ring between his finger and thumb, without scalding himself, he is pronounced victorious.[1] In 1783 a case is recorded as occurring at Benares, in which a Brahman accused a linen-painter of theft, and as there was no other way of settling the dispute, both parties agreed to abide by the result of the ordeal. At that time the East India Company was endeavoring to discountenance this superstition, but could not venture to abolish it forcibly, and as persuasion was unavailing the accused was allowed to undergo the experiment, which resulted in his conviction. Not much confidence, however, seems to have been felt in the trial, as the fine incurred by him was not enforced.[2] Of course, under the influence of English rule, this and all other ordeals are legally obsolete, but the popular belief in them is not easily eradicated. So lately as 1867 the Bombay *Gazette* records a case occurring at Jamnuggur, when a cameldriver named Chakee Soomar, under whose charge a considerable sum of money was lost, was exposed by a local official to the ordeal of boiling oil. The authorities, however, took prompt measures to punish this act of cruelty. The *karbharee* who ordered it escaped chastisement by opportunely dying, but the owner of the treasure, who had urged the trial, was condemned to pay to the camel-driver a pension of 100 rupees during life. In 1868 the Madras *Times* chronicled an attempt to revive the practice among the Brahmans of Travancore. About thirty years before it had been abolished by the British authorities, but previous to that time it was performed by placing a small silver ball in a brazen vessel eight inches deep, filled with boiling ghee. After various religious ceremonies, the accused plunged in his hand, and sometimes was obliged to repeat the attempt several times before he could

---

[1] Ayeen Akbery, II. 498. This work was written about the year 1600 by Abulfazel, vizier of the Emperor Akbar. Gladwin's Translation was published under the auspices of the East India Company in 1800. See also Ali Ibrahim Khan, in Asiatic Researches, I. 398.

[2] Ali Ibrahim Khan, loc cit.

bring out the ball.   The hand was then wrapped up in tender palm leaves and examined after an interval of three days.   In 1866 some Brahmans in danger of losing caste endeavored to regain their position by obtaining permission to undergo a modification of this trial, substituting cold oil for boiling ghee. The authorities made no objection to this, but the holy society refused to consider it a valid purgation.

Christian faith improved on the simplicity of pagan devices, and was able, through the intermediation of men of supreme sanctity, to induce Heaven to render the ordeal still more miraculous.   D'Achery quotes from a contemporary MS. life of the holy Pons, Abbot of Andaone near Avignon, a miracle which relates that one morning after mass, as he was about to cross the Rhone, he met two men quarrelling over a ploughshare, which, after being lost for several days, had been found buried in the ground, and which each accused the other of having purloined and hidden.   As the question was impenetrable to human wisdom, Pons intervened and told them to place the ploughshare in the water of the river, within easy reach.   Then, making over it the sign of the cross, he ordered the disputant who was most suspected to lift it out of the river.   The man accordingly plunged his arm into the stream only to withdraw it, exclaiming that the water was boiling, and showed his hand fearfully scalded, thus affording the most satisfactory evidence of his guilt.[1]   St. Bertrand, Bishop of Comminges, adopted a similar method in a case of disputed paternity.   A poor woman came to him with a starving infant, which the father refused to recognize or provide for, lest such evidence of sin should render him ineligible for an ecclesiastical benefice.   The bishop summoned the offender, who stoutly denied the allegation, until a vessel of cold water was brought and a stone thrown in, when the bishop blessed the water, and ordered the father to take out the stone, saying that the result would show the truth or falsity of his assevera-

---

[1] D'Achery, Not. 119 ad Opp. Guibert. Noviogent.

tions. Full of confidence, the man plunged in his hand and brought out the stone, with his hand scalded as though the water had been boiling. He promptly admitted his guilt, acknowledged the child, and thenceforth provided for it.[1] Similar to this was the incident which drove the holy St. Gengulphus from the world. While yet a warrior and favorite of King Pepin, during his travels in Italy he was attracted by a way-side fountain, and bought it from the owner, who imagined that it could not be removed from his possessions. On his return to France, Gengulphus drove his staff into the ground near his house, in a convenient place, and on its being withdrawn next day, the obedient stream, which had followed him from Italy, burst forth. He soon learned that during his absence his wife had proved unfaithful to him with a priest, and desiring to test her innocence, he took her to the fountain and told her that she could disprove the reports against her by picking up a hair which lay at the bottom of the pool. She boldly did this, but on withdrawing her hand it was fearfully scalded, the skin and flesh hanging in strips from her finger-ends. He pardoned her and retired from the world, but she was implacable, and took her revenge by inciting her paramour to murder him.[2]

CHAPTER III.

THE ORDEAL OF RED-HOT IRON.

In almost all ages there has existed the belief that under the divine influence the human frame was able to resist the action of fire. Even the sceptic Pliny seems to share the superstition as to the families of the Hirpi, who at the annual sacrifice

[1] Vit. S. Bertrandi Convenar. No. 15 (Martene Ampliss. Collect. VI. 1029-30).

[2] Pet. Cantor. Verb. Abbrev. Not. in cap. lxxviii. (Migne's Patrol. T. CCV. p. 471).

made to Apollo, on Mount Soracte, walked without injury over piles of burning coals, in recognition of which, by a perpetual senatus consultum, they were relieved from all public burdens.[1] That fire applied either directly or indirectly should be used in the appeal to God was therefore natural, and the convenience with which it could be employed by means of iron rendered that the most usual form of the ordeal. As employed in Europe, under the name of *judicium ferri* or *juise* it was administered in two essentially different forms. The one (*vomeres igniti, examen pedale*) consisted in laying on the ground at certain distances six, nine, or in some cases twelve, red-hot ploughshares, among which the accused walked barefooted, sometimes blindfolded, when it became an ordeal of pure chance, and sometimes compelled to press each iron with his naked feet.[2] The other and more usual form obliged the patient to carry in his hand for a certain distance, usually nine feet, a piece of red-hot iron, the weight of which was determined by law and varied with the importance of the question at issue or the magnitude of the alleged crime. Thus, among the Anglo-Saxons, in the "simple ordeal" the iron weighed one pound, in the "triple ordeal" three pounds. The latter is prescribed for incendiaries and "morth-slayers" (secret murderers), for false coining, and for plotting against the king's life; while at a later period, in the collection known as the Laws of Henry I., we find it extended to cases of theft, robbery, arson, and felonies in general.[3] In Sweden, for theft, the form known as *trux iarn* was employed, in which

---

[1] Natur. Histor. L. VII. c. 2.

[2] "Si titubaverit, si singulos vomeres pleno pede non presserit, si quantulumcunque læsa fuerit, sententia proferatur."—Annal. Winton. Eccles. (Du Cange, s. v. *Vomeres*). Six is the number of ploughshares specified in the celebrated trial of St. Cunigunda, wife of the emperor St. Henry II. (Mag. Chron. Belgic.). Twelve ploughshares are prescribed by the Swedish law (Legg. Scan. Provin. Lib. VII. c. 99. Ed. Thorsen. p. 170).

[3] Legg. Æthelstan. iv. § 6; Ætheldréd. iii. § 7; Cnut. Secular. § 58; Henrici I. lxvi. 9.

the accused had to carry the red-hot iron and deposit it in a
hole twelve paces from the starting-point; in other cases the
ordeal was called *scuz iarn*, when he carried it nine paces and
then cast it from him. These ordeals were held on Wednesday, after fasting on bread and water on Monday and Tues-
day; the hand or foot was washed, after which it was allowed
to touch nothing till it came in contact with the iron; it was
then wrapped up and sealed until Saturday, when it was
opened in presence of the accuser and the judges.[1] In Spain,
the iron had no definite weight, but was a palm and two
fingers in length, with four feet, high enough to enable the
criminal to lift it conveniently.[2] The episcopal benediction
was ·necessary to consecrate the iron to its judicial use. A
charter of 1082 shows that the Abbey of Fontanelle in Normandy had one of approved sanctity, which, through the
ignorance of a monk, was applied to other purposes. The
Abbot thereupon asked the Archbishop of Rouen to consecrate another, and before the latter would consent the institution had to prove its right to administer the ordeal.[3] The
wrapping up and sealing of the hand was a general custom,
derived from the East, and usually after three days it was uncovered and the decision was rendered in accordance with its
condition.[4] These proceedings were accompanied by the
same solemn observances which have been already described,
the iron itself was duly exorcised, and the intervention of God
was invoked in the name of all the manifestations of Divine
clemency or wrath by the agency of fire—Shadrach, Meshach,
and Abednego, the burning bush of Horeb, the destruction of
Sodom, and the day of judgment.[5] Occasionally, when

1 Legg. Scan. Provin. Lib. VII. c. 99 (Ed. Thorsen, pp. 170–2).

2 Fuero de Baeça, *ap.* Villadiego, Fuero Juzgo, fol. 317*a*.

3 Du Cange, s. v. *Ferrum candens.*

4 Laws of Ethelstan, iv. ₹ 7.—Adjuratio ferri vel aquæ ferventis (Baluz.
II. 656).—Fuero de Baeça (*ubi sup.*).

5 For instance, see various forms of exorcism given by Baluz, II. 651–
654. Also Dom Gerbert (Patrologiæ CXXXVIII. 1127); Goldast. Alamann. Antiquitat. T. II. p. 150 (Ed. Senckenberg).

several criminals were examined together, the same piece of heated iron was borne by them successively, giving a manifest advantage to the last one, who had to endure a temperature considerably less than his companions.[1]

In India this was one of the earliest forms of the ordeal, in use even in the Vedic period, as it is referred to in the Khandogya Upanishad of the Sama Veda, where the head of a hatchet is alluded to as the implement employed for the trial —subsequently replaced by a ploughshare.[2] In the seventh century, A. D., Hiouen Thsang reports that the red-hot iron was applied to the tongue of the accused as well as to the palms of his hands and the soles of his feet, his innocence being designated by the amount of resultant injury.[3] This may have been a local custom, for, according to Institutes of Vishnu, closely followed by Yajnavalkya, the patient bathes and performs certain religious ceremonies; then after rubbing his hands with rice bran, seven green asvattha leaves are placed on the extended palms and bound with a thread. A red-hot iron ball or spear-head, weighing about two pounds and three-quarters, is then brought, and the judge adjures it—

"Thou, O fire, dwellest in the interior of all things like a witness. O fire, thou knowest what mortals do not comprehend.

"This man being arraigned in a cause desires to be cleared from guilt. Therefore mayest thou deliver him lawfully from this perplexity."

The glowing ball is then placed on the hands of the accused, and with it he has to walk across seven concentric circles of cow-dung, each with a radius sixteen fingers' breadth larger than the preceding, and throw the ball into a ninth circle, where it must burn some grass placed there for the purpose.

---

[1] Petri Cantor. Verb. Abbreviat cap. lxxviii. (Patrol. CCV. 233).

[2] Weber's Hist. of Indian Literature, Mann & Zachariae's Translation, p. 73.

[3] Travels of Hiouen Thsang (Wheeler, Hist. of India, III. 262).

If this be accomplished without burning the hands, he gains his cause, but the slightest injury convicts him. A minimum limit of a thousand pieces of silver was established at an early period as requisite to justify the administration of this form of ordeal in a suit.[1] But the robust faith in the power of innocence characteristic of the earlier Hindus seems to have diminished, for subsequent recensions of the code and later lawgivers increase the protection afforded to the hand by adding to the asvattha leaves additional strata of dharba grass and barley moistened with curds, the whole bound around with seven turns of raw silk.[2] Ali Ibrahim Khan relates a case which he witnessed at Benares in 1783 in which a man named Sancar, accused of larceny, offered to be tried in this manner. The court deliberated for four months, urging the parties to adopt some other mode, but they were obstinate, and being both Hindus claimed their right to the ancient forms of law, which was at last conceded. The ordeal took place in presence of a large assemblage, when, to the surprise of every one, Sancar carried the red-hot ball through the seven circles, threw it duly into the ninth where it burnt the grass, and exhibited his hands uninjured. By way of discouraging such experiments for the future, the accuser was imprisoned for a week.[3] Even in 1873, the Bombay *Gazette* states that this ordeal is still practised in Oodeypur, where a case had shortly before occurred wherein a husbandman had been obliged to prove his innocence by holding a red-hot ploughshare in his hands, duly guarded with peepul leaves, turning his face

---

[1] Institutes of Vishnu, XI.—Yajnavalkya II. 103–6 (Stenzler's Translation, p. 61).

It is easy to understand the prescription of Vishnu that the fire ordeal is not to be administered to blacksmiths or to invalids, but not so easy that it was forbidden during summer and autumn (Ib. X. 25–6). Yajnavalkya, moreover, says that the ordeals of fire, water, and poison are for Sudras (II. 98).

[2] Ayeen Akbery, II. 497.—Patetta, Le Ordalie, p. 106.

[3] Asiatic Researches, I. 395.

towards the sun and invoking it: "Thou Sun-God, if I am actually guilty of the crime, punish me; if not, let me escape unscathed from the ordeal!"—and in this instance, also, the accused was uninjured.

A peculiar modification of the hot-iron ordeal is employed by the aboriginal hill-tribes of Rajmahal, in the north of Bengal, when a person believes himself to be suffering from witchcraft. The *Satane* and the *Cherreen* are used to find out the witch, and then the decision is confirmed by a person representing the sufferer, who, with certain religious ceremonies, applies his tongue to a red-hot iron nine times, unless sooner burnt. A burn is considered to render the guilt of the accused indubitable, and his only appeal is to have the trial repeated in public, when, if the same result follows, he is bound either to cure the bewitched person or to suffer death if the latter dies.[1]

In the earlier periods of European law, the burning iron was reserved for cases of peculiar atrocity. Thus we find it prescribed by Charlemagne in accusations of parricide;[2] the Council of Risbach in 799 directed its use in cases of sorcery and witchcraft;[3] and among the Thuringians it was ordered for women suspected of poisoning or otherwise murdering their husbands[4]—a crime visited with peculiar severity in almost all codes. In 848 the Council of Mainz indicates it specially for slaves,[5] while the Council of Tribur, in 895, orders it for all cases of accusation against freemen.[6] Among the Anglo-Saxons the accuser had the right to select the ordeal to be employed,[7] while at a later period in Germany this

---

[1] Lieut. Shaw, in Asiatic Researches, IV. 69.

[2] Capit. Carol. Mag. II. ann. 803, cap. 5.

[3] Concil. Risbach. can. ix. (Hartzheim Concil. German. II. 692).

[4] L. Anglior. et Werinor. Tit. xiv.

[5] Si presbyterum occidit . . . si liber est cum XII. juret; si autem servus per xii. vomeres ignitos se purget.—C. Mogunt, ann. 848 c. xxiv.

[6] Concil. Triburiens. ann. 895 c. 22 (Harduin. Concil. VI. I. 446).

[7] Laws of Ethelred, iv. § 6.

privilege was conferred on the accused.[1]　In England it subsequently became rather an aristocratic procedure as contra-
distinguished from the water ordeals.[2]　On the other hand, in
the Assises de Jerusalem the hot iron is the only form alluded
to as employed in the *roturier* courts;[3] in the laws of Nieu-
port, granted by Philip of Alsace in 1163, it is prescribed as a
plebeian ordeal;[4] and about the same period, in the military
laws enacted by Frederic Barbarossa during his second Italian
expedition, it appears as a servile ordeal.[5]　In the Russian law
of the eleventh century, it is ordered in all cases where the
matter at stake amounts to more than half a *grivna* of gold,
while the water ordeal is reserved for suits of less importance.[6]
In the Icelandic code of the twelfth century it is prescribed
for men, in cases in which women are required to undergo the
hot-water ordeal;[7] while the reverse of this is seen in an
English case occurring in 1201, where six men and a woman
were accused of burglary; the men were ordered to the water
ordeal and the woman to red-hot iron.[8]　A specially severe
form was provided for women in Ireland, who, when accused,

---

[1] The Jus Provin. Alaman. (cap. xxxvii. §§ 15, 16; cap. clxxxvi. §§ 4,
6, 7; cap. ccclxxiv.) allows thieves and other malefactors to select the
ordeal they prefer.　The Jus Provin. Saxon. (Lib. I. art. 39) affords them
in addition the privilege of the duel.

[2] Après les serements des parties soloit lon garder la partie, et luy porter
a la maine une piece de fer flambant sil fuit frank home, ou de mettre le
main ou la pié en eaw boillant s'il ne fuit frank.—Myrror of Justice, cap.
III. sect. 23.—Cf. Glanville, Lib. XIV. c. I.

[3] Baisse Court, cap. 132, 261, 279, 280, etc.

[4] Lesbroussart's Oudegherst, II. 707.

[5] Radevic. de Reb. Frid. Lib. I. cap. xxvi.

[6] Rouskaïa Prawda, Art. 28.

[7] Grágás, Sect. VI. c. lv.

[8] Maitland, Pleas, etc., I. 5.　Again in another case in 1207 (p. 55),
while in yet another a man and woman, accomplices in the same crime, are
both sent to the hot iron (p. 77).　In 1203 a case occurs in which the
court offers the accused the choice between red-hot iron and water, and he
selects the former.—Ib. p. 30.

were obliged to lick with the tongue a bronze axe-head heated to redness in a fire of black-thorn.[1]

Irrespective of these distinctions, we find it to have been the mode usually selected by persons of rank when compelled to throw themselves upon the judgment of God. The Empress Richardis, wife of Charles le Gros, accused in 887 of adultery with Bishop Liutward, offered to prove her innocence either by the judicial combat or the red-hot iron.[2] So when the Emperor St. Henry II. indulged in unworthy doubts of the purity of his virgin-wife St. Cunigunda, she eagerly appealed to the judgment of God, and established her innocence by treading unharmed the burning ploughshares.[3] The tragical tradition of Mary, wife of the Third Otho, contains a similar example, with the somewhat unusual variation of an accuser undergoing an ordeal to prove a charge. The empress, hurried away by a sudden and unconquerable passion for Amula, Count of Modena, in 996, repeated in all its details the story of Potiphar's wife. The unhappy count, unceremoniously condemned to lose his head, asserted his innocence to his wife, and entreated her to clear his reputation. He was executed, and the countess, seeking an audience of the emperor, disproved the calumny by carrying unharmed the red-hot iron, when Otho, convinced of his rashness by this triumphant vindication, immediately repaired his injustice by consigning his empress to the stake.[4] When Edward the

---

[1] O'Curry, *ap*. Pictet, Origines Indo-Européennes, III. 179.

[2] Regino. ann. 886.—Annales Metenses.

[3] Vit. S. Kunegundæ cap. 2 (Ludewig Script. Rer. German. I. 346–7).

[4] Gotfridi Viterbiensis Pars XVII., "De Tertio Othone Imperatore." Siffridi Epit. Lib. I. ann. 998. Ricobaldi Hist. Impp. sub Ottone III.—The story is not mentioned by any contemporary authorities, and Muratori has well exposed its improbability (Annali d'Italia, ann. 996); although he had on a previous occasion argued in favor of its authenticity (Antiq. Ital. Dissert. 38). In convicting the empress of calumny, the Countess of Modena appeared as an accuser, making good the charge by the ordeal; but if we look upon her as simply vindicating her husband's character, the

Confessor, who entertained a not unreasonable dislike for his mother Emma, listened eagerly to the accusation of her criminal intimacy with Alwyn, Bishop of Winchester, she was condemned to undergo the ordeal of the burning shares, and, walking over them barefooted and unharmed, she established beyond peradventure the falsehood of the charge.[1] So when in 943 Arnoul of Flanders had procured the assassination of William Longsword, Duke of Normandy, at Pecquigny, he offered to Louis d'Outremer to clear himself of complicity in the murder by the ordeal of fire.[2] Robert Curthose, son of William the Conqueror, while in exile during his youthful rebellion against his father, formed an intimacy with a pretty girl. Years afterwards, when he was Duke of Normandy, she presented herself before him with two likely youths, whom she asserted to be pledges of his former affection. Robert was incredulous; but the mother, carrying unhurt the red-hot iron, forced him to forego his doubts and to acknowledge the paternity of the boys, whom he thenceforth adopted.[3] Indeed this was the legal form of proof in cases of disputed paternity established by the Scandinavian legislation at this period,[4] and in that of Spain a century later.[5] Remy, Bishop

case enters into the ordinary course of such affairs. Indeed, among the Anglo-Saxons, there was a special provision by which the friends of an executed criminal might clear his reputation by undergoing the triple ordeal, after depositing pledges, to be forfeited in cases of defeat (Ethelred, iii. § 6), just as in the burgher law of Northern Germany a relative of a dead man might claim the duel to absolve him from an accusation (Sachsische Weichbild, art. lxxxvii.). This was not mere sentiment, as in crimes involving confiscation the estate of the dead man was at stake.

[1] Giles states (note to William of Malmesbury, ann. 1043) that Richard of Devizes is the earliest authority for this story.

[2] Dudon. S. Quintini Lib. iv.

[3] Order. Vitalis Lib. x. cap. 13.

[4] Grágás, Sect. VI. cap. 45. Andreas of Lunden early in the 13th century speaks of it as formerly in vogue for these cases, but disused in his time (Legg. Scan. Provin. Ed. P. G. Thorsen, Kjobenhavn, 1853, p. 110).

[5] " E si alguna dixiere que preñada es dalguno, y el varon no la creyere, prenda fierro caliente; e si quemada fuere, non sea creyda, mas si sana

of Dorchester, when accused of treason against William the Conqueror, was cleared by the devotion of a follower, who underwent the ordeal of hot iron.[1] When, in 1098, William Rufus desired to supply his treasury by confiscations, he accused about fifty of his richest Saxon subjects of having killed deer in his forests and hurried them to the hot-iron ordeal, but he was stupefied when after the third day their hands were found to be unhurt.[2] In 1143, Henry I., Archbishop of Mainz, ordered its employment, and administered it himself, in a controversy between the Abbey of Gerode and the Counts of Hirschberg. In the special charter issued to the abbey attesting the decision of the trial, it is recorded that the hand of the ecclesiastical champion was not only uninjured by the fiery metal, but was positively benefited by it.[3] About the same period, Centulla IV. of Béarn caused it to be employed in a dispute with the Bishop of Lescar concerning the fine paid for the murder of a priest, the ecclesiastic, as usual, being victorious.[4] The reward of the church for its faith in adopting these pagan customs was seen in the well-known case by which Bishop Poppo of Slesvick, in 962, succeeded in convincing and converting the Pagan Danes even as, three thousand years earlier, according to the Persian historians, Zoroaster convinced King Gushtashp of the truth of his revelation from Hormazd,[5] and, within seven centuries, Adurabad converted the heretical Mazdeans. The worthy missionary, dining with King Harold Blaatand, denounced, with more zeal than discretion, the indigenous deities as lying devils. The king dared him to prove his faith in his God, and, on his assenting, caused next morning an immense piece of iron to be duly

---

escapare del fierro, de el fijo al padre, e criel assi como fuero es."—Fuero de Baeça (Villadiego, Fuero Juzgo, fol. 317a).

1 Roger of Wendover, ann. 1085.
2 Eadmeri Hist. Novor. Lib. II. (Migne, CLIX. 412).
3 Gudeni Cod. Diplom. Mogunt. T. I. No. liii.
4 Mazure et Hatoulet, Fors de Béarn, p. xxxviii.
5 Hyde Relig. Vet. Persar. cap. xxiv. (Ed. 1760, pp. 320-1).

heated, which the undaunted Poppo grasped and carried around to the satisfaction of the royal court, displaying his hand unscathed by the glowing mass ; or, as a variant of the legend asserts, he drew on an iron gauntlet reaching to the elbow and heated to redness. The miracle was sufficient, and Denmark thenceforth becomes an integral portion of Christendom.[1] Somewhat similar, except in its results, was a case in which a priest involved in a theological dispute with a Jew, and unable to overcome him in argument, offered to prove the divinity of Christ by carrying a burning brand in his naked hand. Invoking the name of Jesus, the faithful ecclesiastic drew the blazing wood from the fire and slowly carried it for a considerable distance, but though he triumphantly exhibited his hand unhurt, his obdurate antagonist refused to be converted, alleging that the miracle was the result of magic.[2] In Norway, the sanctity of St. Olaf the King was attested in the same way, when he thoughtlessly whittled a twig on Sunday, and his attention was respectfully called by one of his courtiers to this violation of the sabbatical rules. By way of penance he collected the chips, placed them on the palm of one hand, and set fire to them, but after they had been

[1] Widukindi Lib. III. cap. 65.—Sigebert. Gemblac. Ann. 966.—Dithmari Chron. Lib. II. cap. viii.—Sáxo. Grammat. Hist. Danic. Lib. X. The annalists of Trèves claim the merit of this for their archbishop Poppo, whose pontificate lasted from 1016 to 1047. According to their legend, Poppo not only drew on an iron gauntlet heated to redness, but entered a fiery furnace clad only in a linen garment soaked in wax, which was consumed by the flames without injury to him.—Gest. Trevir. Archiep. cap. xvi. (Martene Ampliss. Collect. IV. 161).

[2] Guibert. Noviogent. de Incarnat. contra Judæos Lib. III. cap. xi. Guibert states that he had this from a Jew, who was an eye-witness of the fact.

Somewhat similar was a volunteer ordeal related by Gregory of Tours, when a Catholic disputing with an Arian threw his gold ring into the fire and when heated to redness placed it in his palm with an adjuration to God that if his faith was true it should not hurt him, which of course proved to be the case.—Greg. Turon. de Gloria Confess. c. xiv.

reduced to ashes, to the surprise of the bystanders, his hand was found unharmed.[1]

In fact, there was scarcely a limit to the credulity which looked for the constant interference of the divine power. About 1215 some heretics at Cambrai were convicted by the hot iron and sentenced to the stake. One of them was of noble birth, and on the way to the place of execution the priest who had conducted the proceedings exhorted him to repentance and conversion. The condemned man listened willingly, and commenced to confess his errors. As he proceeded his hand commenced to heal, and when he had received absolution there remained no trace of the burn. When he was called in turn to take his place at the stake, the priest interposed, saying that he was innocent, and, on examination of the hand, he was released. About the same time a similar occurrence is recorded at Strassburg, where ten heretics had been thus convicted and condemned to be burnt, and one repenting at the last moment was cured of his burn, and was discharged. In this case, however, on his return to his house near the town, his wife upbraided him for his weakness in betraying the eternal truth to avoid a momentary suffering, and under her influence he relapsed. Immediately the burn on his hand reappeared, and a similar one took possession of his wife's hand, scorching both to the bone and inflicting such excruciating agony that being unable to repress their screams, and fearing to betray themselves, they took to the woods, where they howled like wolves. Concealment was impossible, however. They were discovered, carried to the city, where the ashes of their accomplices were not yet cold, and both promptly shared the same fate.[2] Somewhat similar is a case recorded in York, where a woman accused of homicide was exposed to the ordeal, resulting in a blister the size of a half walnut. She was accordingly convicted by a jury of knights,

---

[1] Legend. de S. Olavo (Langebek II. 548).
[2] Cæsar. Heisterbach. Dial. Mirac. Dist. III. c. xvi. xvii.

but on her offering a prayer at the tomb of St. William of
York the blister disappeared.   Thereupon the royal justiciaries
dismissed her as innocent, and declared the jury to be at the
king's mercy for rendering a false verdict.[1]

No form of ordeal was more thoroughly introduced throughout the whole extent of Europe.   From Spain to Constantinople, and from Scandinavia to Naples, it was appealed to
with confidence as an unfailing mode of ascertaining the will of
Heaven.   The term *judicium*, indeed, was at length understood to mean an ordeal, and generally that of hot iron, and
in its barbarized form, *juise*, may almost always be considered
to indicate this particular kind.   In the Swedish law of the
early 13th century, the red-hot iron was used in a large
number of crimes, and the ferocity of its employment is ex-
emplified in the formula prescribed for homicide.   A person
accused of murder on suspicion was always obliged to justify
himself by carrying the hot iron for nine steps ; and if he did
not appear to stand his trial when duly summoned, he might
be forced to undergo a preliminary ordeal to prove that he
had been unavoidably detained.   If he failed in this, he was
condemned as guilty, but if he succeeded in enduring it he
was forced to perform the second ordeal to clear him of the
crime itself; while the heir of the murdered man, so long as
no one succumbed in the trial, could successively accuse ten
men ; for the last of whom, however, the nine burning ploughshares were substituted.[2]   In the code of the Frankish kingdoms of the East, it is the only mode alluded to, except the
duel, and it there retained its legal authority long after it had
become obsolete elsewhere.   The Assises de Jerusalem were in
force in the Venetian colonies until the sixteenth century, and
the manuscript preserved officially in the archives of Venice,
described by Morelli as written in 1436, retains the primitive

[1] Raine's Church of York (English Historical Review, No. 9, p. 159).
[2] Legg. Scan. Provin. Lib. v. c. 57 (Ed. Thorsen, pp. 139–40).

directions for the employment of the *juise*.[1] Even the Venetian translation, commenced in 1531, and finished in 1536, is equally scrupulous, although an act of the Council of Ten, April 10, 1535, shows that these customs had fallen into desuetude and had been formally abolished.[2] In Hungary, the judicial records of Waradin from 1209 to 1235 contain 389 judgments, of which a large part were determined by the hot-iron ordeal.[3]

This ordeal even became partially naturalized among the Greeks, probably as a result of the Latin domination at Constantinople. In the middle of the thirteenth century, the Emperor Theodore Lascaris demanded that Michael Paleologus, who afterwards wore the imperial crown, should clear himself of an accusation in this manner; but the Archbishop of Philadelphia, on being appealed to, pronounced that it was a custom of the barbarians, condemned by the canons, and not to be employed except by the special order of the emperor.[4] Yet George Pachymere speaks of the custom as one not uncommon in his youth, and he describes at some length the ceremonies with which it was performed.[5]

In Europe, even as late as 1310, in the proceedings against the Order of the Templars, at Mainz, Count Frederic, the master preceptor of the Rhenish provinces, offered to substantiate his denial of the accusations by carrying the red-hot iron.[6] In Modena in 1329, in a dispute between the German soldiers of Louis of Bavaria and the citizens, the Germans offered to settle the question by carrying a red-hot bar; but when the townsfolks themselves accomplished the feat, and

---

[1] This text is given by Kausler, Stuttgard, 1839, together with an older one compiled for the lower court of Nicosia.

[2] Pardessus, Us et Coutumes de la Mer, I. 268 sqq.

[3] Patetta, Le Ordalie, p. 475.

[4] Du Cange, s. v. *Ferrum Candens.*

[5] Pachymeri Hist. Mich. Palæol. Lib. I. cap. xii.

[6] Raynouard, Monuments relatifs à la Condamn. des Chev. du Temple, p. 269.

triumphantly showed that no burn had been inflicted, the Germans denied the proof, and asserted that magic had been employed.[1]

Though about this time it may be considered to have disappeared from the ordinary proceedings of the secular courts, there was one class of cases in which its vitality still continued for a century and a half.   The mysterious crime of witchcraft was so difficult of proof that judicial ingenuity was taxed to its utmost to secure conviction, and the Devil was always ready to aid his followers and baffle the ends of justice.   The Inquisitor Sprenger, writing in 1487, therefore recommends that, when a witch cannot be forced to confess her guilt by either prayers or torture, she shall be asked whether she will undergo the ordeal of red-hot iron; to this she will eagerly assent, knowing that she can rely on the friendly assistance of Satan to carry her through it unscathed, and this readiness will be good evidence of her guilt.   He warns inexperienced judges moreover not to allow the trial to take place, and thus afford to Satan the opportunity of triumph, and instances a case which occurred in 1484 before the Count of Furstenberg. A well-known witch was arrested and tried, but no confession could be extorted from her by all the refinements of torture. Finally she offered to prove her innocence with the red-hot iron, and the Count being young and unwary accepted the proposal, sentencing her to carry it three paces.   She carried it for six paces and offered to hold it still longer, exhibiting her hand uninjured.   The Count was forced to acquit her, and at the time that Sprenger wrote she was still living, to the scandal of the faithful.[2]

After the judicial use of the red-hot iron had at last died out, the superstition on which it was based still lingered, and men believed that God would reverse the laws of nature to

---

[1] Bonif. de Morano Chron. Mutinense. (Muratori Antiq. Ital. Diss. 38).

[2] Malleus Maleficar. Francof. 1580, pp. 523–31.

accomplish a special object. About 1670 Georg Frese, a merchant of Hamburg, distinguished for piety and probity, published an account, the truth of which was vouched for by many respectable eye-witnesses, stating that a friend of his named Witzendorff, who had bound himself to a young woman by terrible oaths, and then had proved false and caused her death, fell into a despairing melancholy. He accused himself of the sin against the Holy Ghost, declared that his salvation was impossible, and refused to hope unless he could see a miracle wrought in his behalf. Frese at length asked him what miracle he required, and on his replying that he must see that fire would not burn, the intrepid consoler went to a blazing fire, picked out the burning coals and also a red-hot ring, which he brought to the sinner with uninjured hands and convinced him that he could be saved by repentance. The moral drawn from the facts by the narrator to whom we owe them, is that he who under Divine influence undertakes such ordeals will be preserved unharmed.[1]

Even as we have seen that Heaven sometimes interposed to punish the guilty by a reversal of the hot-water ordeal, so the industrious belief of the Middle Ages found similar miracles in the hot-iron trial, especially when Satan or some other mysterious influence nullified the appeal to God. Early in the thirteenth century a case is related in which a peasant to revenge himself on a neighbor employed a vagabond monk to burn the house of the latter. The hot-iron ordeal was vainly employed on all suspected of the crime; the house was rebuilt, the monk again bribed, burnt it a second time, and again the ordeal proved vain. The owner again rebuilt his house, and kept in it the ordeal-iron, ready for use. The monk, tempted

---

[1] P. Burgmeister, who relates this in his thesis for the Doctorate (De Probat. per aquam, &c. Ulmæ, 1680), vigorously maintains the truth of the miracle against the assaults of a Catholic controversialist who impugned its authenticity. The affair seems to have attracted considerable attention at the time, as a religious question between the old Church and the Lutherans.

with fresh promises, paid him another visit, and was hospitably received as before, when seeing the piece of iron, his curiosity was aroused and he asked what it was. The host handed it to him, explaining its use, but as soon as the wretch took it, it burned him to the bone, when the other seeing in him the incendiary, seized him; he was duly tried, confessed his guilt, and was broken on the wheel.[1] A variant of this story relates how a man accused of arson offered to prove his innocence by the red-hot iron, which he carried for a long distance and then showed his hand uninjured. The ordeal-iron mysteriously vanished and could not be found, until a year afterwards, when a laborer who was mending the highway came upon it under a layer of sand. It was still glowing fiercely, and when he attempted to pick it up, it burnt him severely. The bystanders at once suspected him of the crime, and on the appropriate means being taken he was forced to confess his guilt, which was duly punished by the wheel.[2] A less tragical example of the same form of miracle was that wrought by the holy Suidger, Bishop of Munster, who suspected his chamberlain of the theft of a cup. As the man stoutly denied his guilt, Suidger ordered him to pick up a knife from the table, after he had mentally exorcised it. The cold metal burnt the culprit's hand as though it had been red-hot, and he promptly confessed his crime.[3]

[1] Cæsar. Heisterb. Dial. Mirac. Dist. x. c. xxxvi.

[2] Godelmanni de Magis Lib. III. cap. v. § 19.

[3] Annalista Saxo ann. 993.

CHAPTER IV.

THE ORDEAL OF FIRE.

THE ordeal of fire, administered directly, without the intervention either of water or of iron, is one of the most ancient
forms, as is shown by the allusions to it in both the Hindu
Vedic writings, the adventure of Siawush, and the passage in
the Antigone of Sophocles (pp. 266, 267, 270). In this, its
simplest form, it may be considered the origin of the proverbial expression, "J'en mettrois la main au feu," as an
affirmation of positive belief,[1] showing how thoroughly the
whole system engrained itself in the popular mind. In
India, as practised in modern times, its form approaches
somewhat the ordeal of the burning ploughshares. A trench
is dug nine hands in length, two spans in breadth, and one
span in depth. This is filled with peepul wood, which is then
set on fire, and the accused walks into it with bare feet.[2] A
more humane modification is described in the seventh century
by Hiouen-Thsang as in use when the accused was too tender
to undergo the trial by red-hot iron. He simply cast into
the flames certain flower-buds, when, if they opened their
leaves, he was acquitted; if they were burnt up, he was condemned.[3]

An anticipation of the fire ordeal may be found in the Rab-
binical story of Abraham when he was cast into a fiery fur-

---

[1] Thus Rabelais, "en mon aduiz elle est pucelle, toutesfoys ie nen vould-
roys mettre mon doigt on feu" (Pantagruel, Liv. II. chap. xv.); and the
Epist. Obscur. Virorum (P. II. Epist. 1) " Quamvis M. Bernhardus diceret,
quod vellet disputare ad ignem quod hæc est opinio vestra."

[2] Ali Ibrahim Khan (Asiatic Researches, I. 390).

[3] Wheeler's Hist. of India, III. 262.

nace by Nimrod, for reproving the idolatry of the latter, and escaped unharmed from the flames ;[1] as well as the similar experience of Shadrach, Mesach, and Abednego, when they were saved from the wrath of Nebuchadnezzar.[2] Miraculous interposition of this kind was expected as a matter of course by the early Christians. About the year 400 Rufinus, in his account of his visit to the monks of the Nitrian desert, tells an adventure of the hermit Copres as related to him by that holy man himself. On visiting a neighboring city he engaged in a disputation with a Manichæan who was perverting the people. Finding the heretic not easily overcome by argument, he proposed that a fire should be built in the public square, into which both should enter. The populace was delighted with the idea and speedily had a roaring pyre ready, when the Manichæan insisted that the Christian should enter first. Copres assented and remained unhurt in the flames for half an hour; his antagonist still held back, when the crowd seized him and tossed him into the fire, where he was severely scorched, and was ejected with disgrace from the city.[3] Almost identical is the story related in 597 A. D., under the Emperor Anastasius, of a Catholic bishop, who, after being worsted in a theological dispute by the subtle logic of an Arian, offered to test the soundness of their respective doctrines by together entering a blazing fire. The prudent Arian declined the proposition, when the enthusiastic Catholic jumped into the burning pile, and thence continued the controversy without suffering the least inconvenience.[4] In the less impressive form of filling the lap with burning coals and carrying them uninjured till they grew cold this ordeal seems to have been a favorite with holy men accused of unchastity. It is related of St. Brice, the successor of St. Martin in the

---

[1] Targum of Palestine, Gen. xi. (Etheridge's Translation, I. 191-2).— Shalshelet Hakkabala fol. 8a. (Wagenseilii Sota p. 192-3).

[2] Daniel, iii. 19-28.

[3] Rufini Historia Monachorum cap. ix.

[4] Theodori Lector. H. E. Lib. II.

see of Tours, of St. Simplicius of Autun, and of Montano bishop of Toledo in the sixth century.[1]

The earliest legal allusion to this form of ordeal in Europe occurs in the code of the Ripuarian Franks, where it is prescribed as applicable to slaves and strangers, in some cases of doubt.[2] From the phraseology of these passages, we may conclude that it was then administered by placing the hand of the accused in a fire. As a legal ordeal this is perhaps the only allusion to it in European jurisprudence, but it was repeatedly resorted to by enthusiasts as a voluntary trial for the purpose of establishing the truth of accusations or of substantiating their position. In these cases it was conducted on a larger and more impressive scale; huge pyres were built, and the individual undergoing the trial literally walked through the flames, as Siawush did. The celebrated Petrus Igneus gained his surname and reputation by an exploit of this kind, which was renowned in its day. Pietro di Pavia, Bishop of Florence, unpopular with the citizens, but protected by Godfrey, Duke of Tuscany, was accused of simony and heresy. Being acquitted by the Council of Rome, in 1063, and the offér of his accusers to prove his guilt by the ordeal of fire being refused, he endeavored to put down his adversaries by tyranny and oppression. Great disturbances resulted, and at length, in 1067, the monks of Vallombrosa, who had borne a leading part in denouncing the bishop, and who had suffered severely in consequence (the episcopal troops having burned the monastery of St. Salvio and slaughtered the cenobites), resolved to decide the question by the ordeal, incited thereto by no less than three thousand enthusiastic Florentines who assembled there for the purpose. Pietro Aldobrandini, a monk of Vallombrosa, urged by his superior, the holy S. Giovanni Gualberto, offered himself to undergo the trial. After im-

[1] Greg. Turon. Hist. Francor. II. 1.—Ejusd. de Gloria Confess. 76.—S. Hildefonsi Toletani Lib. de Viris Illustribus c. iii.

[2] Quodsi servus in ignem manum miserit, et læsam tulerit, etc.—Tit. xxx. cap. i.; also Tit. xxxi.

posing religious ceremonies, he walked slowly between two
piles of blazing wood, ten feet long, five feet wide, and four
and a half feet high, the passage between them being six feet
wide and covered with an inch or two of glowing coals. The
violence of the flames agitated his dress and hair, but he
emerged without hurt, even the hair on his legs being unsinged,
barelegged and barefooted though he was. Desiring to return
through the pyre, he was prevented by the admiring crowd,
who rushed around him in triumph, kissing his feet and garments, and endangering his life in their transports, until he
was rescued by his fellow monks. A formal statement of the
facts was sent to Rome by the Florentines, the papal court
gave way, and the bishop was deposed; while the monk who
had given so striking a proof of his steadfast faith was marked
for promotion, and eventually died Cardinal of Albano.[1]

An example of a similar nature occurred in Milan in 1103,
when the Archbishop Grossolano was accused of simony by
a priest named Liutprand, who, having no proof to sustain
his charge, offered the ordeal of fire. All the money he could
raise he expended in procuring fuel, and when all was ready
the partisans of the archbishop attacked the preparations and
carried off the wood. The populace, deprived of the promised
exhibition, grew turbulent, and Grossolano was obliged not
only to assent to the trial, but to join the authorities in providing the necessary materials. In the Piazza di S. Ambrogio
two piles were accordingly built, each ten cubits long, by four
cubits in height and width, with a gangway between them of
a cubit and a half. As the undaunted priest entered the
blazing mass, the flames divided before him and closed as he
passed, allowing him to emerge in safety, although with two
slight injuries, one a burn on the hand, received while sprink-
ling the fire before entering, the other on the foot, which he
attributed to a kick from a horse in the crowd that awaited his

[1] Vit. S. Johannis Gualberti c. lx.–lxiv.—Berthold. Constantiens. Annal.
ann. 1078.

exit. The evidence was accepted as conclusive by the people, and Grossolano was obliged to retire to Rome. Pascal II., however, received him graciously, and the Milanese suffragans disapproved of the summary conviction of their metropolitan, to which they were probably all equally liable. The injuries received by Liutprand were exaggerated, a tumult was excited in Milan, the priest was obliged to seek safety in flight, and Grossolano was restored for a time, but the adverse party prevailed and in spite of papal support he was forced to exile.[1]

A volunteer miracle of somewhat the same character, which is recorded as occurring in Paris early in the thirteenth century, may be alluded to as illustrating the belief of the period. A loose woman in the household of a great noble was luring the youthful retainers to sin, when the chaplain remonstrated with his master, and threatened to depart unless she was removed. When she was taxed with her guilt she defended herself by saying that the priest had accused her because she had refused his importunities, and offered to prove it. Approaching him as a penitent, she sought to seduce his virtue, finally threatening to kill herself unless he would gratify her despairing love, until, to prevent her suicide, he finally made an appointment with her. Secretly announcing her triumph to the noble, she went to the place of meeting, where she found the chaplain mounted on a bed of plank, surrounded by straw and dry wood, to which he set fire on her appearance, and invited her to join him. Covered by the flames, the sinless man felt nothing but a cool, refreshing breeze, and when the pile had burnt out, he emerged unhurt, even his garments and hair being untouched.[2]

But the experiment was not always so successful for the rash enthusiast. In 1098, during the first crusade, after the cap-

---

[1] Landulph. Jun. Hist. Mediol. cap. ix. x. xi. (Rer Ital. Script. T. V.).—Muratori, Annal. Ann. 1103, 1105.

[2] Cæsar. Heisterb. Dial. Mirac. Dist. x. c. xxxiv.—The same incident is related of St. Francis of Assisi (Vita et Admiranda Historia Seraphici S. P. Francisci, Augsburg, 1694, xxiii.).

ture of Antioch, when the Christians were in turn besieged in that city, and, sorely pressed and famine-struck, were well-nigh reduced to despair, an ignorant peasant named Peter Bartholomew, a follower of Raymond of Toulouse, announced a series of visions in which St. Andrew and the Saviour had revealed to him that the lance which pierced the side of Christ lay hidden in the church of St. Peter. After several men had dug in the spot indicated, from morning until night, without success, Peter leaped into the trench, and by a few well-directed strokes of his mattock exhumed the priceless relic, which he presented to Count Raymond. Cheered by this, and by various other manifestations of Divine assistance, the Christians gained heart, and defeated the Infidels with immense slaughter. Peter became a man of mark, and had fresh visions on all important conjunctures. Amid the jealousies and dissensions which raged among the Frankish chiefs, the possession of the holy lance vastly increased Raymond's importance, and rival princes were found to assert that it was merely a rusty Arab weapon, hidden for the occasion, and wholly undeserving the veneration of which it was the object. At length, after some months, during the leisure of the siege of Archas, the principal ecclesiastics in the camp investigated the matter, and Peter, to silence the doubts expressed as to his veracity, offered to vindicate the identity of the relic by the fiery ordeal. He was taken at his word, and after three days allowed for fasting and prayer, a pile of dry olive-branches was made, fourteen feet long and four feet high, with a passage-way one foot wide. In the presence of forty thousand men all eagerly awaiting the result, Peter, bearing the object in dispute, and clothed only in a tunic, boldly rushed through the flames, amid the anxious prayers and adjurations of the multitude. As the chroniclers lean to the side of the Neapolitan Princes or of the Count of Toulouse, so do their accounts of the event differ; the former asserting that Peter sustained mortal injury in the fire; the latter assuring us that he emerged safely, with but one or two slight burns, and that the crowd enthusiastically pressing around him in triumph, he was thrown down, trampled on, and injured so severely that he died in a few days, asseverating with his latest breath the truth of his revelations. Raymond persisted in upholding the sanctity of his relic, but it was subsequently lost.[1]

Even after the efforts of Innocent III. to abolish the ordeal, and while the canons of the Council of Lateran were still fresh, St. Francis of Assisi, in 1219, offered himself to the flames for the propagation of the faith. In his missionary trip to the East, finding the Soldan deaf to his proselyting eloquence, he proposed to test the truth of their respective religions by entering a blazing pile in company with some imams, who naturally declined the perilous experiment. Nothing daunted, the enthusiastic saint then said that he would traverse the flames alone if the Soldan would bind himself, in the event of a triumphant result, to embrace the Christian religion and to force his subjects to follow the example. The Turk, more wary than the Dane whom Poppo converted, declined the

---

1 Fulcher. Carnot. cap. x.; Radulf. Cadomensis cap. c. ci. cii. cviii.; Raimond. de Agiles (Bongars, I. 150–168). The latter was chaplain of the Count of Toulouse, and a firm asserter of the authenticity of the lance. He relates with pride, that on its discovery he threw himself into the trench and kissed it while the point only had as yet been uncovered. He officiated likewise in the ordeal, and delivered the adjuration as Peter entered the flames: " Si Deus omnipotens huic homini loquutus est facie ad faciem, et beatus Andreas Lanceam Dominicam ostendit ei, cum ipse vigilaret, transeat iste illæsus per ignem. Sin autem aliter est, et mendacium est, comburatur iste cum lancea quam portabit in manibus suis." Raoul de Caen, on the other hand, in 1107 became secretary to the chivalrous Tancred, and thus obtained his information from the opposite party. He is very decided in his animadversions on the discoverers. Foulcher de Chartres was chaplain to Baldwin I. of Jerusalem, and seems impartial, though sceptical.

The impression made by the incident on the popular mind is manifested in the fact that the Nürnberg Chronicle (fol. cxcv.) gives a veritable representation of the lance-head.

proposition, and St. Francis returned from his useless voyage unharmed.[1]

In this St. Francis endeavored unsuccessfully to emulate the glorious achievement of Boniface, the Apostle of Russia, who, according to the current martyrologies, converted the King of Russia to the true faith by means of such a bargain and ordeal.[2] It is a little curious that Peter Cantor, in his diatribe against the judgment of God, presents the supposition of a trial such as this as an unanswerable argument against the system—the Church, he says, could not assent to such an experiment, and therefore it ought not to be trusted in affairs of less magnitude.[3]

Somewhat irregular as a judicial proceeding, but yet illustrating the general belief in the principles of the ordeal of fire, was an occurrence related about the year 1220 by Cæsarius of Heisterbach as having taken place a few years before in Arras. An ecclesiastic of good repute decoyed a goldsmith into his house, and murdered him to obtain possession of some valuables, cutting up the body, with the assistance of a younger sister, and hiding the members in a drain. The crime was proved upon them, and both were condemned to the stake. On the way to the place of punishment, the girl demanded a confessor, and confessed her sins with full contrition, but the brother was obdurate and impenitent. Both were tied to the same stake; the brother was promptly reduced to ashes, while the flames were deliciously cool to the sister, and only burnt the rope with which she was tied, so that she quietly walked down from the pile. The judges, thus convinced of her innocence, dismissed her without further trouble.[4]

From every point of view, however, both as to date and as to consequences, the most remarkable recourse to the fire ordeal was that which proved to be the proximate cause of the

---

[1] Raynaldi Annal. Eccles. ann. 1219, c. 56.

[2] Martyrol. Roman. 19 Jun.—Petri Damian. Vit. S. Romualdi c. 27.

[3] Petri Cantor. Verb. Abbreviat. cap. lxxviii. (Patrol. CCV. 229).

[4] Cæsar. Heisterbach. Dial. Mirac. Dist. III. c. xv.

downfall of Savonarola. Long after the ordeal system had been superseded in European jurisprudence, and occurring in the centre of the New Learning, it was a most noteworthy illustration of the superstition which formed a common bond between sceptics and religious enthusiasts. In 1498 Savonarola had been silenced by command of Alexander III., his influence with the people was waning, and his faithful follower Fra Domenico da Pescia was desperately struggling in the pulpit to maintain the cause against the assaults of the Franciscans led by the eloquent Fra Francesco della Puglia. Domenico in a sermon offered to prove the truth of his leader's utterances by throwing himself from the roof of the Palazzo de' Signori, by casting himself in the river, or by entering fire. This burst of rhetoric might have passed unheeded had not Fra Francesco taken it up and offered to share the ordeal with Savonarola himself. Savonarola declined, except under impossible conditions, but Domenico accepted the challenge and affixed to the portal of Santa Croce a paper in which he offered to prove by argument or miracle the truth of sundry propositions bearing upon his teacher's mission. To this Fra Francesco replied that he would enter fire with Fra Domenico ; that he fully expected to be burnt, but that he would willingly suffer if he could disabuse the people of their false idol. Popular excitement rose to such a height that the Signoria sent for both disputants, and made them sign a written agreement to undergo the ordeal. In this Fra Francesco wisely provided that, although he was willing to enter fire with Savonarola himself, if Domenico was to act he would only produce a champion, who was readily found in the person of Fra Giuliano Rondinelli. On the side of the Dominicans the enthusiasm was so great that all the friars of Savonarola's convent of San Marco, nearly three hundred in number, eagerly signed a pledge to submit to the ordeal, and he assured them that in such a cause they could do so without danger. In fact, when, on the day before the trial, he preached on the subject in San Marco, the whole audience rose as one man and offered to take Domenico's place.

April 7th was the day fixed for the *Sperimento del Fuoco*. In the Piazza de' Signori a huge pile of wood, plentifully reinforced with gunpowder, sulphur, oil, and spirits, was built with a gangway through which the champions were to pass ; it was to be lighted at one end, and after they entered fire was to be set at the other to preclude retreat. All Florence assembled to witness the spectacle, and patiently endured the peltings of a terrible storm. The day was spent, however, in wrangling over questions skilfully raised by the Franciscans, the chief one being whether Fra Domenico should carry in his hand a consecrated host. It had been revealed to one of his brethren that this was indispensable, and Savonarola adhered to it firmly. When evening came the Signoria announced that the ordeal was abandoned. The crowd was enraged at the loss of the promised exhibition ; the Dominicans had so confidently promised a miracle that the drawn battle was universally regarded as their defeat, an armed guard was required to protect their return to their convent, and Savonarola's power over the Florentine populace was gone. His enemies lost no time in pushing their advantage. The next evening the mob assailed San Marco ; he was seized and conveyed to prison, and after prolonged and repeated tortures he was hanged and burnt on May 23d.[1]

It will be observed that the ordeal of fire was principally affected by ecclesiastics in church affairs, perhaps because it was of a nature to produce a powerful impression on the spectators, while at the same time it could no doubt in many instances be so managed as to secure the desired results by those who controlled the details. In like manner, it was occasionally employed on inanimate matter to decide points

---

[1] Luca Landucci, Diario Fiorentino, pp. 166–9.—Burlamacchi, Vita di Savonarola (Baluz. et Mansi I. 559–63).—Processo Autentico (Baluz. et Mansi I. 535–42.—Villari, Storia di Gir. Savonarola, II. App. lxxi. lxxv. lxxx. lxxxiii. xc.–xciii.— Diarium Burchardi ann. 1498.—Guicciardini, III. vi.

of faith or polity. Thus, in the question which excited great commotion in Spain, in 1077, as to the substitution of the Roman for the Gothic or Mozarabic rite, after a judicial combat had been fought and determined in favor of the national ritual, the partisans of the Roman offices continued to urge their cause, and the ordeal of fire was appealed to. A missal of each kind was committed to the flames, and, to the great joy of all patriotic Castilians, the Gothic offices were unconsumed.[1] More satisfactory to the orthodox was the result of a similar ordeal during the efforts of St. Dominic to convert the Albigenses. In a dispute with some heretics he wrote out his argument on the points of faith, and gave it to them for examination and reply. That night, as they were seated around the hearth, the paper was produced and read, when one of them proposed that it should be cast into the flames, when, if it remained unconsumed, they would see that its contents were true. This was promptly done, when the saintly document was unharmed. One, more obstinate than the rest, asked for a second and then for a third trial, with the same result. The perverse heretics, however, closed their hearts against the truth, and bound themselves by oath to keep the affair secret; and so glorious a victory for the true faith would have remained unknown but for the indiscretion of one of them, a knight, who had a covert inclination towards orthodoxy.[2] A somewhat similar instance occurred in Constantinople as late as the close of the thirteenth century, when Andronicus II., on his accession, found the city torn into factions relative to the patriarchate, arising from the expulsion of Arsenius, a former patriarch. All attempts to soothe the dissensions proving vain, at length both parties agreed to write out their respective statements and arguments, and, committing both books to the flames, to abide by the result, each side hoping that its manuscript would be preserved by

---

[1] Roderici Toletani de Reb. Hispan. VI. xxvi. (see ante p. 132).
[2] Pet. Val. Cernaii Hist. Albigens. cap. III.

the special interposition of Heaven. The ceremony was conducted with imposing state, and, to the general surprise, both
books were reduced to ashes. Singularly enough, all parties
united in the sensible conclusion that God had thereby commanded them to forget their differences and to live in peace.[1]

About the same period as this last example, Samaritan
tradition related that the comparative claims of Mt. Gerizim
and Al-Qods (Jerusalem) as the sole seats of Yahveh-worship
were settled before Nebuchadnezzar, by the ordeal of fire,
applied respectively to the Pentateuch and to the later books
of the Jewish canon, Sanballat appearing for Ephraim, and
Zerubbabel for Judah. The later books were promptly consumed, but the law of Moses emerged twice from the flames
unhurt. Zerubbabel, in despair, then spat upon some pages of
the index, and cast the Law a third time into the fire, when
the leaves thus polluted were burnt, but the book itself leaped
unscathed into the bosom of the king, who promptly slew the
representatives of Judah, and gave an unhesitating verdict in
favor of the Samaritans.[2]

The genuineness of relics was often tested in this manner
by exposing them to the action of fire. This custom, like the
ordeal itself as a judicial process, finds its original home in
the East. When, for instance, the sacred tooth-relic of
Buddha was carried to the court of King Pandu at Patali-
putta, and its holiness was questioned by the Niganthas, or
worshippers of Siva, they tested it by casting it into a pit
filled with glowing charcoal " bright and horrid as the hell
Roruva"—when the tooth, in place of being consumed to
ashes, rose out of the fiery mass resting on a lotus the size of
a chariot-wheel.[3] Even Roman unbelief accepted a similar
faith respecting the superfluous thumb which ornamented the
right foot of King Pyrrhus, the touch of which cured diseases

---

[1] Niceph. Gregor. Lib. VI.

[2] Chron. Samaritan. c. xlv. (Ed. Juynboll, Lug. Bat. 1848, p. 183).

[3] Dathavansa, chap. III. 11–13 (Sir M. Coomara Swamy's Translation,
London, 1874).

of the spleen, and which remained unharmed on the funeral pyre which consumed the rest of his body to ashes. The indestructible supplementary member was thereupon inclosed in a casket, and reverently placed in a temple—the first relic, probably, on record in the western world.[1] At how early an age Christianity adopted the belief which led to this is manifested by the story of the swaddling-cloth of Christ in one of the apocryphal Gospels. The Virgin, being unable, on account of poverty, to make a return for the offerings of the Magi who came to worship the infant Saviour, presented them with one of his swaddling-bands. On their return they placed it in the sacred fire of their altar, and though the flames eagerly embraced it, they left it unharmed and unaltered, whereupon the Magi venerated it, and laid it away among their treasures.[2] On the conversion of the Spanish Arians the experiment was tried on a larger scale. It seems that doubts were felt by the orthodox as to the relics preserved in their churches, and a general regulation was adopted by the Council of Saragossa in 592 that they should be all brought before the bishops and tested by fire—with what result is not recorded.[3]

In such cases the ceremony of the ordeal was conducted with appropriate religious services, including the following prayer, which would seem to show that in its regular form it was not the relic itself, but the cloth in which it was wrapped that was exposed to the test—

Lord Jesus Christ, who art king of kings and lord of lords, and lover of all believers in thee, who art a just judge, strong and powerful, who hast revealed thy holy mysteries to thy priests, and who didst mitigate the flames to the Three Children; concede to us thy unworthy servants and grant our prayers that this cloth or this thread in which are wrapped those bodies of saints, if they are not genuine let them be burned by this fire, and if they are genuine let them escape, so that iniquity shall not prevail over injustice but falsehood shall

---

[1] Plinii Hist. Natur. L. VII. c. ii.

[2] Gospel of the Infancy, III.

[3] Concil. Cæsar-August. II. ann. 592 c. 2.

succumb to truth, so that thy truth shall be declared to thee and be manifested to us, believers in thee, that we may know thee to be the blessed God in ages everlasting.   Amen.[1]

Numerous instances of this superiority of relics to fire are narrated by the pious chroniclers of the middle ages.   In 1015 some monastic pilgrims, hospitably received at Monte Cassino on their return from Jerusalem, offered at the shrine of St. Benedict a fragment of the towel with which the Saviour had washed the feet of his disciples.   Some of the monks, being incredulous, placed it on burning coals, when it turned fiery red, but, on being removed, returned to its original color, and all doubts as to its authenticity were dispelled.[2] When, in 1065, the pious Egelwin, Bishop of Durham, miraculously discovered the relics of the holy martyr King Oswyn, he gave the hair to Judith, wife of Tosti, Earl of Northumberland, and she with all reverence placed it on a raging fire, whence it was withdrawn, not only uninjured, but marvellously increased in lustre, to the great edification of all beholders.[3]   A similar miracle attested the sanctity of King Olaf the Saint, of Norway, when his hair was laid on a pan of live coals, consecrated by Bishop Grimkel, to satisfy the incredulity of Queen Alfifa.[4]   Guibert de Nogent likewise relates that, when his native town became honored with the possession of an arm of St. Arnoul, the inhabitants, at first doubting the genuineness of the precious relic, cast it into the flames; when it vindicated its sanctity, not only by being fireproof, but also by leaping briskly away from the coals, testimony which was held to be incontrovertible.[5]   The historian of the monastery of Andres informs us that when in 1084 the long-lost remains of the holy virgin Rotruda were miraculously found, and Baldwin I., Count of Guisnes, desired to take the

---

[1] Martene de Antiquis Ecclesiæ Ritibus Lib. III. c. viii. ¿ 2.

[2] Chron. Casinensis Lib. II. c. xxxiv.

[3] Matthew of Westminster, ann. 1065.

[4] Olaf Haraldss. Saga, ch. 258 (Laing's Heimskringla, II. 349).

[5] Guibert. Noviogent. de Vita sua Lib. III. cap. xxi.

sacred treasure to his town of Guisnes, it refused to be removed until he proposed to place it on a wagon and allow a team of oxen to be divinely guided to the spot where the saint desired to rest. This was accordingly done, and the oxen carried the relics to a little chapel dedicated to St. Medard, where steps were immediately taken to found an abbey. The Seigneur of Andres, however, Baldwin Bochard, on whose lands the chapel lay, foreseeing that a powerful monastery would be a troublesome neighbor, and being an irreligious man, circulated defamatory libels impugning the authenticity of the relics, and finally pursuaded Count Baldwin to have them tested by the ordeal of fire. This was accordingly done, and the genuineness of the holy remains was proved to the satisfaction of all. Bochard and his descendants continued inveterately hostile to St. Rotruda and her monks, but all, without exception, were compelled, upon their death-beds, to contribute a portion of their substance to her honor.[1] The custom continued even until the sixteenth century was well advanced. In the Jeronymite monastery of Valdebran in Catalonia, a piece of the true cross bears inscription that its genuineness was tested with fire by Archbishop Miralles on October 2, 1530.[2]

The persistency of popular belief in this method of ascertaining guilt or innocence is seen as recently as 1811, when a Neapolitan noble, suspecting the chastity of his daughter, exposed her to the ordeal of fire, from which she barely escaped with her life.[3]

---

[1] Chron. Andrensis Monast. (D'Achery Spicileg. II. 782).

[2] Villanueva, Viage Literario, T. XIX. p. 42.

[3] Patetta, Le Ordalie, p. 34.

CHAPTER V.

THE ORDEAL OF COLD WATER.

THE cold-water ordeal (*judicium aquæ frigidæ*) differed from most of its congeners in requiring a miracle to convict the accused, as in the natural order of things he escaped. The preliminary solemnities, fasting, prayer, and religious rites, were similar to those already described; holy water sometimes was given to the accused to drink; the reservoir of water, or pond, was then exorcised with formulas exhibiting the same combination of faith and impiety, and the accused, bound with cords, was slowly lowered into it with a rope, to prevent fraud if guilty, and to save him from drowning if innocent.[1] According to Anglo-Saxon rule, the length of rope allowed under water was an ell and a half;[2] in one ritual it is directed that a knot be made in the rope at a distance of a long hair from the body of the accused, and if he sinks so as to bring the knot down to the surface of the water, he is cleared;[3] but in process of time nice questions arose as to the precise amount of submergence requisite for acquittal. Towards the close of the twelfth century we find that some learned doctors insisted that sinking to the very bottom of the water was indispensable; others decided that if the whole person were submerged it was sufficient; while others again reasoned that

---

[1] Hincmar. de Divort. Lothar. Interrog. vi.   It may readily be supposed that a skilful management of the rope might easily produce the appearance of floating, when a conviction was desired by the priestly operators.

[2] L. Æthelstani I. cap. xxiii.

[3] Martene de Antiq. Eccles. Ritibus Lib. III. c. vii. Ordo 8.

as the hair was an accident or excrement of the body, it had the privilege of floating without convicting its owner, if the rest of the body was satisfactorily covered.[1]

The basis of this ordeal was the belief, handed down from the primitive Aryans, that the pure element would not receive into its bosom any one stained with the crime of a false oath, another form of which is seen in the ancient superstition that the earth would eject the corpse of a criminal, and not allow it to remain quietly interred. The manner in which the church reconciled it to orthodoxy is clearly set forth by Hincmar : "He who seeks to conceal the truth by a lie will not sink in the waters over which the voice of the Lord hath thundered ; for the pure nature of water recognizes as impure, and rejects as incompatible, human nature which, released from falsehood by the waters of baptism, becomes again infected with untruth."[2] The baptism in the Jordan, the passage of the Red Sea, and the crowning judgment of the Deluge, were freely adduced in support of this theory, though these latter were in direct contradiction to it ; and the most figurative language was boldly employed to give some show of probability to the results expected. Thus, in the elaborate formula which passes under the name of St. Dunstan, the prayer offered over the water metaphorically adjures the Supreme Being—"Let not the water receive the body of him who, released from the weight of goodness, is upborne by the wind of iniquity!"[3]

In India the ordeal of cold water became simply one of endurance. The stream or pond was exorcised with the customary Mantras :—

"Thou O water dwellest in the interior of all things like a witness. O water thou knowest what mortals do not comprehend.

"This man being arraigned in a cause desires to be cleared

---

[1] Petri Cantor. Verb. Abbreviat. cap. lxxviii. (Patrol. CCV. 233).

[2] De Divort. Lothar. Interrog. vi.

[3] Ordo S. Dunstani Dorobern. (Baluze II. 650).

from guilt. Therefore mayest thou deliver him lawfully from this perplexity."

The patient stood in water up to his middle, facing the East, caught hold of the thighs of a man "free from friendship or hatred" and dived under, while simultaneously an arrow of reed without a head was shot from a bow, 106 fingers' breadth in length, and if he could remain under water until the arrow was picked up and brought back, he gained his cause, but if any portion of him could be seen above the surface he was condemned. Yajnavalkya says this form of ordeal was only used on the Sudras, or lowest caste, while the Ayeen Akbery speaks of it as confined to the Vaisyas, or caste of husbandmen and merchants. According to the Institutes of Vishnu, it was not to be administered to the timid or those affected with lung diseases, nor to those who gained their living by the water, such as fishermen or boatmen, nor was it allowed during the winter.[1]

Although, as we have seen (p. 268), the original cold-water ordeal in India, as described by Manu, was precisely similar to the European form, inasmuch as the guilty were expected to float and the innocent to sink, and although in this shape it prevailed everywhere throughout Europe, and its tenacity of existence rendered it the last to disappear in the progress of civilization, yet it does not make its appearance in any of the earlier codes of the Barbarians. The first allusions to it occur in the ninth century, and it was then so generally regarded as a novelty that documents almost contemporaneous ascribe its invention to the popes of that period. One story is that when

---

[1] Institutes of Vishnu IX. 29-30, XII.—Yajnavalkya II. 98, 108-9.—Ayeen Akbery, II. 497.—Some unimportant variations in details are given by Ali Ibrahim Khan (As. Researches, I. 390). Hiouen Thsang describes a variant of this ordeal in which the accused was fastened into one sack and a stone in another; the sacks were then tied together and cast into a river, when if the man sank and the stone rose he was convicted, while if he rose and the stone sank he was acquitted (Wheeler's Hist. of India, III. 262).

Leo III. fled in 799 from his rebellious subjects to Charle-magne, and returned to Rome under the latter's protection, the cold-water ordeal was introduced for the purpose of trying the rebels or recovering a treasure which they had stolen.[1] Another version asserts that Eugenius II., who occupied the pontifical throne from 824 to 827, invented it at the request of Louis le Débonnaire, for the purpose of repressing the preva-lent sin of perjury.[2] It is further worthy of note that St. Agobard, Archbishop of Lyons, in his treatises against the judg-ments of God, written a few years before the accession of Euge-nius, while enumerating and describing the various methods in use at that time, says nothing about that of cold water.[3] But for the evidence of its pre-existence in the East, we there-fore should be justified in assuming that it was an innovation invented by the Church of the ninth century. That it was a novelty is proved by the necessity felt to adduce authority for its use.[4]

At first, its revival promised to be but temporary. Only a few years after its introduction it was condemned by Louis

[1] Canciani Legg. Barbar. T. I. pp. 282-3.—Martene de Antiq. Eccles. Ritibus Lib. III. c. vii. Ord. 9, 16.

[2] Baluze II. 646.—Mabillon Analect. pp. 161-2 (ap. Cangium).—Mura-tori Antiq. Ital. Diss. 38.—Jureti Observat. ad Ivon. Epist. 74. An Ordo printed by Dr. Patetta from an early tenth century MS. (Archivio Giuridico, Vol. XLV.) mixes up Popes Eugenius and Leo, the Emperor Leo and Charlemagne in a manner to show how exceedingly vague were the notions concerning the introduction of the ordeal, " Incipit juditium aqua frigida. Quod dominus eugenius et leo imperator et episcopi vel abbati sive comiti fecerunt . . . . Similiter fecit domnus carolus imperator pro domnus leo papa, etc."

[3] Lib. adv. L. Gundobadi cap. ix.—Lib. contra Judic. Dei. c. i.

[4] Arguments for its earlier use in Europe have been drawn from certain miracles related by Gregory of Tours (Mirac. Lib. I. c. 69-70), but these relate to innocent persons unjustly condemned to drowning, who were pre-served, and therefore these cases have no bearing on the matter. The Epistle attributed by Gratian to Gregory I. (c. 7 § 1 Caus. II. q. v.), in which the cold-water ordeal is alluded to, has long since been restored to its true author, Alexander II. (Epist. 122).

le Débonnaire at the Council of Worms, in 829 ; its use was strictly prohibited, and the *missi dominici* were instructed to see that the order was carried into effect, regulations which were repeated by the Emperor Lothair, son of Louis.[1] These interdictions were of little avail. The ordeal found favor with popular superstition, and Hincmar contents himself with remarking that the imperial prohibition was not confirmed by the canons of authoritative councils.[2] The trial by cold water spread rapidly throughout Europe, and by all the continental races it was placed on an equal footing with the other forms of ordeal. Among the Anglo-Saxons, indeed, its employment has been called in question by some modern writers ; but the Dooms of Ethelstan sufficiently manifest its existence in England before the Conquest, while as late as the close of the twelfth century its use would seem to have been almost universal. The assizes of Clarendon in 1166, confirmed at Northampton in 1176, direct an inquest to be held in each shire, and all who are indicted for murder, robbery, harboring of malefactors, and other felonies are to be at once, without further trial, passed through the water ordeal to determine their guilt or innocence.[3]

As we have seen in the case of the iron ordeal, those of water, both cold and hot, were variously described as patrician or plebeian in different times and places. Thus Hincmar, in the ninth century, alludes to the water ordeals as applicable to persons of servile condition ;[4] a constitution of the Emperor St. Henry II., about A. D. 1000, in the Lombard law, has a similar bearing ;[5] in the eleventh century an Alsatian document,[6] in the twelfth Glanville's treatise on the laws of Eng-

---

[1] Capit. Wormat. ann. 829, Tit. II. cap. 12.—L. Longobard. Lib. II. Tit. lv. § 31.

[2] De Divort. Lothar. Interrog. vi.

[3] Assisa facta apud Clarendune §§ 1, 2.—Assisa apud Northamtoniam (Gesta Henrici II. T. II. p. cxlix. ; T. I. p. 108.—M. R. Series).

[4] Opusc. adv. Hincmar. Laudun. cap. xliii.

[5] L. Longobard. Lib. I. Tit. ix. § 39.

[6] Recess. Convent. Alsat. anno 1051, § 6 (Goldast. Constit. Imp. II. 48).

land,[1] and in the thirteenth the laws of Scotland[2] all assume the same position. This, however, was an innovation ; for in the earliest codes there was no such distinction, a provision in the Salic law prescribing the *æneum*, or hot-water ordeal, even for the Antrustions, who constituted the most favored class in the state.[3] Nor even in later times was the rule by any means absolute. In the tenth century, Sanche, Duke of Gascony, desirous of founding the monastery of Saint Sever, claimed some land which was necessary for the purpose, and being resisted by the possessor, the title was decided by reference to the cold-water ordeal.[4] In 1027, Welf II., Count of Altorf, ancestor of the great houses of Guelf in Italy and England, having taken part in the revolt of Conrad the Younger and Ernest of Suabia, was forced by the Emperor Conrad the Salic to prove his innocence in this manner.[5] About the same period Othlonus relates an incident in which a man of noble birth accused of theft submitted himself to the cold-water ordeal as a matter of course ;[6] while in 1068, at the Council of Vich, in Catalonia, held for the purpose of enforcing the Truce of God, all persons accused of being directly concerned in its violation are directed to be tried by the cold-water ordeal in the Church of San Pedro, without

---

[1] De Legg. Angliæ Lib. XIV. cap. i.

We have seen above (p. 292), however, that this rule was by no means invariable. In addition to the cases there adduced another may be cited when in 1177 a citizen of London who is qualified as "nobilissimus et ditissimus," accused of robbery, was tried by the water ordeal, and on being found guilty offered Henry II. five hundred marks for a pardon. The dazzling bribe was refused, and he was duly hanged.—Gesta Henrici II. T. I. p. 156.

[2] Regiam Majestatem Lib. IV. cap. iii. § 4.

[3] Text. Herold. Tit. LXXVI.

[4] Mazure et Hatoulet, Fors de Béarn, p. xxxi.

[5] Conrad. Ursperg. sub. Lothar. Saxon.

[6] Quidam illustris vir. — Othlon. de Mirac. quod nuper accidit etc. (Migne's Patrol. T. CXL. p. 242).

distinction of rank.[1] Nearly two centuries later, indeed, when all the vulgar ordeals were falling into disuse, the water ordeal was established among the nobles of Southern Germany, as the mode of deciding doubtful claims on fiefs, and in Northern Germany, for the settlement of conflicting titles to land.[2]

In 1083, during the deadly struggle between the Empire and the Papacy, as personified in Henry IV. and Hildebrand, the imperialists related with great delight that some of the leading prelates of the papal court submitted the cause of their chief to this ordeal. After a three days' fast, and proper benediction of the water, they placed in it a boy to represent the emperor, when to their horror he sank like a stone. On referring the result to Hildebrand, he ordered a repetition of the experiment, which was attended with the same result. Then, throwing him in as a representative of the pope, he obstinately floated during two trials, in spite of all efforts to force him under the surface, and an oath was exacted from all concerned to maintain inviolable secrecy as to the unexpected result.[3]

Perhaps the most extensive instance of the application of this form of ordeal was that proposed when the sacred vessels were stolen from the cathedral church of Laon, as related by a contemporary. At a council convened on the subject, Master Anselm, the most learned doctor of the diocese, suggested that, in imitation of the plan adopted by Joshua at Jericho, a young child should be taken from each parish of the town and be tried by immersion in consecrated water. From each house of the parish which should be found guilty, another child should be chosen to undergo the same process. When the house of the criminal should thus be discovered, all its inmates should be submitted to the ordeal, and the

---

1 Concil. Ausonens. ann. 1068 can. vii. (Aguirre, IV. 433).

2 Juris Feud. Alaman. cap. lxxvii. § 2.—Jur. Prov. Saxon. Lib. III. c. 21.

3 MS. Brit. Mus. quoted by Pertz in Hugo. Flaviniac. Lib. II.

author of the sacrilege would thus be revealed. This plan would have been adopted had not the frightened inhabitants rushed to the bishop and insisted that the experiment should commence with those whose access to the church gave them the best opportunity to perpetrate the theft. Six of these latter were accordingly selected, among whom was Anselm himself. While in prison awaiting his trial, he caused himself to be bound hand and foot and placed in a tub full of water, in which he sank satisfactorily to the bottom, and assured himself that he should escape. On the day of trial, in the presence of an immense crowd, in the cathedral which was chosen as the place of judgment, the first prisoner sank, the second floated, the third sank, the fourth floated, the fifth sank, and Anselm, who was the sixth, notwithstanding his previous experiment, obstinately floated, and was condemned with his accomplices, in spite of his earnest protestations of innocence.[1]

Although the cold-water ordeal disappears from the statute-book in civil and in ordinary criminal actions together with its kindred modes of purgation, there was one class of cases in which it maintained its hold upon the popular faith to a much later period. These were the accusations of sorcery and witchcraft which form so strange a feature of mediæval and modern society; and its use for this purpose may apparently be traced to various causes. For such crimes, drowning was the punishment inflicted by the customs of the Franks, as soon as they had lost the respect for individual liberty of action which excluded personal punishments from their original code;[2] and in addition to the general belief that the pure element refused to receive those who were tainted with crime, there was in this special class of cases a widely spread superstition that adepts in sorcery and magic

---

[1] Hermann. de Mirac. S. Mariæ Laudun. Lib. III. cap. 28.

[2] Lodharius . . . Gerbergam, *more maleficorum*, in Arari mergi præcepit.—Nithardi Hist. Lib. I. ann. 834.

lost their specific gravity.   Pliny mentions a race of en-
chanters on the Euxine who were lighter than water—"eos-
dem præterea non posse mergi ne veste quidam degravatos;"[1]
and Stephanus Byzantinus describes the inhabitants of Thebe
as magicians who could kill with their breath, and floated
when thrown into the sea.[2]   To the concurrence of these
notions we may attribute the fact that when the cold-water
ordeal was abandoned, in the thirteenth century, as a judicial
practice in ordinary cases, it still maintained its place as a
special mode of trying those unfortunate persons whom their
own folly, or the malice and fears of their neighbors, pointed
out as witches and sorcerers.[3]   No less than a hundred years
after the efforts of Innocent III. had virtually put an end to
all the other forms of vulgar ordeals, we find Louis Hutin
ordering its employment in these cases.[4]   At length, however,
it fell into desuetude, until the superstitious panic of witchcraft which took possession of the popular mind caused its
revival in the second half of the sixteenth century.   In 1487,
Sprenger, while treating of every possible detail concerning
witchcraft and its prosecution, and alluding to the red-hot
iron ordeal, makes no reference whatever to cold water or to
the faculty of floating possessed by witches, thus showing that
it had passed completely out of remembrance as a test in these
cases, both popularly and judicially.[5]   In 1564, Wier discusses
it as though it were in ordinary use in Western Germany, and
mentions a recent case wherein a young girl falsely accused
was tested in this manner and floated, after which she was
tortured until the executioner himself wondered at her power

[1] Plinii Natur. Histor. L. VII. c. ii.

[2] Ameilhon, de l'Épreuve de l'Eau Froide.

[3] In earlier times, various other modes of proof were habitually resorted
to.   Among the Lombards, King Rotharis prescribed the judicial combat
(L. Longobard. Lib. I. Tit. xvi. § 2).   The Anglo-Saxons (Æthelstan.
cap. VI.) direct the triple ordeal, which was either red-hot iron or boiling
water.

[4] Regest. Ludovici Hutini (ap. Cangium).

[5] Mall. Maleficarum.

of endurance. As no confession could be extracted, she was discharged, which shows how little real confidence was reposed in the ordeal.[1] Twenty years later, Scribonius, writing in 1583, speaks of it as a novelty, but Neuwald assures us that for eighteen years previous it had been generally employed throughout Westphalia,[2] and in 1579 Bodin alludes to it as a German fashion which, though he believes in its efficacy, he yet condemns as savoring of magic.[3] The crime was one so difficult to prove judicially, and the ordeal offered so ready and so satisfactory a solution to the doubts of timid and conscientious judges, that its resuscitation is not to be wondered at. The professed demonographers, Bodin, Binsfeld, Godelmann, and others, opposed its revival for various reasons, but still it did not lack defenders. In 1583, Scribonius, on a visit to Lemgow, saw three unfortunates burnt as witches, and three other women, the same day, exposed to the ordeal on the accusation of those executed. He describes them as stripped naked, hands and feet bound together, right to left, and then cast upon the river, where they floated like logs of wood. Profoundly impressed with the miracle, in a letter to the magistrates of Lemgow he expresses his warm approbation of the proceeding, and endeavors to explain its rationale, and to defend it against unbelievers. Sorcerers, from their intercourse with Satan, partake of his nature; he resides within them, and their human attributes become altered to his; he is an imponderable spirit of air, and therefore they likewise become lighter than water. Two years later, Hermann Neuwald published a tract in answer to this, gravely confuting the arguments advanced by Scribonius, who, in 1588, returned to the attack with a larger and more elaborate treatise in favor of the ordeal. Shortly after this, Bishop Binsfeld, in his

---

[1] Wieri de Præstigiis Dæmonum pp. 589, 581.

[2] Scribonii Epist. de Exam. Sagarum. Newald Exegesis Purgat. Sagarum. These tracts, together with Rickius's "Defensio Probæ Aquæ Frigidæ," were reprinted in 1686 at Leipsic, in 1 vol. 4to.

[3] De Magor. Dæmonomania, Basil. 1581, pp. 372, 385.

exhaustive work on witchcraft, states that the process was one in common use throughout Westphalia, and occasionally employed in the Rhinelands. He condemns it, however, on the score of superstition, and the prohibition of all ordeals by the popes, and concludes that any judge making use of it, or any one believing in it, is guilty of mortal sin. Rejecting the explanation of Scribonius, he argues that the floating of the witch is caused by the direct interposition of the Devil himself, who is willing to sacrifice a follower occasionally in order to damn the souls of those who participate in a practice condemned by the Church.[1] Wier, who denied witchcraft, while believing in the active interposition of the Devil, argues likewise that those who float are borne up by demons, but he attributes it to their desire to confirm the popular illusions concerning witchcraft.[2] Another demonographer of the period, Godelmann, does not hesitate to say that any judge resorting to this mode of proof rendered himself liable to a retaliatory action; and he substantiates his opinion as to the worthlessness of the trial by a case within his own experience. In 1588 he was travelling from Prussia to Livonia, when at the castle of a great potentate his host happened to mention that he had condemned a most wicked witch to be burnt the next day. Godelmann, desirous to know whether the proof could be relied on, asked whether the water ordeal had been tried, and on being answered in the negative, urged the experiment. His request was granted, and the witch sank like a stone. Subsequently the noble wrote to him that he had tried it with six other indubitable witches, and that it had failed with all, showing that it was a false indication, which might deceive incautious judges.[3] Oldenkop, on the other hand, relates that he was present when some suspected women

---

[1] Binsfeldi Tract. de Confess. Malefic. pp. 287–94 (Ed. 1623). He argues that, as the proceeding was unlawful, confessions obtained by means of it were of no legal weight.

[2] Wieri *op. cit.* p. 589.

[3] Godelmanni de Magis Lib. III. cap. v. §§ 30, 35.

were tried in this manner, who all floated, after which one of the spectators, wholly innocent of the crime, to satisfy the curiosity of some nobles who were present, allowed himself for hire to be tied and thrown in, when he likewise floated and could not be made to sink by all the efforts of the officiating executioner.[1] In 1594, a more authoritative combatant entered the arena—Jacob Rickius, a learned jurisconsult of Cologne, who, as judge in the court of Bonn, had ample opportunity of considering the question and of putting his convictions into practice. He describes vividly the perplexities of the judges hesitating between the enormity of the crime and the worthlessness of the evidence, and his elaborate discussions of all the arguments in favor of the ordeal may be condensed into this: that the offence is so difficult of proof that there is no other certain evidence than the ordeal; that without it we should be destitute of absolute proof, which would be an admission of the superiority of the Devil over God, and that anything would be preferable to such a conclusion. He states that he never administered it when the evidence without it was sufficient for conviction, nor when there was not enough other proof to justify the use of torture; and that in all cases it was employed as a prelude to torture— "præparandum et muniendum torturæ viam"—the latter being frequently powerless in consequence of diabolical influences. The deplorable examples which he details with much complacency as irrefragable proofs of his positions show how frequent and how murderous were the cases of its employment, but would occupy too much space for recapitulation here; while the learning displayed in his constant citations from the Scriptures, the Fathers, the Roman and the Canon Law, is in curious contrast with the fatuous cruelty of his acts and doctrines.

[1] P. Burgmeister Dissert. de Probat. per aquam, etc. Ulmæ, 1680, § 44. Burgmeister adopts the explanation of Binsfeld to account for the cases in which witches floated.

In France, the central power had to be invoked to put an end to the atrocity of such proceedings. In 1588, an appeal was taken to the supreme tribunal from a sentence pronounced by a Champenois court, ordering a prisoner to undergo the experiment, and the Parlement, in December, 1601, registered a formal decree against the practice ; an order which it found necessary to repeat, August 10, 1641.[1] That this latter was not uncalled for, we may assume from the testimony of Jeiôme Bignon, who, writing nearly at the same time, says that, to his own knowledge, within a few years, judges were in the habit of elucidating doubtful cases in this manner.[2] In England, James I. gratified at once his conceit and his superstition by eulogizing the ordeal as an infallible proof in such cases. His argument was the old one, which pronounced that the pure element would not receive those who had renounced the privileges of the water of baptism,[3] and his authority no doubt gave encouragement to innumerable judicial murders. In Scotland, indeed, the indecency of stripping women naked for the immersion was avoided by wrapping them up in a sheet before binding the thumbs and toes together, but a portion of the Bay of St. Andrews is still called the " Witch Pool," from its use in the trial of these unfortunates.[4]

How slowly the belief was eradicated from the minds of even the educated and enlightened may be seen in a learned inaugural thesis presented by J. P. Lang, in 1661, for the Licentiate of Laws in the University of Bâle, in which, dis-

[1] Königswarter, *op. cit.* p. 176.—Bochelli Decr. Eccles. Gallicanæ, Paris, 1609, p. 1211.

[2] " Porro, nostra memoria, paucis abhinc annis, solebant judices reos maleficii accusatos mergere, pro certo habentes incertum crimen hac ratione patefieri."—Notæ ad Legem Salicam.

[3] Tanquam aqua suum in sinum eos non admitteret, qui excussa baptismi aqua se omni illius sacramenti beneficio ultro orbarunt.—Dæmonologiæ Lib. III. cap. vi.

[4] Rogers' Scotland, Social and Domestic, p. 266 (Grampian Club, 1869).

cussing incidentally the question of the cold-water ordeal for
witches, he concludes that perhaps it is better to abstain from
it, though he cannot question its efficaciousness as a means of
investigation.[1] In 1662, N. Brant, in a similar thesis, offered
at Giessen, speaks of it as used in some places, chiefly in
Westphalia, and argues against it on the ground of its uncertainty.[2] P. Burgmeister, in a thesis presented at Ulm in 1680,
speaks of the practice as still continued in Westphalia, and
that it was defended by many learned men, from whose
opinions he dissents; among them was Hermann Conring, one
of the most distinguished scholars of the time, who argued
that if prayers and oaths could obtain the divine interposition,
it could reasonably be expected in judicial cases of importance.[3]
Towards the close of the century it was frequently practised
in Burgundy, not as a judicial process, but when persons
popularly reputed as sorcerers desired to free themselves from
the damaging imputation. In these cases they are frequently
reported as floating in spite of repeated efforts to submerge
them, and though this evidence of guilt did not lead to a
formal trial they would have to abandon the neighborhood.
A notarial act of June 5, 1696, records such a trial at Montigny-
le-Roi, when six persons offered themselves to the ordeal in the
River Senin; two sank and four floated for about half an hour,
with hands and feet tied.[4] F. M. Brahm, in 1701, alludes to
the ordeal as no longer in use;[5] but in 1714, J. C. Nehring
describes it as nearly, though not quite obsolete, and considers
it worthy of an elaborate discussion. He disapproves of it,
though he records a case which occurred a few years previously,
in which a woman accused of witchcraft managed to escape

[1] Dissert. Inaug. de Torturis Th. XVIII. § xi. Basil. 1661.

[2] N. Brandt de Legitima Maleficos et Sagas investigandi et convincendi
ratione, Giessen, 1662.

[3] P. Burgmeister Dissert. de Probat. per aquam ferventem et frigidam,
§§ 29, 39-41, Ulmæ, 1680.

[4] Le Brun, Histoire critique des Pratiques Superstitieuses, pp. 526-36
(Rouen, 1702).

[5] F. M. Brahm de Fallacibus Indiciis Magiæ, Halæ Magdeburg. 1709.

fro n her chains, and went into the water to try herself, and
could not be submerged. Notwithstanding this he declares
that even when a prisoner demands the ordeal, the judge who
grants it is guilty of mortal sin, for the Devil often promises
witches to save them in this manner, and, though he very
rarely keeps his promise, still he thus succeeds in retaining
men in superstitious observances. The success of the ordeal
thus is uncertain, and his conclusion is that laws must be made
for the generality of cases, and not for exceptional ones.[1]   In
1730 thirteen persons were exposed to the cold-water ordeal at
Szegedin, in Hungary, and though their guilt was proved by it,
any remaining doubts were settled by submitting them to the
balance ;[2] and five years later Ephraim Gerhardt alludes to it
as everywhere in daily use in such cases.[3]   Even in the middle
of the century, the learned and pious Muratori affirms his
reverent belief in the miraculous convictions recorded by the
mediæval writers as wrought in this manner by the judgment
of God ; and he further informs us that it was common in his
time throughout Transylvania, where witches were very
numerous ;[4] while in West Prussia, as late as 1745, the Synod
of Culm describes it as a popular abuse in frequent use, and
stringently forbids it for the future.[5]

Although, within the last hundred years, the cold-water
ordeal has disappeared from the authorized legal procedures
of Europe, still the popular mind has not as yet altogether
overcome the superstitions and prejudices of so many ages,

---

[1] J. C. Nehring de Indiciis, Jenæ, 1714.

[2] J. H. Böhmer, Jur. Eccles. Protestant. T. V. p. 608.

[3] Per aquam, tum frigidam ut hodiernum passim in sagarum inquisitionibus.
—Eph. Gerhardi Tract. Jurid. de Judic. Duellico, cap. i. ₰ 4 (Francof.
1735).

[4] Antiq. Ital. Dissert. 38.

[5] Qui ex levi suspicione, in tali crimine delatas, nec confessas, nec con-
victas, ad torturas, supernatationem aquarum, et alia eruendæ veritatis
media, tandem ad ipsam mortem condemnare . . . non verentur, exempla
proh dolor ! plurima testantur.—Synod. Culmens. et Pomesan. ann. 1745,
c. v. (Hartzheim Concil. German. X. 510).

and occasionally in some benighted spot a case occurs to show us that mediæval ignorance and brutality still linger amid the triumphs of modern civilization. In 1815 and 1816, Belgium was disgraced by trials of the kind performed on unfortunates suspected of witchcraft;[1] and in 1836, the populace of Hela, near Dantzic, twice plunged into the sea an old woman reputed to be a sorceress, and as the miserable creature persisted in rising to the surface, she was pronounced guilty, and was beaten to death.[2] Even in England it is not many years since a party of credulous people were prosecuted for employing the water ordeal in the trial of a woman whom they believed to be a witch.[3]

In Montenegro and Herzegovina the practice continued till the middle of the present century. Any unusual mortality of children was attributed to sorcery by women : in such cases the head of a village assembled all the men and exhorted them to bring next morning their wives and mothers to the nearest water—a lake or a river, or if necessary a well. The women were then examined one by one, by passing a rope under the arms and tossing them in, without divesting them of their clothes. Those who were so ill-advised as not to sink were pronounced guilty, and were liable to lapidation if they would not swear to abandon their evil practices. The belief even extended to the dominant Turks who, in 1857 at Trebinje, compelled the Christians to bring all their women to the river and cast them in. Buoyed up by their garments seven floated, and these were only saved from stoning by the archimandrite Eustache, who administered to them a solemn oath of abstinence from witchcraft. Austrian domination has rendered all such proceedings unlawful of late years, but in the remoter districts they are said to be still occasionally practised.[4]

---

[1] Meyer, Institutions Judiciaires, I. 321.
[2] Königswarter, op. cit. p. 177.
[3] Spottiswoode Miscellany, Edinburgh, 1845, II. 41.
[4] V. Bogisic, in Mélusine, T. II. pp. 6–7.

Perhaps we may class as a remnant of this superstition a custom described by a modern traveller as universal in Southern Russia. When a theft is committed in a household, the servants are assembled, and a sorceress, or *vorogeia*, is sent for. Dread of what is to follow generally extorts a confession from the guilty party without further proceedings, but if not, the *vorogeia* places on the table a vase of water and rolls up as many little balls of bread as there are suspected persons present. Then, taking one of the balls, she addresses the nearest servant—"If you have committed the theft, this ball will sink to the bottom of the vase, as will your soul in Hell; but if you are innocent, it will float on the water." The truth or falsehood of this assertion is never tested, for the criminal invariably confesses before his turn arrives to undergo the ordeal.[1]

CHAPTER VI.

THE ORDEAL OF THE BALANCE.

WE have seen above that a belief existed that persons guilty of sorcery lost their specific gravity, and this superstition naturally led to the use of the balance in the effort to discover and punish the crime of witchcraft, which all experts assure us was the most difficult of all offences on which to obtain evidence. The trial by balance, however, was not a European invention. Like nearly all the other ordeals, it can be traced back to India, where, at least as early as the time of the Institutes of Vishnu, it was in common use. It is described there as reserved for women, children, old men, invalids, the blind, the lame, and the privileged Brahman caste, and not to be undertaken when a wind was blowing. After proper ceremonies the patient was placed in one scale, with an equivalent

---

[1] Hartausen, Études sur la Russie (Du Boys, Droit Criminel des Peuples Modernes, I. 256).

weight to counterbalance him in the other, and the nicety of
the operation is shown by the prescription that the beam must
have a groove with water in it, evidently for the purpose of
detecting the slightest deflection either way. The accused
then descended and the judge addressed the customary adjuration to the balance :—

"'Thou, O balance, art called by the same name as holy
law (dharma) ; thou, O balance, knowest what mortals do not
comprehend.

"This man, arraigned in a cause, is weighed upon thee.
Therefore mayest thou deliver him lawfully from this perplexity."

Then the accused was replaced in the scale, and if he were
found to be lighter than before he was acquitted. If the scale
broke, the trial was to be repeated.[1]

It will be seen here that lightness was an evidence of innocence, but in Europe the ordeal was reversed in consequence
of the belief that sorcerers became lighter than water.
Rickius, writing in 1594, speaks of this mode of trial being
commonly used in many places in withcraft cases, and gravely
assures us that very large and fat women had been found to
weigh only thirteen or fifteen pounds ;[2] but even this will
scarcely explain the modification of the process as employed
in some places, which consisted in putting the accused in one
scale and a Bible in the other.[3] Kœnigswarter assures us that
the scales formerly used on these occasions are still to be seen
at Oudewater in Holland.[4] In the case already referred to as
occurring July 30, 1728, at Szegedin in Hungary, thirteen persons, six men and seven women, were burnt alive for witch-

[1] Institutes of Vishnu, X.—In the code of Yajnavalkya (II. 100–102)
there are some differences in the process, but the statement in the text is
virtually the same as that in the Ayeen Akbery (II. 486) as in force in the
seventeenth century.

[2] Rickii Defens. Probæ Aq. Frigidæ, § 41.

[3] Collin de Plancy, Dict. Infernal, s. v. *Bibliomancie.*

[4] Kœnigswarter, *op. cit.* p. 186.

craft, whose guilt had been proved, first by the cold-water ordeal and then by that of the balance. We are told that a large and fat woman weighed only one and a half drachms and her husband five drachms and the rest varied from a penny-weight to three drachms and under. One of the victims was a man of 82, a local judge, who had previously borne an un-blemished character.[1] The use of the Bible as a counterpoise is on record even as lately as the year 1759, at Aylesbury in England, where one Susannah Haynokes, accused of witch-craft, was formally weighed against the Bible in the parish church.[2]

CHAPTER VII.

THE ORDEAL OF THE CROSS.

THE ordeal of the cross (*judicium crucis, stare ad crucem*) was one of simple endurance and differed from all its con-geners, except the duel, in being bilateral. The plaintiff and defendant, after appropriate religious ceremonies and prepara-tion, stood with uplifted arms before a cross, while divine ser-vice was performed, victory being adjudged to the one who was able longest to maintain his position. An ancient formula for judgments obtained in this manner in cases of disputed titles to land prescribes the term of forty-two nights for the trial.[3] It doubtless originated in the use of this exercise by the Church both as a punishment and as a penance.[4] Of its use as an ordeal the earliest instance which I have observed occurs in a Capitulary of Pepin le Bref, in 752, where it is prescribed in cases of application by a wife for dissolution of

---

[1] J. H. Böhmer, Jur. Eccles. Protestant. T. V. p. 608.

[2] E. B. Tylor in Macmillan's Magazine, July, 1876.

[3] Formulæ Bignonianæ, No. xii.

[4] Vit. S. Lamberti (Canisii et Basnage, II. 140).—Pseudo Bedæ Lib. de Remed. Peccator. Prologus (Wasserschleben, Bussordnungen, Halle, 1851, p. 248).

marriage.[1] Charlemagne appears to have regarded it with much favor, for he not only frequently refers to it in his edicts, but, when dividing his mighty empire, in 806, he directs that all territorial disputes which may arise in the future between his sons shall be settled in this manner.[2] An example occurring during his reign shows the details of the process. A controversy between the bishop and citizens of Verona, relative to the building of certain walls, was referred to the decision of the cross. Two young ecclesiastics, selected as champions, stood before the sacred emblem from the commencement of mass; at the middle of the Passion, Aregaus, who represented the citizens, fell lifeless to the ground, while his antagonist, Pacificus, held out triumphantly to the end, and the bishop gained his cause, as ecclesiastics were wont to do.[3]

When a defeated pleader desired to discredit his own compurgators, he had the right to accuse them of perjury, and the question was then decided by this process.[4] In a similar spirit, witnesses too infirm to undergo the battle-trial, by which in the regular process of law they were bound to substantiate their testimony, were allowed, by a Capitulary of 816, to select the ordeal of the cross, with the further privilege, in cases of extreme debility, of substituting a relative or other champion, whose robustness promised an easier task for the Divine interference.[5]

A slight variation of this form of ordeal consisted in standing with the arms extended in the form of a cross, while certain portions of the service were recited. In this manner St. Lioba, Abbess of Bischoffsheim, triumphantly vindicated the purity of her flock, and traced out the offender, when

[1] Capit. Pippini ann. 752, § xvii.

[2] Chart. Division. cap. xiv. Capit. ann. 779, § x.; Capit. IV. ann. 803, §§ iii. vi.; in L. Longobard. Lib. II. Tit. xxviii. § 3; Tit. lv. § 25, etc.

[3] Ughelli Italia Sacra T. V. p. 610 (Ed. 1653).

[4] Capit. Car. Mag. incerti anni c. x. (Hartzheim. Concil. German. I. 426).

[5] Capit. Lud. Pii ann. 816, § 1 (Eccardi L. Francorum, pp. 183, 184).

the reputation of her convent was imperilled by the discovery of a new-born child drowned in a neighboring pond.[1]

The sensitive piety of Louis le Débonnaire was shocked at
this use of the cross, as tending to bring the Christian sym-
bol into contempt, and in 816, soon after the death of Charlemagne, he prohibited its continuance, at the Council of Aix-
la-Chapelle ;[2] an order which was repeated by his son, the
Emperor Lothair.[3] Baluze, however, considers, with apparent reason, that this command was respected only in the
Rhenish provinces and in Italy, from the fact that the manuscripts of the Capitularies belonging to those regions omit the
references to the ordeal of the cross, which are retained in the
copies used in the other territories of the Frankish empire.[4]
Louis himself would seem at length to have changed his
opinion ; for, in the final division of his succession between
his sons, he repeats the direction of Charlemagne as regards

[1] Rudolph. Fuldens. Vitæ S. Liobæ cap. xv. (Du Cange, s. v. *Crucis
Judicium*).

[2] Concil. Aquisgran. cap. xvii.

[3] L. Longobard. Lib. ii. Tit. lv. ¿ 32.

[4] Not. ad Libb. Capit. Lib. i. cap. 103. This derives additional probability from the text cited immediately above, relative to the substitution of
this ordeal for the duel, which is given by Eckhardt from an apparently
contemporary manuscript, and which, as we have seen, is attributed to
Louis le Débonnaire in the very year of the Council of Aix-la-Chapelle.
It is not a simple Capitulary, but an addition to the Salic Law, which
invests it with much greater importance. Lindenbruck (Cod. Legum
Antiq. p. 355) gives a different text, purporting likewise to be a supplement to the Law, made in 816, which prescribes the duel in doubtful cases
between laymen, and orders the ordeal of the cross for ecclesiastical causes
—" in Ecclesiasticis autem negotiis, crucis judicio rei veritas inquiratur"—
and allows the same privilege to the " imbecillibus aut infirmis qui pugnare
non valent." Baluze's collection contains nothing of the kind as enacted
in 816, but under date of 819 there is a much longer supplement to the
Salic law, in which cap. x. presents the same general regulations, almost
verbatim, except that in ecclesiastical affairs the testimony of witnesses only
is alluded to, and the *judicium crucis* is altogether omitted. The whole
manifestly shows great confusion of legislation.

the settlement of disputed boundaries.[1] The procedure, how-ever, appears to have soon lost its popularity, and indeed never to have obtained the wide and deeply-seated hold on the veneration of the people enjoyed by the other forms of ordeal, though there is extant a formula for confirming disputed titles to real estate decided in this manner.[2] We see little of it at later periods, except the trace it has left in the proverbial allu-sion to an *experimentum crucis*.

In India a cognate mode is adopted by the people of Ramgur to settle questions of disputed boundaries between villages. When agreement by argument or referees is found impossible, each community chooses a champion, and the two stand with one leg buried in the earth until weariness or the bites of insects cause one of them to yield, when the territory in litigation is adjudged to the village of the victor.[3]

CHAPTER VIII.

THE CORSNÆD.

THE ordeal of consecrated bread or cheese (*judicium offæ, panis conjuratio, pabulum probationis*, the *corsnæd* of the Anglo-Saxons) was administered by presenting to the accused a piece of bread (generally of barley) or of cheese, about an ounce in weight,[4] over which prayers and adjurations had been pronounced. After appropriate religious ceremonies, includ-ing the communion, the morsel was eaten, the event being determined by the ability of the accused to swallow it. This depended of course on the imagination, and we can readily understand how, in those times of faith, the impressive ob-

---

[1] Chart. Divisionis ann. 837, cap. 10.

[2] Meyer, Recueil d'Anciens Textes, Paris, 1874, p. 12.

[3] Sir John Shore, in Asiatic Researches, IV. 362.

[4] Half an ounce, according to a formula in a MS. of the ninth century, printed by Dom Gerbert (Migne's Patrolog. CXXXVIII. 1142).

servances which accompanied the ordeal would affect the criminal, who, conscious of guilt, stood up at the altar, took the sacrament, and pledged his salvation on the truth of his oath. The mode by which a conviction was expected may be gathered from the forms of the exorcism employed, of which a number have been preserved.

" O Lord Jesus Christ, ... grant, we pray thee, by thy holy name, that he who is guilty of this crime in thought or in deed, when this creature of sanctified bread is presented to him for the proving of the truth, let his throat be narrowed, and in thy name let it be rejected rather than devoured. And let not the spirit of the Devil prevail in this to subvert the judgment by false appearances. But he who is guilty of this crime, let him, chiefly by virtue of the body and blood of our Lord which he has received in communion, when he takes the consecrated bread or cheese tremble, and grow pale in trembling, and shake in all his limbs ; and let the innocent quietly and healthfully, with all ease, chew and swallow this morsel of bread or cheese, crossed in thy holy name, that all may know that thou art the just Judge," etc.[1]

And even more forcible in its devout impiety is the following :—

" O God Most High, who dwellest in Heaven, who through thy Trinity and Majesty hast thy just angels, send, O Lord, thy Angel Gabriel to stick in the throat of those who have committed this theft, that they may neither chew nor swallow this bread and cheese created by Thee. I invoke the patriarchs, Abraham, Isaac, and Jacob, with twelve thousand Angels and Archangels. I invoke the four evangelists, Matthew, Mark, Luke, and John. I invoke Moses and Aaron, who divided the sea. That they may bind to their throats the tongues of the men who have committed this theft, or consented thereto. If they taste this bread and cheese created by Thee, may they tremble like a trembling tree, and have no rest, nor keep the bread and cheese in their mouths ; that all may know Thou art the Lord, and there is none other but Thee !"[2]

[1] Baluze II. 655.

[2] Muratori, Antiq. Ital. Dissert. 38.—For three other formulas see *Fasciculus Rerum Expetendarum et Fugiendarum*, Ed. 1690, II. 910.

As the efficiency of the ordeal depended upon the effect produced on the imagination of the patient clerical ingenuity exhausted itself in devising tremendous and awe-inspiring exorcisms. One like the following, for instance, could hardly fail to constrict the throat of the most hardened sinner :—

" I exorcise thee, accursed and most filthy dragon, basilisk, evil serpent, by the Word of truth, by almighty God, by the spotless Lamb begotten of the Highest, conceived of the Holy Ghost, born of the Virgin Mary, whose coming Gabriel announced, whom when John saw he cried aloud This is the Son of the living God, that thou may'st have no power over this bread or cheese, but that he who committed this theft may eat in trembling and vomit forth by Thy command, Holy Father and Lord, almighty and eternal God . . . . May he who has stolen these things or is an accomplice in this, may his throat and his tongue and his jaws be narrowed and constricted so that he cannot chew this bread or cheese, by the Father and the Son and the Holy Ghost, by the tremendous Day of Judgment, by the four Evangels, by the twelve Apostles, by the four and twenty elders who daily praise and worship Thee, by that Redeemer who deigned for our sins to stretch his hands upon the cross, that he who stole these things cannot chew this bread or cheese save with a swelled mouth and froth and tears, by the aid of our Lord Jesus Christ, to whom is honor and glory forever and forever."[1]

Yet Boccaccio's story of Calendrino, which turns upon the mixing of aloes with the bread administered in the *corsnæd*, perhaps affords a more rationalistic explanation of the expected miracle.[2]

A striking illustration of the superstitions connected with this usage is found in the story related by most of the English chroniclers concerning the death of Godwin, Duke of Kent, father of King Harold, and in his day the king-maker of England. As he was dining with his royal son-in-law, Edward the Confessor, some trivial circumstance caused the king to repeat an old accusation that his brother Alfred had met his

---

[1] Martene de Antiq. Eccles. Ritibus Lib. III. c. vii. Ordo 15.
[2] Decam. Giorn. VIII. Nov. 6.

death at Godwin's hands. The old but fiery duke, seizing a
piece of bread, exclaimed : " May God cause this morsel to
choke me if I am guilty in thought or in deed of this crime !"
Then the king took the bread and blessed it, and Godwin,
putting it in his mouth, was suffocated by it, and fell dead.[1]
A poetical life of Edward the Confessor, written in the
thirteenth century, gives a graphic picture of the death of the
duke and the vengeful triumph of the king :—

> " L'aleine e parole pert
> Par le morsel ki ferm s'ahert.
> Morz est li senglant felun ;
> Mut out force la benaicun,
> Ke duna a mors vertu,
> Par unc la mort provée fu.
> ' Atant' se escrie li rois,
> ' Treiez hors ceu chen punois.' "[2]

This form of ordeal never obtained the extended influence
which characterized some of the other modes, and it seems
to have been chiefly confined to the populations allied to the
Saxon race. In England, before the Conquest, it was enjoined on the lower orders of the clergy who were unable to

[1] This account, with unimportant variations, is given by Roger of Wendover, ann. 1054, Matthew of Westminster, ann. 1054, the Chronicles of
Croyland, ann. 1053, Henry of Huntington, ann. 1053, and William of
Malmesbury, Lib. II. cap. 13, which shows that the legend was widely
spread and generally believed, although the Anglo-Saxon Chronicle, ann.
1052, and Roger de Hoveden, ann. 1053, in mentioning Godwin's death,
make no allusion to its being caused in this manner. A similar reticence
is observable in an anonymous Life of Edward (Harleian MSS. 526, p. 408
of the collection in M. R. Series), and although this is perhaps the best
authority we have for the events of his reign, still the author's partiality for
the family of Godwin renders him not altogether beyond suspicion.

No great effort of scepticism is requisite to suggest that Edward, tired of
the tutelage in which he was held, may have made way with Godwin by
poison, and then circulated among a credulous generation the story related
by the annalists.

[2] Lives of Edward the Confessor, p. 119 (M. R. Series).

procure conjurators,[1] and it may be considered as a plebeian mode of trial, rarely rising into historical importance. Its vitality, however, is demonstrated by the fact that Lindenbruck, writing in 1613, states that it was then still in frequent use.[2]

Aimoin relates a story which, though in no sense judicial, presents us with a development of the same superstition. A certain renowned knight named Arnustus unjustly occupied lands belonging to the Benedictine Abbey of Fleury. Dining at the usurped property one day, and boasting of his contempt for the complaints of the holy monks, he took a pear and exclaimed—"I call this pear to witness that before the year is out I will give them ample cause for grumbling." Choking with the first morsel, he was carried speechless to bed, and miserably perished unhouselled, a warning to evildoers not to tempt too far the patience of St. Benedict.[3] Stories such as this are by no means uncommon, and are not without interest as a portion of the armory by which the clergy defended themselves against their unquiet neighbors. Of kindred nature is an occurrence related about the year 1090, when Duke Henry of Limburg was involved in a quarrel with Engilbert, Archbishop of Trèves, and treated with contempt the excommunication and anathema inflicted upon him. Joking upon the subject with his followers one day at dinner, he tossed a fragment of food to his dog, remarking that if the animal ate it, they need not feel apprehensive of the episcopal curse. The dog refused the tempting morsel, though he manifested his hunger by eagerly devouring food given him by another hand, and the duke, by the advice of his counsellors, lost no time in reconciling himself with his ghostly adversary. This is the more remarkable, as Engilbert himself was under excommunication by Gregory VII.,

---

[1] Dooms of Ethelred, IX. § 22; Cnut. Eccles. Tit. v.

[2] Alium examinis modum, nostro etiamnunc sæculo, sæpe malo modo usitatum.—Cod. Legum Antiq. p. 1418.

[3] De Mirac. S. Benedicti. Lib. I. c. v.

being a stanch imperialist, who had received his see from
Henry IV., and his pallium from the antipope Guiberto.[1]

In India, this ordeal is performed with a kind of rice called
sathee, prepared with various incantations. The person on
trial eats it, with his face to the East, and then spits upon a
peepul leaf. "If the saliva is mixed with blood, or the
corners of his mouth swell, or he trembles, he is declared to
be a liar."[2] A slightly different form is described for cases in
which several persons are suspected of theft. The consecrated rice is administered to them all, is chewed lightly, and
then spit out upon a peepul leaf. If any one ejects it either
dry or tinged with blood, he is adjudged guilty.[3]

Based on the same theory is a ceremony performed by the
pre-Aryan hill-tribes of Rajmahal, when swearing judges into
office preparatory to the trial of a case. In this a pinch of
salt is placed upon a *tulwar* or scimitar, and held over the
mouth of the judge, to whom is addressed the adjuration,
"If thou decidest contrary to thy judgment and falsely, may
this salt be thy death!" The judge repeats the formula, and
the salt is washed with water into his mouth.[4]

CHAPTER IX.

THE EUCHARIST AS AN ORDEAL.

FROM ancient times in India there has been in common use
an ordeal known as *cosha*, consisting of water in which an
idol has been washed. The priest celebrates solemn rites "to
some tremendous deity," such as Durga or the Adityas, whose
image is then bathed in water. Three handfuls of this water
are then drunk by the accused, and if within fourteen days he

---

[1] Gesta Treverorum, continuat. I. (Migne's Patrol. CLIV. 1205-6).

[2] Ayeen Akbery, II. 498.

[3] Ali Ibrahim Khan (Asiatic Researches, I. 391-2).

[4] Lieut. Shaw in As. Researches, IV. 80.

is not visited with some dreadful calamity from the act of the deity or of the king, "he must indubitably be acquitted."[1]

In adapting the ordeal system to Christianity the natural substitute for this pagan ceremony was the administration of the Eucharist. This, indeed, formed a portion of the preparatory rites in all the judgments of God, the Host being given with the awful adjuration, "May this body and blood of our Lord Jesus Christ be a judgment to thee this day !" The apostle had said that "he that eateth and drinketh unworthily eateth and drinketh damnation to himself" (I. Corinth. xi. 28, 29), and the pious veneration of the age accepted the admonition literally. Mediæval literature is full of legends showing the miraculous power of the Eucharist in bringing sinners to repentance and exposure, even without any special invocation; and the absolute belief in this fetishism, even by the irreligious, is fairly illustrated by the case of a dissolute priest of Zurich, in the fourteenth century. An habitual drunkard, gambler, and fornicator, he yet celebrated mass daily with exemplary regularity. On being warned of the dangers to which he was thus exposing himself in partaking of the Eucharist, he at length confessed that he never consecrated the host, but that he carried about him a small round piece of wood, resembling the holy wafer, which he exhibited to the people and passed it off for the body of Christ. The honest chronicler fairly explodes with indignation in relating the subterfuge, and assures us that while the priest succeeded in escaping one danger he fell into a much greater, as he was the cause of leading his flock into the unpardonable sin of idolatry. Apparently his parishioners thought so too, for though they had patiently endured the scandals of his daily life, as soon as this trick became known they drove him away unceremoniously.[2] What this pastor, but for his ingenious device, might have reasonably dreaded

---

[1] Institutes of Vishnu, XIV.—Yajnavalkya, II. 112–13.
[2] Vitodurani Chron. ann. 1336.

is to be learned from the story of a volunteer miracle vouchsafed to an unchaste priest at Lindisfarne, who being suddenly
summoned to celebrate mass without having had time to
purify himself, when he came to partake of the sacramental
cup, saw the wine change to an exceeding blackness. After
some hesitation he took it, and found it bitter to the last
degree. Hurrying to his bishop, he confessed his sin, underwent penance, and reformed his life.[1] Even more edifying
was a case related as happening in France about the year
1200. A priest yielded to the temptation of the flesh immediately before celebrating mass on Christmas eve, when, after
consecrating the body and blood, and before he could touch
them with his polluted lips, a white dove appeared which
drank the wine and carried off the wafer. It happened that
he could find no one to replace him during the ceremonies of
the festival, and, though appalled by the miracle, he could
not refuse to perform his functions without exposure, so that
a second and a third time he went through the canon with
the same result. Finally he applied to an abbot, and confessed his sin with due contrition. The abbot postponed
inflicting penance until the priest should officiate again, when
the dove reappeared, bearing in its beak the three wafers, and
returning to the chalice all the wine it had taken. Filled
with rejoicing at this evidence that his contrition was accepted, the priest cheerfully undertook three years' pilgrimage
in the Holy Land, prescribed for him by the abbot, and on
his return entered a convent.[2]

A still more striking manifestation of the interposition of
God by means of the Eucharist to vindicate innocence is to
be found in the case of Erkenbald de Burban, a noble of
Flanders, who was renowned for his inflexible administration
of justice. While lying on his death-bed, his favorite nephew
and heir endeavored to violate one of the maidens of the

[1] Roger of Wendover, ann. 1051.
[2] Cæsar. Heisterbacens. Dial. Mirac. Dist. II. c. v.

castle. Erkenbald ordered him to be hanged, but his followers were afraid to execute the sentence; so, when after
an interval, the youth approached his uncle for a reconciliation, the latter put his arm affectionately round his neck, and
drove a dagger up to the hilt in his throat. When Erkenbald
made his final confession preparatory to the last sacrament, he
refused to include this deed among his sins, claiming that it
was an act of righteousness, and his bishop consequently refused to administer the Host. The dying man obdurately
allowed him to depart; then ordering him recalled, asked
him to see whether he had the wafer in his pyx. On the
latter being opened it was found empty, and Erkenbald exhibited it to him in his mouth. The Eucharist which man
had refused, God had ministered to the righteous judge.[1]

It is, therefore, easy to understand the superstition of the
ages of faith which believed that, when the consecrated wafer
was offered under appropriate adjurations, the guilty could
not receive it; or that, if it were taken, immediate convulsions and speedy death, or some other miraculous manifestation would ensue, thus constituting its administration for such
purposes a regular and recognized form of ordeal. This is
well illustrated by a form of exorcism preserved by Mansi:
"We humbly pray thy Infinite Majesty that this priest, if
guilty of the accusation, shall not be able to receive this venerated body of thy Son, crucified for the salvation of all, and
that what should be the remedy of all evil shall prove to him
hurtful, full of grief and suffering, bearing with it all sorrow
and bitterness."[2] What might be expected under such circumstances is elucidated by a case which occurred in the
early part of the eleventh century, as reported by the contemporary Rodolphus Glaber, in which a monk, condemned to
undergo the trial, boldly received the sacrament, when the
Host, indignant at its lodgment in the body of so perjured a
criminal, immediately slipped out at the navel, white and pure

---

[1] Ibid. Dist. IX. c. xxxviii.   [2] Baluz. et Mansi Miscell. II. 575.

as before, to the immense consternation of the accused, who forthwith confessed his crime.[1]

The antiquity of this mode of trial is shown in its employment by Cautinus, Bishop of Auvergne, towards the close of the sixth century. A certain Count Eulalius was popularly accused of parricide, whereupon he was suspended from communion. On his complaining of thus being punished without a trial, the bishop administered the sacrament under the customary adjuration, and Eulalius, taking it without harm, was relieved from the imputation.[2] It was usually, however, a sacerdotal form of purgation, as is shown by the Anglo-Saxon laws,[3] and by the canons of the council of Worms in 868, embodied in the *Decretum* of Gratian.[4] Thus, in 941, Frederic, Archbishop of Mainz, publicly submitted to an ordeal of this kind, to clear himself of the suspicion of having taken part in an unsuccessful rebellion of Henry, Duke of Bavaria, against his brother, Otho the Great.[5] After the death of Henry, slander assailed the fame of his widow, Juthita, on account of an alleged intimacy between her and Abraham, Bishop of Freisingen. When she, too, died, the bishop performed her funeral rites, and, pausing in the mass, he addressed the congregation : " If she was guilty of that whereof she was accused, may the Omnipotent Father cause the body and blood of the Son to be my condemnation to just perdition, and perpetual salvation to her soul !"—after which he took the sacrament unharmed, and the people acknowledged the falsity of their belief.[6] In 1050, Subico, Bishop of Speyer, sought to clear himself of a similar accusation at the council of Mainz, in the same manner, when according to one version he succeeded, while another less friendly account assures us that

---

[1] Rod. Glabri Hist. Lib. v. cap. i.

[2] Greg. Turon. Hist. Lib. x. cap. 8.

[3] Dooms of Ethelred, x. § 20; Cnut. Eccles. Tit. v.

[4] C. 23, 26 Caus. II. q. v.

[5] Reginonis Continuat. ann. 941.

[6] Dithmari Chron. Lib. II.

his jaw became paralyzed in the very act, and remained so till the day of his death.[1]

Perhaps the most striking instance recorded of its administration was, however, in a secular matter, when in 869 it closed the unhappy controversy between King Lothair and his wives, to which reference has been already made. To reconcile himself to the Church, Lothair took a solemn oath before Adrian II. that he had obeyed the ecclesiastical mandates in maintaining a complete separation from his pseudo-wife Waldrada, after which the pontiff admitted him to communion, under an adjuration that it should prove the test of his truthfulness. Lothair did not shrink from the ordeal, nor did his nobles, to whom it was given on their declaring that they had not abetted the designs of the concubine; but leaving Rome immediately afterwards, the royal *cortége* was stopped at Piacenza by a sudden epidemic which broke out among the courtiers, and there Lothair died, August 8th, with nearly all of his followers—an awful example held out by the worthy chroniclers as a warning to future generations.[2]

In this degradation of the Host to the level of daily life there was a profanity repugnant to a reverential mind, and we are therefore not surprised to find King Robert the Pious, in the early part of the eleventh century, raising his voice against its judicial use, and threatening to degrade the Archbishop of Sens for employing it in this manner, especially as his biographer informs us that the custom was daily growing in favor.[3] Robert's example was soon afterwards imitated by Alexander II., whose pontificate lasted from 1061 to 1073.[4] The next pope, however, the impetuous Hildebrand, made use of it on a memorable occasion. When, in 1077, the Emperor Henry IV. had endured the depths of humiliation before the castle

[1] Hist. Archiep. Bremens. ann. 1051.—Lambert. Hersfeld. ann. 1050.—Hartzheim. Concil. German. III. 112.

[2] Regino ann. 869.—Annal. Bertiniani.

[3] Helgaldi Epitome Vitæ Roberti Regis.

[4] Duclos, Mémoire sur les Épreuves.

gate of Canossa, and had at length purchased peace by submitting to the exactions demanded of him, the excommunication under which he had lain was removed in the chapel.
Then Gregory, referring to the crimes imputed to himself by
the emperor's partisans, said that he could easily refute them
by abundant witnesses ; " but lest I should seem to rely rather
on human than on divine testimony, and that I may remove
from the minds of all, by immediate satisfaction, every scruple,
behold this body of our Lord which I am about to take. Let
it be to me this day a test of my innocence, and may the
Omnipotent God this day by his judgment absolve me of the
accusations if I am innocent, or let me perish by sudden death
if guilty !" Swallowing the wafer, he turned to the emperor,
and demanded of him the same refutation of the charges urged
against him by the German princes. Appalled by this unexpected trial, Henry in an agony of fear evaded it, and consulted
hurriedly with his councillors how to escape the awful test,
which he finally declined on the ground of the absence of
both his friends and his enemies, without whose presence the
result would establish nothing.[1] In estimating the mingled
power of imagination and conscience which rendered the proposal insupportable to the emperor, we must allow for the influence which a man like Hildebrand with voice and eye can
exert over those whom he wishes to impress. At an earlier
stage of his career, in 1055, he improvised a very effective
species of ordeal, when presiding as papal legate at the Council of Lyons, assembled for the repression of simony. A
guilty bishop had bribed the opposing witnesses, and no testimony was obtainable for his conviction. Hildebrand addressed
him : " The episcopal grace is a gift of the Holy Ghost. If,
therefore, you are innocent, repeat, ' Glory to the Father, and
to the Son, and to the Holy Ghost !' " The bishop boldly
commenced, "Glory to the Father, and to the Son, and to—"

---

[1] Lambert. Hersfeld. ann. 1077.

here his voice failed him, he was unable to finish the sentence ; and, confessing the sin, he was deposed.[1]

Henry's prudence in declining the Eucharistic ordeal was proved by the fate of the unfortunate Imbrico, Bishop of Augsburg, who, in the same year, 1077, after swearing fealty to Rodolph of Suabia, abandoned him and joined the emperor. Soon after, while saying mass before Henry, to prove the force of his loyal convictions, he declared that the sacrament he was about to take should attest the righteousness of his master's cause ; and the anti-imperialist chronicler duly records that a sudden disease overtook him, to be followed by speedy death.[2] In the case of William, Bishop of Utrecht, as related by Hugh of Flavigny, the Eucharist was less an ordeal than a punishment. He dared, at the Assembly of Utrecht, in 1076, to excommunicate Gregory, at the command of Henry IV. ; but when, at the conclusion of the impious ceremony, he audaciously took the Host, it turned to fire within him, and, shrieking " I burn ! I burn !" he fell down and miserably died.[3]

According to a Spanish theologian in the sixteenth century, when the Eucharist was administered as an ordeal it was to be taken without previous sacramental confession—presumably in order that the accused might not escape in consequence of absolution.[4] After the Reformation, the Protestants who denied the real presence naturally rejected this form of ordeal, but Del Rio, writing in 1599, compares them to frogs swelling themselves against an elephant ; and Peter Kluntz, in 1677, assures us that it was still commonly used in his day.[5]

---

[1] This anecdote rests on good authority. Peter Damiani states that he had it from Hildebrand himself (Opusc. XIX. cap. vi.), and Calixtus II. was in the habit of relating it (Pauli Bernried. Vit. Greg. VII. No. 11).

[2] Bernald. Constant. Chron. ann. 1077.

[3] Hugon. Flaviniac. Chron. Lib. II. ann. 1080.—Lambert. Hersfeld. ann. 1076.

[4] Ciruelo, Reprovacion de las Supersticiones, P. II. cap. vii. Barcelona, 1628. The first edition appeared in 1539 at Salamanca.

[5] Del Rio Disquis. Magic. L. IV. c. iv. q. 3.—P. Kluntz Dissert. de Probat. per S. Eucharist. Ulmæ, 1677.

CHAPTER X.

THE ORDEAL OF THE LOT.

THE appeal to chance, as practised in India, bears several forms, substantially identical in principle. One mode consists in writing the words *dherem* (consciousness of innocence) and *adherem* (its opposite) on plates of silver and lead respectively, or on pieces of white and black linen, which are placed in a vessel that has never held water. The person whose cause is at stake inserts his hand and draws forth one of the pieces, when if it happens to be *dherem* it proves his truth.[1] Another method is to place in a vessel a silver image of Dharma, the genius of justice, and one in iron or clay of Adharma; or else a figure of Dharma is painted on white cloth and another on black cloth, and the two are rolled together in cow-dung and thrown into a jar, when the accused is acquitted or convicted according to his fortune in drawing Dharma.[2]

In adapting to Christian usage the ordeal of the lot, attempts were made to invest it with similar sacred symbolism, but it was not well adapted to display the awful solemnity which rendered the other forms so impressive. Notwithstanding the ample warrant for it in Scripture, and its approval by St. Augustin,[3] it was therefore in less favor with the Church, and it seems not to have retained among the people, after their conversion, the widespread popularity and confidence

---

[1] Ayeen Akbery, II. 498. This form of ordeal is allowed for all the four castes.

[2] Ali Ibrahim Khan (As. Researches I. 392).

[3] " Sors enim non aliquid mali est, sed res est in dubitatione humana divinam indicans voluntatem."—S. Augustini Enarrat. in Psal. xxx. Serm. ii. § 13.—Gratian. c. I Caus. xxvi. q. ii.—Gratian, however, gives an ample array of other authorities condemning it.

enjoyed by the other ordeals. Indeed, as a judicial process, it is only to be found prescribed in the earlier remains of the Barbarian laws and customs, and no trace of it is to be met with in the latter legislation of any race. Thus mention of it is made in the Ripuarian code,[1] and in some of the earlier Merovingian documents its use is prescribed in the same brief manner.[2] As late as the middle of the eighth century, Ecgberht, Archbishop of York, quotes from the canons of an Irish Council a direction for its employment in cases of sacrilegious theft, as a means of determining the punishment to be inflicted;[3] but not long after, the Council of Calchuth condemned the practice between litigants as a sacrilege and a remnant of paganism.[4] This was ineffectual, for about 850 Leo IV. describes it as in universal use in England, and forbids it as mere divination.[5]

No explanation is given of the details of the process by which this appeal to fortune was made, and I know of no contemporary applications by which its formula can be investigated; but in the primitive Frisian laws there is described an ordeal of the lot, which may reasonably be assumed to show us one of the methods in use. When a man was killed in a chance-medley and the murderer remained unknown, the friends had a right to accuse seven of the participants in the brawl. Each of these defendants had then to take the oath of denial with twelve conjurators, after which they were

---

1 Ad ignem seu ad sortem se excusare studeat.—Tit. XXXI. § 5.

2 Pact. Childeberti et Chlotarii, ann. 593, § 5 : " Et si dubietas est, ad sortem ponatur." Also § 8 : " Si litus de quo inculpatur ad sortem ambulaverit." As in § 4 of the same document the *æneum* or hot-water ordeal is provided for freemen, it is possible that the lot was reserved for slaves. This, however, is not observed in the Decret. Chlotarii, ann. 595, § 6, where the expression, " Si de suspicione inculpatur, ad sortem veniat," is general in its application, without reservation as to station.

3 Ecgberti Excerpt. cap. lxxxiv. (Thorpe, II. 108).

4 Conc. Calchuth. can. 19 (Spelman. Concil. Brit. I. 300).

Leon. PP. IV. Epist. VIII. c. 4 (Gratian, c. 7. Caus. XXVI. q. v.).

admitted to the ordeal. Two pieces of twig, precisely similar, were taken, one of which was marked with a cross; they
were then wrapped up separately in white wool and laid on
the altar; prayers were recited, invoking God to reveal the
innocence or guilt of the party, and the priest, or a sinless
youth, took up one of the bundles. If it contained the
marked fragment, the defendants were absolved; if the un-
marked one, the guilty man was among them. Each one
then took a similar piece of stick and made a private mark
upon it; these were rolled up as before, placed on the altar,
taken up one by one, and unwrapped, each man claiming his
own. The one whose piece was left to the last was pronounced
guilty, and was obliged to pay the wer-gild of the murder.[1]
Among the ancient Irish the lot or *crannchur* was employed
by mingling white and black stones, when if the accused drew
a black one he was adjudged guilty.[2]

The various modes of ecclesiastical divination, so frequently
used in the Middle Ages to obtain an insight into the future,
sometimes assumed the shape of an appeal to Heaven to
decide questions of the present or of the past.[3] Thus, when
three bishops, of Poitiers, Arras, and Autun, each claimed
the holy relics of St. Liguaire, and human means were una-

[1] L. Frision. Tit. XIV. §§ 1, 2. This may not improbably be derived
from the mode of divination practised among the ancient Germans, as described by Tacitus, De Moribus German. cap. x.

[2] Sullivan, *ap.* Pictet, Origines Indo-Européennes, III. 179.

[3] When used for purposes of divining into the future, these practices
were forbidden. Thus, as early as 465, the Council of Vannes denounced
those who "sub nomine fictæ religionis quas sanctorum sortes vocant divi-
nationis scientiam profitentur, aut quarumcumque scripturarum inspectione
futura promittant," and all ecclesiastics privy to such proceedings were to
be expelled from the church (Concil. Venet. can. xvi.). This canon is
repeated in the Council of Agde in 506, where the practice is denounced
as one "quod maxime fidem catholicæ religionis infestat" (Conc. Agathens.
can. xlii.); and a penitential of about the year 800 prescribes three years'
penitence for such acts.—Ghaerbaldi Judicia Sacerdotalia c. 29 (Martene
Ampl. Coll. VII. 33).

vailing to reconcile their pretensions, the decision of the Supreme Power was resorted to, by placing under the altar-cloth three slips with their respective names inscribed, and after a becoming amount of prayer, on withdrawing one of them, the see of Poitiers was enriched with the precious remains by Divine favor.[1]

That such appeals to chance were regarded by the Church with disfavor is shown by Gratian, who argues that the Hebrew examples were not precedents to be observed under the New Law.[2] Yet the second council of Barcelona in 599 had decreed that when an episcopal vacancy was to be filled two or three candidates should be chosen by the clergy and people, and from among these the metropolitan and his suffragans should select one by lot, after due fasting and prayer.[3]

One of the most interesting applications of the lot on record was that by which the founders of the Bohemian Brethren determined upon the future existence of the sect. At an assembly of deputies held at Lhotka, in 1467, the lot was resorted to to ascertain whether it was the will of God that they should separate themselves from the Roman presbyterate and seek consecration from the Waldenses, when the response was in the affirmative. Then nine men were chosen, from among whom three or two, or one, or none should be drawn as candidates for the episcopate. Twelve cards were taken, three inscribed " is" and nine " is not," and nine of them were distributed among the men selected. Three were found to be drawn ; one of them was sent to an Austrian community of Waldenses for episcopal consecration, and the " Unitas Fratrum" was then organized.[4] This same pious dependence on the will of God is still preserved by the Mennonites in the choice of pastors. As described in the journals of 1884 an election of this kind in Lancaster County, Pennsylvania,

---

[1] Baldric. Lib. I. Chron. Camerac. cap. 21 (Du Cange, s. v. *Sors*).

[2] Decret. Caus. XXVI. q. ii.

[3] Concil. Barcinon. II. ann. 599 c. 3.

[4] Goll, Quellen und Untersuchungen, II. 99–105.

where there were twenty candidates, was conducted by three bishops. After divine service twenty books with clasps were taken in one of which was inserted a slip of paper inscribed *Ein Diener des Wort;* the books were placed in a row on a table and each applicant selected one. Bishop Shenk proceeded to open the books, and in the eleventh, held by Menno Zimmerman, the paper was found, entitling him to the position.

Closely related to the lot are the appeals to chance, to settle doubtful questions or ascertain guilt. Such was that made by the pious monks of Abingdon, about the middle of the tenth century, to determine their right to the meadows of Beri against the claims of some inhabitants of Oxfordshire. For three days, with fasting and prayer, they implored the Divine Omnipotence to make manifest their right; and then, by mutual assent, they floated on the Thames a round buckler, bearing a handful of wheat, in which was stuck a lighted taper. The sturdy Oxonians gaped at the spectacle from the distant bank, while a deputation of the more prudent monks followed close upon the floating beacon. Down the river it sailed, veering from bank to bank, and pointing out, as with a finger, the various possessions of the Abbey, till at last, on reaching the disputed lands, it miraculously left the current of the stream, and forced itself into a narrow and shallow channel, which in high water made an arm of the river around the meadows in question. At this unanswerable decision, the people with one accord shouted "Jus Abbendoniæ, jus Abbendoniæ!" and so powerful was the impression produced, that the worthy chronicler assures us that thenceforth neither king, nor duke, nor prince dared to lay claim to the lands of Beri, showing conclusively the wisdom of the abbot who preferred thus to rely upon his right rather than on mouldy charters or dilatory pleadings.[1]

A more prosaic form of the ordeal of chance is the trial by

[1] Hist. Monast. de Abingdon. Lib. I. (M. R. Series I. 89).

Bible and key which is of old Teutonic origin.[1] It is still in common use in England, where it may even yet "be met with in many an out-of-the-way-farm-house." In cases of theft a key is secured at Psalm 50, 18 : "When thou sawest a thief, then thou consentedst with him, and hast been partaker with adulterers ;"[2] and the mode in which it is expected to reveal guilt is manifested in a case recorded in the London *Times* as occurring at Southampton in 1867, where a sailor boy on board a collier was brought before court on a charge of theft, the only evidence against him being that afforded by securing a key in a Bible opposite the first chapter of Ruth. The Bible was then swung round while the names of several suspected persons were repeated, and on the mention of the prisoner's name the book fell on the floor. A somewhat different method is recounted in a case reported by the journals in 1879, where a woman in Ludlow, who had lost a sheet, perambulated the streets of the town with a Bible and key, and brought a prosecution against a person whose guilt she had thus discovered. It was explained in court that the key was placed at Ruth 1. 16, the investigator holding his fingers crossed, and when the thief was named the key would spontaneously move. In this case the prosecutrix declared that when she came to the defendant's house "the Bible turned completely round and fell out of her hands." A variant of this, described in two MSS. of the twelfth century, consisted in placing a piece of wood over the verse of the Psalm, "Thou art just, O Lord, and thy judgment is true ;" the book was then securely bound so that the head of the wood protruded, and it was suspended, while a priest uttered an adjuration and the accused was questioned, the result being apparently determined by the motion or rest of the book. Still another form consisted of suspending a small loaf of bread which had been placed behind the altar during mass and at its conclusion blessed and marked

[1] Grimm's Teutonic Mythology, Stallybrass's Translation, p. 1109.
[2] E. B. Tylor on Ordeals and Oaths (Macmillan's Mag. July, 1876).

with a cross by the priest.   At the trial he uttered a conjura-
tion, when if the bread turned the accused was held guilty.[1]

Closely akin to the Bible and key is the sieve-driving or
sieve-turning by which criminals were detected by the tilting
or falling of a sieve when, in repeating the names of those suspected, that of the culprit was mentioned.   The sieve required
to be an heirloom in the family ; it was balanced on the point
of a pair of scissors, or was laid upon a pair of tongs, or the
point of a pair of scissors was driven into the rim and it was
suspended by the ring to the middle finger of the right hand.
This was of ancient origin and was extensively practised in
France and Germany even in the sixteenth and seventeenth
centuries.[2]   The existence of the same belief in England is
shown in 1554, when William Haselwood, on being cited before the ecclesiastical court of the diocese of London, said that
having lost his purse " remembering that he being a chylde dyd
hear his mother declare that when any man had lost anything,
then they wolde use a syve and a payre of sheers to bring to
knowledge who hadd the thing lost ; and so he did take a
seve and a payre of sheeres and hanged the seve by the pointe
of the sheeres and sayd these words : By Peter and Paule he
hath yt, namying the party whom he in that behalf suspected."[3]
Evidently at this time the Church regarded the process as
sorcery.

[1] Patetta, Le Ordalie, p. 216.

[2] Grimm's Teutonic Mythology, pp. 1108–9. Grimm quotes Theocritus
and Lucian to show that similar forms of divination with a sieve were
familiar in classical antiquity.

[3] Inderwick, Side-lights on the Stuarts, p. 152.

CHAPTER XI.

BIER-RIGHT.

THE belief that at the approach of the murderer the corpse of the slain would bleed or give some other sign has, under the names of *jus feretri, jus cruentationis, bahr-recht,* and "bier-right," been a resource eagerly seized by puzzled jurists. Its source is not easily traced. There is no evidence of its existence among the Eastern Aryans, nor is it alluded to in any of the primitive "Leges Barbarorum," though Russian legends render probable that it was current among the Slavs at an early day.[1] Enthusiastic explorers into antiquity quote Aristotle for it,[2] while others find in

[1] Patetta, Le Ordalie, p. 158.

[2] Carena, Tractatus de Officio Sanctiss. Inquisit. P. II. Tit. xii. § xxii. In Carena's first edition (Cremona, 1636) there is no allusion to the subject. His attention apparently was attracted to it by a case occurring at Cremona in 1636, where he was acting as criminal judge. In this, Gonsalvo de Cremona, the clerical governor of Cremona, applied to the Council of Milan in February for instructions and received an unsatisfactory reply. He returned to the charge in June and was effectually snubbed by the following:—

"Philippus IV. Hispaniarum Rex et Mediolani Dux.

"Dilectiss. Noster: satis fuit responsum litteris quas die 28 Febr. proxime præteriti scripsistis ad magnificum Senatus nostri præsidem de nece Juliæ Bellisellæ et Jo. Baptisti Vicecomitis, cujus ex vulneribus sanguis exivit in conspectu Vespasiani Schitii, non autem Gasparis Picenardi, pariter suspectorum eius facinoris. Igitur novissimis litteris quibus petiistis vobis dici quid de ea re sentiamus nihil est quod præterea respondeamus nisi ut meliora quæratis indicia et juxta ea procedatis ad expeditionem causæ, referendo referenda.

"Mediolani 3 Julii, 1636."

Lucretius evidence that it was shared by cultured Romans.[1]
Possibly its origin may be derived from a Jewish custom
under which pardon was asked of a corpse for any offences
committed against the living man, the offender laying hold of
the great toe of the body as prepared for sepulture, and it is
said to be not uncommon, where the injury has been grievous,
for the latter to respond to the touch by a copious nasal hem-
orrhage.[2]

The earliest allusion I have met with to this belief occurs
in 1189, and shows that already it was rooted in popular credulity. It is the well-known story that when Richard Cœur
de Lion hastened to the funeral of his father, Henry II., and
met the procession at Fontevraud, the blood poured from the
nostrils of the dead king, whose end he had hastened by his
rebellion and disobedience.[3] Although it never seems to have
formed part of English jurisprudence, its vitality in the popular mind is shown in Shakespeare's Richard III., where Glos-
ter interrupts the obsequies of Henry VI. and Lady Anne
exclaims :—

> " O gentlemen, see, see! dead Henry's wounds
> Open their congealed mouths and bleed afresh !"

---

[1] Marsilii Ficini de Immortal. Animæ Lib. XVI. c. 5.—Del Rio, Magicarum Disquisit. Lib. I. cap. iii. Q. 4, ¶ 6.—C. C. Oelsner de Jure Feretri
cap. I. § 6 (Jenæ, 1711).

The passage relied on has usually a much less decent significance ascribed to it—

> " Idque petit corpus mens, unde 'st saucia amore :
> Namque omnes plerumque cadunt in volnus et illam
> Emicat in partem sanguis unde icimur ictu,
> Et si cominus est hostem ruber occupat humor."
>
> De Rer. Nat. IV. 1041–44.

[2] Gamal. ben Pedazhur's Book of Jewish Ceremonies, London, 1738,
p. 11.

[3] Roger de Hoveden, ann. 1186; Roger of Wendover; Benedicti Ab-
batis Gesta Henricii II. ann. 1189.

And in the ballad of "Earl Richard"—

> "Put na the wite on me, she said,
>   It was my may Catherine.
> Then they hae cut baith fern and thorn,
>   To burn that maiden in.
>
> "It wadna take upon her cheik,
>   Nor yet upon her chin,
> Nor yet upon her yellow hair
>   To cleanse that deadly sin.
>
> "The maiden touched that clay-cauld corpse,
>   A drap it never bled.
> The ladye laid her hand on him,
>   And soon the ground was red."[1]

This indicates that the belief was equally prevalent in Scotland. Indeed King James VI. gave it the stamp of his royal authority,[2] and cases on record there show that it was occasionally received as judicial evidence, and even sometimes prescribed as an ordeal for detection. Thus in 1611, doubts arising as to the mode by which a person had met his death, the vicinage was summoned, as we are told according to custom, to touch the body which had been exhumed for the purpose. The murderer, whose rank relieved him of suspicion, kept away, but his little daughter, attracted by curiosity, approached the corpse, when it began to bleed and the crime was proved.[3] One of the most noted cases in which crime was detected in this manner was that of Philip Standsfield, tried in 1688 for the murder of his father, Sir James Standsfield of New Milne. In this the indictment sets forth that after the body had been found in a pond and an autopsy had been performed by a surgeon, "James Row, merchant, having lifted the left side of Sir James, his head and shoulder, and the said Philip the right side, his father's body, though care-

---

[1] Scott's Minstrelsy of the Scottish Border.

[2] Nam ut in homicidio occulto sanguis e cadavere, tangente homicida, erumpit, quasi cœlitus poscens ultionem.—Demonologiæ Lib. III. c. vi.

[3] Scott's notes to the ballad of Earl Richard.

fully cleaned, as said is, did (according to God's usual mode of discovering murders), blood afresh upon him and defiled all his hands, which struck him with such a terror that he immediately let his father's head and body fall with violence and fled from the body and in consternation and confusion cryed Lord have mercy upon me! and bowed himself down over a seat in the church (where the corp were inspected), wiping his father's innocent blood off his own murdering hands upon his cloaths." When such was the spirit of the prosecution it need not surprise us that though the defence showed that in the autopsy an incision had been made in the neck, where there was a large accumulation of extravasated blood, and though high authorities were quoted to prove that such bleeding was not evidence sufficient even to justify torture, Philip Standsfield was condemned and executed in spite of the insufficiency of circumstantial evidence.[1] A similar incident is recorded in the indictment of Christian Wilson, tried for witchcraft at Edinburgh in 1661.[2] These cases are typical, inasmuch as they illustrate the two forms, the existence of which differentiates this from other ordeals. Sometimes, as in others, suspects were brought, under judicial order, to view or touch the body. Frequently, however, the occurrence is spontaneous, and serves to excite or direct suspicion where none existed before.

The belief extended throughout all the nationalities of Europe. Although there is no reference to it in the German municipal codes of the thirteenth century, there is ample store of cases both of its spontaneous occurrence and of its judicial employment. In 1261, at Forchheim, a manifestation of this kind brought home to the Jews the lingering death of a young girl slain by them according to their hellish custom, and the guilty were promptly broken on the wheel.[3] More serious

---

[1] Cobbett's State Trials, XI. 1371.
[2] Spottiswoode Miscellanies, II. 69.
[3] Alphonsi de Spina Fortalicium Fidei Lib. III. consid. vii.

was an affair at Ueberlingen in 1331. The body of a child
was found in a pond and from the character of the wounds it
was recognized that Jewish fanaticism had caused the murder.
The corpse was therefore carried in front of the houses of the
principal Jews and when it began to bleed the evidence was
deemed sufficient. The burgomaster endeavored to calm the
populace, but his efforts were ascribed to Hebrew gold, and
condign punishment was resolved upon. All the Jews of the
town were skilfully decoyed into a large stone house and when
they had been securely locked in the upper stories it was set
on fire. Those that succeeded in throwing themselves from
the roof were dispatched by the mob, and the rest, to the
number of three hundred, were consumed by the avenging
flames. Though sundry miracles ratified the justice of the act,
yet the godless Emperor, Louis of Bavaria, punished the pious
townsfolk by dismantling their walls and levying a heavy fine
upon them.[1] The judicial employment of the ordeal is seen
in a case in 1324, when Reinward, a canon of Minden, was
murdered by a drunken soldier and the crime was proved by
a trial of this kind.[2] More satisfactory, as showing how through
the influence of imagination the ordeal sometimes resulted in
substantial justice, was a case in Lucerne in 1503, when Hans
Speiss of Etiswiler murdered his wife. She was duly buried,
but suspicion arose, and after three weeks the body was exhumed and he was brought before it. As he approached, it
flushed with color and immediately began to bleed. He had
hitherto defiantly asserted his innocence, but at this sight he
fell on his knees, confessed the crime, and begged for mercy.
He was broken on the wheel and died most penitently.[3]
Numerous cases are on record of its use throughout Germany
in the seventeenth century, of which it will suffice to refer to
one in which the corpse manifested a discrimination greatly

---

[1] Vitodurani Chron. ann. 1331.
[2] Swartii Chron. Ottbergensis ᶻ xlvii. (Paullini Antiq. Germ. Syntagma).
[3] Val. Anshelm, Berner-Chronik, ann. 1503 (Bern, 1886, II. 393).

impressing the authorities. It had been dead for thirty-six hours and refused to bleed on the approach of two persons suspected. Then three others were brought, one of whom, George, had planned the murder and been present, but had not taken personal part in it: for him the corpse bled at the mouth. Then came Lorenz, who had held the victim when the blow was struck: for him the mouth frothed and the wound bled. Finally Claus, who had inflicted the blow, came, and for him the blood gushed forth from the wound.[1]

The extent to which popular credulity was prepared to accept this miraculous manifestation is shown in a story which obtained wide currency. An Austrian noble journeying to Vienna passed through a wood in which his dogs scratched up some bones. Their whiteness struck his fancy; he carried them to the city and sent them to a cutler to be worked up into some ornament, when as soon as they were brought into the presence of the artificer they became covered with blood. The noble reported the fact to the magistrates, the cutler was arrested and confessed that twenty years before he had slain a comrade and buried the body where the bones were found.[2] We may trace a more poetic form of this sympathy in the legend which relates the welcome given by the bones of Abelard to Heloise when, twenty years after his death, her body was consigned to his tomb.

In Denmark, though this form of trial finds no place in the codes of law, we are told that it was generally used during the seventeenth century in all appropriate cases.[3] In Holstein

---

[1] Oelsner de Jure Feretri c. iii. § 8. This little thesis was written in 1680. It seems to have met with approval, for it was reprinted in 1711 and 1735.

[2] Oelsner *op. cit.* cap. iii. § 7. A variant of this story is told by Scott in his notes to the "Minstrelsy of the Scottish Border." In this the bone chances to be fished up from a river, where it had lain for fifty years, and the murderer, then an old man, happens to touch it, when it streams with blood. He confesses the crime and is duly condemned.

[3] Carena, *op. cit.* P. II. Tit. xii. § 22.

there was a custom known as *Scheingehen*, in which, when a murderer remained undiscovered, a hand was severed from the corpse with provident care and preserved as a touchstone for the future. A celebrated case is related in the books in which a dead body was found and buried, and the hand was hung up in the prison of Itzehoe. Ten years later a thief was arrested and brought there, when the hand immediately began to bleed freely, and the thief confessed the murder.[1]

Italy shared fully in the belief. The most distinguished exponent of the New Learning in the fifteenth century, Marsiglio Ficino, the Platonist, does not hesitate to adduce it as a fact well known to judges, in his argument to prove the immortality of the soul against the Averrhoism fashionable in his day.[2] Equally distinguished as a jurist was Hippolito de' Marsigli (died in 1528), who relates that in his youth he was governor of Alberga, near Genoa, when a murder occurred without affording evidence as to the perpetrator. By the advice of an old citizen he had the body brought before him and summoned all liable to suspicion to pass near it one by one. When the homicide approached, to the surprise of Marsigli, the wounds burst out afresh, but his incredulity was such that he did not consider this to warrant even an arrest until he had collected sufficient collateral evidence, when the culprit confessed without torture.[3] In Venice this ordeal was sometimes used and likewise in Piedmont, though in the latter region some magistrates regarded it as fallacious, for their experience showed that blood had not flowed in the presence of those

---

[1] Oelsner, cap. iii. § 6. Joh. Christ. Nehring de Indiciis, Jenæ, 1714, p. 19.—Königswarter (*op. cit.* p. 183) tells us that this custom was observed also in the Netherlands and throughout the North.

[2] Unde forte contingit ut occisi hominis vulnus etiam jacente cadavere, in eum qui vulneraverat, si modo ille comminus instet, vulnus ipsum inspiciens, sanguinem rursus ejiciat, quod quidem evenire nonnunquam Lucretius affirmavit et judices observarunt.—De Immortalitate Animæ Lib. XVI. c. 5.

[3] Marsil. Pract. Criminal. (*ap.* Binsfeld, de Confess. Maleficar. pp. 111–12).

subsequently proved to be guilty.[1] In Corsica the belief, if not still existent, has been widely diffused until within a few years.[2]

France seems to have been even more addicted to this superstition. About 1580 President Bertrand d'Argentré, in his Commentaries on the Customs of Brittany, treats it as an indisputable fact and one affording good evidence.[3] In Picardy we are told it was constantly used by magistrates, it was approved by the courts in Bordeaux, and Chassanée, whose authority in Burgundy was great, argues that its occurrence justifies the torture of the accused without further videence.[4] Spain likewise was not exempt from it. A celebrated case is cited in the books as occurring in Aragon, where the accused was brought before the corpse of the victim in the public square and appealed to God to perform a miracle if he were guilty, whereupon the body raised its right arm, pointed with its fingers to the several wounds and then to the accused ; this was regarded as sufficient proof, and under sentence of the Council of Aragon the culprit was executed. Another case which occurred at Ledesma, near Salamanca, shows the existence of the belief in Castile.[5]

English colonists brought the superstition across the Atlantic, where it has never been fairly eradicated from the popular mind. In January, 1680, in Accomac County, Virginia, a new-born illegitimate child of " Mary, daughter of Sarah, wife of Paul Carter" died and was buried. It was nearly six weeks before suspicion was aroused, when the coroner impannelled a jury of twelve matrons, whose verdict recorded that

---

[1] Carena, *loc. cit.*   [2] Patetta, Le Ordalie, p. 34.

[3] Cujus rei rationem petunt e causis naturalibus et reddere conatur Petrus Apponensis; quæ qualescunque tandem hæ sint, constat evenisse sæpe, et magnis autoribus tradita exempla.—B. d'Agentré Comment. in Consuet. Britann. p. 145 (Ed. Antverp. 1644).

[4] Carena, *loc. cit.*—Oelsner, *op. cit.* c. iv. § 2.

[5] Carena, *loc. cit.* A similar dramatic exhibition by a corpse is recorded in a case occurring in Germany in 1607.—Oelsner, c. iii. § 5.

Sarah Carter was brought to touch the corpse without result, but when Paul Carter touched it "immediately whilst he was stroaking ye childe ye black and settled places above ye body of ye childe grew fresh and red so that blud was ready to come through ye skin of ye childe." On the strength of this verdict an indictment was found against Paul Carter, but with what result the records do not show.[1] Nearly a century later, in 1767, the coroner's jury of Bergen County, N. J., was summoned to view the body of one Nicholas Tuers, whose death had led to suspicion of murder. Johannes Demarest, the coroner, attests that he had no belief in bier-right and paid no attention to the experiment, when one of the jury touched the body without result. At length a slave named Harry, who had been suspected without proof, was brought forward for the trial when he heard an exclamation "He is the man," and was told that the body had bled when touched by Harry. He then ordered the slave to place his hand on its face, when about a tablespoonful of blood flowed from each nostril, and Harry confessed the murder.[2] So recently as 1833 a man named Getter was hanged in Pennsylvania for the murder of his wife, and among the evidence which was allowed to go to the jury on the trial was that of a female witness, who swore "If my throat was to be cut I could tell, before God Almighty, that the deceased smiled when he (the murderer) touched her. I swore this before the justice, and also that she bled considerably. I was sent for to dress her and lay her out. He touched her twice. He made no hesitation about doing it. I also swore before the justice that it was observed by other people in the house."[3] This is perhaps the latest instance in which bier-right has figured in regular judicial proceedings, but the popular belief in it is by no means eradicated. In 1860 the

---

[1] I owe this account to the kindness of L. S. Joynes, M.D., of Richmond, who informs me that he found it while examining the Accomac County records.

[2] Annual Register for 1767, pp. 144–5.

[3] Dunglison's Human Physiology, 8th Edition, II. 657.

Philadelphia journals mention a case in which the relatives of a deceased person, suspecting foul play, vainly importuned the coroner, six weeks after the interment, to have the body exhumed in order that it might be touched by a person whom they regarded as concerned in his death.   In 1868 at Verdiersville, Virginia, a suspected murderer was compelled to touch the body of a woman found murdered in a wood ; and in 1869, at Lebanon, Illinois, the bodies of two murdered persons were exhumed and two hundred of the neighbors were marched past and made to touch them in the hope of identifying the criminals.[1]

In Germany, in the seventeenth century, there was a recognized formula for the administration of the ordeal.   The corpse was exposed to the open air for some hours, with breast and stomach bare to insure the thorough coagulation of the blood.   The person suspected was then brought forward and required to repeat certain adjurations read to him, and then he was made to touch with two fingers the mouth, the navel, and the wounds, if there were any.   If the corpse manifested any signs of sensation, if there was frothing at the mouth, or bleeding from any orifices or wounds it was considered an evidence of guilt.[2]   The trial was not a mere popular experiment, but was a judicial proceeding, under the order of a magistrate.

Although bier-right, in comparison with other ordeals, plays so inconspicuous a part in the history of jurisprudence, it is especially interesting in one respect.   As a judicial expedient, it did not spring into notice until after the other vulgar ordeals had been discredited and banished from the courts.   It escaped the censure of the Church and was a survival of the Judgment of God, reaching its fullest development in the seventeenth century.   It thus became the subject of investigation and debate in an age of critical tendencies and comparative

[1] Phila. Bulletin, April 19, 1860.—N. Y. World, June 5, 1868.—Phila. North American, March 29, 1869.

[2] Oelsner, *op. cit.* cap. i. § 10; c. iii. § 8.

intelligence. Among those who had faith in it there was much fruitless speculation to account for the result, and there was by no means a consensus of opinion as to the causes at work. In 1487 the inquisitor Sprenger takes a materialistic view and uses it as the basis of an argument on the wonderful properties of inanimate matter. He explains that air is introduced into the wound when it is inflicted, and that it rushes out when agitated by the presence of the slayer, bringing blood with it, but he adds that others believe it to be the cry of blood from the earth against the murderer, as related of the first homicide, Cain.[1] About a century later Del Rio tells us that some looked upon it as a miracle, others as an accident, while he himself can see no better reason than the violent antipathy conceived by the slain for the slayer.[2] Carena holds it to be the mysterious Judgment of God, unless it happens to be the work of the demon, and in this uncertainty concludes that if there are no other proofs it only justifies further investigation and not torture.[3] Oelsner informs us that learned men disputed whether it was occasioned by antipathy or sympathy, by the remains of the soul in the body, by wandering spirits of the dead, or by the spirit of enmity, and he concludes that the causes are sometimes natural and sometimes supernatural.[4] It is significant that, among so many theories framed by believers in the fact, there were so few who assented to the direct interposition of God.

Among jurists there was lively debate as to the exact weight of the evidence when the experiment was successful. Criminal lawyers were naturally loath to admit that it was decisive, for the corollary followed that if no bleeding occurred the suspect must be innocent, which was contradicted by the numerous

---

[1] Malleus Maleficarum, Francof. 1580, pp. 21, 32.

[2] Magicarum Disquisit. Lib. I. cap. iii. Q. 4, ¶ 6.

[3] Tract. de Officio Sanctiss. Inquisit. P. II. Tit. xii. § 22.—" Sed utcunque sit certum est in judiciis passim fuisse practicatum indicium istud sanguinis emissi sufficere ad torturam si doctoribus nostris credendum est."

[4] De Jure Feretri, cap. ii.

cases in which an accused successfully passed through the
ordeal and was subsequently proved to be guilty. This de-
cisiveness was the essence of the older ordeals, and was wholly
opposed to the current inquisitorial system in which certainty
was aimed at by the habitual use of torture. Almost with
unanimity, therefore, the legists held that it was only one of
the indications pointing to guilt, and that its failure could not
be alleged as a proof of innocence. They differed, however,
as to the weight of the indication which it afforded. Authoritative names were cited in favor of the opinion that it sufficed
by itself to justify the subjection of the accused to torture, as
in a case at Marburg in 1608, where on this ground alone
several suspects were tortured, when they confessed and were
executed. Others took the position that it did not of itself
warrant the use of torture, and that it required to be supported
by other proof. Among these was the great criminal jurist
Carpzov, who states that in cases submitted to him and his
colleagues he had seen many in which no bleeding occurred
when the murderers touched the corpse, while in others it did
occur when innocents were exposed to the trial.[1] When the
discussion had reached this stage the ordeal became a super-
fluity which was bound to disappear from the courts in spite
of the persistence of popular credulity, and a school of jurists
arose who denied that it deserved the name of evidence, and
declared that it must be wholly disregarded. It was only a
question of time when this opinion should triumph, and the
first quarter of the eighteenth century probably witnessed the
disappearance of this survival of mediævalism from recognized
judicial procedure.[2]

[1] Oelsner, *op. cit.* c. iv. §§ 2, 3.   Cf. Zangeri Tract. de Quæstionibus cap.
ii. n. 160.—It is perhaps worthy of remark that the earlier jurists made no
allusion to it. Angelus Aretinus, Albertus de Gandavo, and Bonifacius
de Vitellinis, in discussing the proofs requisite to justify torture, do not mention it.

[2] As late as 1678, an anonymous *Praxis Criminalis*, printed at Alten-
burg, speaks of it as a recognized process, gives instructions as to the cautions

CHAPTER XII.

OATHS AS ORDEALS.

THE oath naturally formed an integral portion of the ordeal. Even as in the battle trial both parties, on entering the lists, were compelled to swear to the truth of their assertions, so in the other ordeals the accuser and accused took an oath immediately prior to the administration of the test.[1] Sometimes, however, the oath of the accused was regarded as a sufficient ordeal in itself. We have seen above how, among many and diverse races, disculpatory oaths are administered with ceremonies which render them practically ordeals in view of the popular belief that misfortune will follow perjury. The anthropomorphic mythology of Hellas presents this idea in its most concrete form by the most solemn oath of the gods, taken on the water of Styx brought in a vase for the purpose, perjury on which was followed by a year of stupor and nine years of segregation from all fellowship with the brother immortals.[2] We have also seen (pp. 29 sqq.) that in Christendom the Church set little store by simple oaths, but reckoned their obligation by the holiness of the material objects on which they were taken; and when these were relics of peculiar sanctity they were held to have the power of punishing the perjurer, thus rendering the oath administered upon them an absolute ordeal. This belief developed itself at an early

requisite, and says the record must be sent to the magistrate (Ib. c. i. § 11). —In 1714, Nehring (De Indiciis, Jenæ, 1714, pp. 42–3) still quotes authorities in favor of its justifying torture, and feels obliged to argue at some length to demonstrate its inadequacy.

[1] Martene de antiq. Ecclesiæ Ritibus, Lib. III. c. vii. Ordo 8, 16.
[2] Hesiodi Theogonia, v. 794–806.

period in the history of the Church.   St. Augustin relates
that at Milan a thief, who swore upon some holy relics with
the intention of bearing false witness, was forced irresistibly
to confess himself guilty of the offence which he designed to
fasten upon another ; and Augustin himself, when unable to
decide between two of his ecclesiastics who accused each
other of revolting crime, sent them both to the shrine of St.
Felix of Nola, in the full expectation that the judgment of
God would bring to light the truth as between them.[1]
Gregory the Great shows the same belief when he alludes
to a simple purgatorial oath taken by a bishop on the relics
of St. Peter in terms which expressly convey the idea that
the accused, if guilty, had exposed himself to no little danger,
and that his performance of the ceremony unharmed had sufficiently proved his innocence.   Gregory, moreover, in one
of his Homilies, assumes that perjury committed on the relics
of the saints is punished by demoniacal possession.[2]

This was not a belief likely to be allowed to die out for lack
of nourishment.   When, in the tenth century, Adaulfus, Bishop
of Compostella, was accused of a nameless crime, and was sentenced by the hasty judgment of the king to be gored to death
by a wild bull, he had taken the precaution, before appearing
at the trial, to devoutly celebrate mass in his full pontificals.
The bull, maddened with dogs and trumpets, rushed furiously
at the holy man ; then, suddenly pausing, advanced gently
towards him and placed its horns in his hands, nor could any
efforts of the assistants provoke it to attack him.   The king
and his courtiers, awed by this divine interposition in favor
of innocence, threw themselves at the feet of the saint, who
pardoned them and retired to the wildest region of the Astu-

---

[1] August. Epist. lxxviii. §§ 2, 3 (Ed. Benedict.).—" Ut quod homines
invenire non possunt de quolibet eorum divino judicio propaletur."

[2] Decreti c. 6, Caus. II. q. v.—Gregor. PP. I. Homil XXXII. in Evangel.
cap. 6.

Dr. Patetta (Ordalie, p. 15) informs us that in some parts of Piedmont it
is still believed that a perjurer will die within the year.

rias, where he passed the rest of his days as an anchorite.
He left his chasuble behind him, however, and this garment
thenceforth possessed the miraculous power that, when worn
by any one taking an oath, it could not be removed if he
committed perjury.[1]

In other cases the shrines of saints convicted the perjurer by
throwing him down in an epileptic fit, or by fixing him rigid
and motionless at the moment of his invoking them to witness
his false oath.[2] The monks of Abingdon boasted a black cross
made from the nails of the crucifixion, said to have been given
them by the Emperor Constantine, a false oath on which was
sure to cost the malefactor his life; and the worthy chronicler
assures us that the instances in which its miraculous power had
been triumphantly exhibited were too numerous to be specified.[3]
At the priory of Die, dependent on the great Benedictine abbey
of Fleury, there was preserved an arm-bone of St. Maur, which
was possessed of somewhat similar properties.   On one occasion a steward of the priory named Joscelin was accused of
embezzlement, and offered to rebut the evidence against him
by an oath taken on the arm of St. Maur.   Rejoiced at passing through the test triumphantly, he removed his hand from
the relic, and stroking his long beard with it he exclaimed,
" By this beard, the oath I swore was true !" when suddenly
the beard came off in his hand, and his chin, thenceforth hair-
less, was the evidence alike of his guilt and his perjury, so that
he and his descendants were at once proclaimed ineligible to
the stewardship.[4]   Less serious in its consequences was a false
oath taken by a peasant on the altar of St. Martial of Limoges.
The offender was deprived of speech, and could only bellow

[1] Munionis Histor. Compostellan. Lib. I. cap. 2, § 2.

[2] Gregor. Turon. De Gloria Martyrum cap. 58, 103.

[3] Sancta enim adeo est, ut nullus, juramento super eam præstito, im-
pune et sine periculo vitæ suæ possit affirmare mendacium.—Hist. Monast.
Abing. Lib. I. c. xii. (M. R. Series).

[4] Radulph. Tortarii Mirac. S. Benedicti cap. xxii. (Migne's Patrol. T.
CLX. p. 1210).

like an ox until he had prayed over the tomb of the saint, and
his throat had received the sign of the cross from a priest.[1]
Even at the present day the jaw-bone of St. Patrick is preserved near Belfast, and is used extra-judicially as an ordeal,
in the full conviction that the slightest variation from the truth
will bring instantaneous punishment on the perjurer,[2] and in
Sardinia a similar oath on relics is believed when false to flay
the hand of the accused.[3] In the Middle Ages these dangerous
relics were common, and however we may smile at the simplicity of the faith reposed in them, we may rest assured that
on many occasions they were the means of eliciting confessions
which could have been obtained by no devices of legal subtlety
according to modern procedures.

Nor did it always require death to confer the sanctity requisite to perform these miracles, as was attested during the life
of St. Bertrand of Comminges. A woman accused of adultery
went to the saint and laying her hand on him swore to her innocence, when the hand immediately withered and remained
a permanent witness of her guilt and her perjury.[4]

Even without any special sanctity in the administration of
the oath, Heaven sometimes interposed to protect the rights of
the Church. About the year 1200 Cæsarius of Königswinter,
a knight, who had borrowed twenty marcs of his brother,
Hirminold Dean of the Chapter of Bonn, denied the loan
after his brother's death. As the money belonged to the
Church, the chapter summoned the knight, and having no
proof, were obliged to content themselves with his oath.
Having accomplished his perjury, Cæsarius mounted his
horse and returned homewards, but when he had accom-

---

[1] Gregor. Turon. de Glor. Confess. c. xxix.

[2] Chambers's Book of Days, I. 384.

[3] Patetta, Le Ordalie, p. 34. In Tonga and Samoa false oaths taken on
certain sacred articles are likewise believed to be followed by speedy death
(Ib. p. 63).

[4] Vit. S. Bertrandi Convenar. No. 26 (Martene Ampliss. Collect. VI.
1035).

plished the half of his journey his horse was suddenly fixed immovable to the earth, and he found himself deprived of the use of the tongue which he had thus abused. Recognizing the source of the trouble, he prayed to Abraham, promising to retrace his steps and confess his sin. He was immediately released, returned to Bonn, made restitution, and accepted penance. He subsequently entered the monastery of Heisterbach as a novice, and related the story of himself.[1]

CHAPTER XIII.

POISON ORDEALS.

THE poison ordeal, which forms the basis of judicial proceedings among so many of the African tribes, seems not to have been brought into Europe by the Aryan invaders, although it was in use among their kindred who remained in the East. Possibly this may have arisen from the fact that in their migrations they could no longer obtain the substances which they had been accustomed to use, and before they had familiarized themselves with the resources of their new homes the custom may have fallen into desuetude amid the abundance of other methods. A lingering remnant of it may perhaps be detected in the trial of the priestess of the Gæum in Achaia, already alluded to, but substantially the poison ordeal may be regarded as obsolete in the West.

In the East, however, it has continued in use. The poison prescribed is that known as *sringa*, produced by a tree which grows in the Himalayas, and the judge invokes it—

" On account of thy venomous and dangerous nature thou art destruction to all living creatures ; thou, O poison, knowest what mortals do not comprehend.

" This man being arraigned in a cause desires to be cleared

---

[1] Cæsar. Heisterbach. Dial. Mirac. Dist. IV. c. lviii.

from guilt. Therefore mayest thou deliver him lawfully from
this perplexity."

Seven grains of the substance, mixed with clarified butter,
are then administered ; if no evil symptoms follow during the
day, at evening the accused is dismissed as innocent.[1] A more
recent authority describes a somewhat different form.   A
specified quantity of some deadly article, varying in amount
with its activity, is mixed with thirty times its weight of *ghee*,
or clarified butter.   The patient takes this, standing with his
face to the north, and if it produces no effect upon him while
the bystanders can clap their hands five hundred times, he is
pronounced innocent and antidotes are at once administered
to him.[2] A slight variation of this is recorded by a writer of
the last century.   After appropriate religious ceremonies, seven
barleycorns of the deadly root *vishanaga*, or of arsenic, are
mingled with thirty-two times its bulk of *ghee*, and eaten by
the accused from the hand of a Brahman.   If it produces no
effect, he is acquitted.[3] Much more humane was the custom
described by Hiouen Thsang in the seventh century, when the
experiment was performed vicariously on a bullock, even as a
hen is used among the Niam-Niam of equatorial Africa.   The
animal was fed with poisoned food, and poison was likewise
inserted in a wound made for the purpose in the right leg,
while the fate of the accused was determined by the death or
survival of the unlucky beast.[4]

Still another form in modern times seems to have been
invented as a combination of the hot-water and poison ordeals.
A *naga* or cobra is dropped into a deep earthen pot along with
a coin or ring, which the person on trial must remove with his
hand.   If he is bitten, he is condemned ; if he escapes scath-
less, he is acquitted.[5]

---

[1] Institutes of Vishnu XIII.—Yajnavalkya, II. 110-111.   Yajnavalkya
classes it among the ordeals reserved for the Sudra caste (Ib. II. 98).

[2] Ayeen Akbery, II. 497.

[3] Ali Ibrahim Khan (As. Researches, I. 391).

[4] Wheeler's India, III. 262.   [5] Ali Ibrahim Khan, *ubi sup.*

CHAPTER XIV.

IRREGULAR ORDEALS.

THE devout dependence upon Heaven, exhibited in the ordeal, did not exhaust itself on the forms of trial described above, but was manifested in various other expedients, sometimes adopted as legal processes, and sometimes merely the outcome of individual credulous piety. While therefore they cannot be regarded as forming part of the recognized institutions of Europe, still they illustrate too clearly the tendency of thought and belief to be entirely passed over.

Among these may be classed a practice which was substantially an appeal to God to regulate the amount of punishment requisite for the expiation of a crime. One or more bands of iron were not infrequently fastened around the neck or arm of a murderer, who was banished until by pilgrimage and prayer his reconciliation and pardon should be manifested by the miraculous loosening of the fetter, showing that soul and body were both released from their bonds.[1] A case is related of a Pole thus wandering with a circlet tightly clasped to each arm. One fell before the intercession of St. Adalbert, the apostle of Prussia, but the other retained its hold until the sinner came to the shrine of St. Hidulf near Toul. There, joining in the worship of the holy monks, the remaining band flew off with such force that it bounded against the opposite wall, while the pardoned criminal fell fainting to the ground, the blood pour-

---

[1] Fratricidas autem et parricidas sive sacerdotum interfectores . . . per manum et ventrem ferratos de regno ejiciat ut instar Cain jugi et profugi circueant terram.—Leg. Bracilai Boœmor (Annal. Saxo ann. 1039). So also a century earlier for the murder of a chief.—Concil. Spalatens. ann. 927, can. 7 (Batthyani, I. 331).

ing from his liberated arm: a miracle gratefully recorded by
the spiritual children of the saint.[1] Equally melodramatic in
its details is a similar instance of an inhabitant of Prunay
near Orléans, laden with three iron bands for fratricide. His
weary pilgrimage was lightened of two by the intercession of
St. Peter at Rome, and the third released itself in the most
demonstrative manner through the merits of St. Bertin and
St. Omer.[2] If the legend of St. Emeric of Hungary be true,
the pope himself did not disdain to prescribe this ordeal to
the criminal whose miraculous release caused the immediate
canonization of the saint by a synod in 1073.[3] In France at
one time we are told that this penance or punishment was
habitual in cases of parricide or fratricide, when the rings or
chains were wrought from the sword with which the crime
had been committed.[4] Repentant sinners also frequently
bound themselves with iron rings and chains by way of
penance, and the spontaneous disruption of these, which sometimes occurred, was regarded as a sign that God had pardoned
the penitent.[5] The shrine of St. Nicetius at Lyons had a
special reputation in these cases, and the pile of broken rings
and chains exhibited there in the sixth century testified to the
power of the saint's intercession.[6]

The spirit of the age is likewise manifested in an appeal to
Heaven which terminated a quarrel in the early part of the
twelfth century between St. Gerald, Archbishop of Braga, and

[1] De Successoribus S. Hidulfi cap. xviii. (Patrolog. CXXXVIII. p. 218).
A similar case attested the sanctity of St. Mansuetus (Vit. S. Mansueti Lib.
II. c. 17.—Martene et Durand. Thesaur. III. 1025).

[2] Folcardi Mirac. S. Bertin. Lib. I. c. 4.

[3] Batthyani, Legg. Eccles. Hung. T. I. p. 413. See also Mirac. S.
Swithuni c. ii. § 32.—Mirac. S. Yvonis c. 21 (Patrol. CLV. 76, 91).
Various other instances may be found in Muratori, Antiq. Med. Ævi, Diss.
23. Charlemagne seems to have considered it a deception to be restrained
by law.—Car. Mag. cap. I. ann. 789, § lxxvii.

[4] Martene de antiquis Ecclesiæ Ritibus Lib. I. cap. vi. art. 4 n. 12.

[5] Cæsar. Heisterb. Dial. Mirac. Dist. XI. c. xxvii. xxix.

[6] Greg. Turonens. Vitæ Patrum, Cap. viii. n. 10.

a magnate of his diocese, concerning the patronage of a church. Neither being inclined to yield, at length the noble prayed that God would decide the cause by not permitting the one who was in the wrong to live beyond the year, to which St. Gerald assented; and in six months the death of the unhappy noble showed how dangerous it was to undertake such experiments with a saint.[1] This, indeed, may be held to have warrant of high authority, for when, in 336, Alexander Bishop of Constantinople was about to engage in disputation with the arch-heretic Arius, he underwent a long fast, and shut himself up for many days and nights alone in his church praying to God, and finally supplicating that if his faith were wrong he might not live to see the day of contest, while if Arius were in error he likewise might be taken off in advance; and the orthodoxy of the Nicene creed was confirmed miraculously by the sudden and terrible death of Arius within a few days.[2]

The error of the Arian doctrine of the Trinity was demonstrated by another volunteer miracle about the year 510, when Deuterius the Arian Bishop of Constantinople undertook to baptize a convert in the name of the Father through the Son in the Holy Ghost, and was rebuked for using this heretical formula by the sudden disappearance of all the water in the font.[3]

With these examples may be classed a trial of faith proposed by Herigarius, one of the earliest Christian converts of Sweden, as conclusive, though not so dangerous as that of Bishop Poppo. After frequent disputes with his Pagan neighbors, he one day suggested, when a storm was approaching, that they

---

[1] Bernald. Vit. S. Gerald. cap. xv. (Baluz et Mansi I. 134).

[2] Socratis Hist. Eccles. Lib. I. c. 25.

[3] Theodori Lector. H. E. Lib. II. When, about the year 500, St. Avitus bishop of Vienne was disputing with the Arians before King Gundobald, he offered to leave the decision as to the rival faiths to Heaven by both parties going to the tomb of St. Justus and appealing to him, but the Arians prudently refused to imitate Saul and practise necromantic arts.—Collatio Episcoporum coram R. Gundebaldo (Migne's Patrologia, LIX. 391).

should stand on one side and he on the other, and see which of them would get wet. The rain came down in torrents and nearly drowned the heathen scoffers, while Herigarius and a boy in his company serenely looked on, untouched by a single drop.[1]

When, at the end of the ninth century, the attacks of Rollo and his Normans drove the monks of St. Martin of Tours to seek safety for themselves and the priceless relics of their saint at Auxerre, the body of St. Martin was deposited in the church of St. Germain near the tomb of the latter. The miracles wrought by the newcomer speedily caused a large influx of oblations which the strangers took to themselves. The monks of St. Germain claimed an equal share on the ground that the miracles were wrought by the combined merits of both saints. The Touraingeois resisted the demand, and finally offered to decide the question by taking a leper and placing him for a night between the rival reliquaries. If he should in the morning be entirely cured, they agreed to admit that both saints were concerned in the miracles, and that the receipts should be shared; but if only one side of him was restored to health then the saint on whose side he was cured should have the credit and his monks the money. This was agreed to; the leper was placed between the tombs, and both parties spent the night in prayer. In the morning he was found with the half of him towards St. Martin sound and well, while the side towards St. Germain had not been in the least benefited. To remove any lingering doubts, he was then turned around, and the other side was cured. The result was beyond further question, and the monks of St. Martin were permitted to enjoy in peace thenceforth the offerings of the faithful.[2]

It occasionally happened that the direct interference of Heaven, without the use of formulas, was volunteered to stay

---

[1] Remberti Vit. St. Anscharii c. xvi. (Langebek I. 458–9).

[2] Gesta Consul. Andegavens. c. iii. § 16 (D'Achery III. 241).

the blundering hand of human justice. In 1219, near Cologne, a man was condemned for theft and promptly hanged, but when the spectators supposed him comfortably dead, he suddenly exclaimed, "Your labor is vain; you cannot strangle me, for my lord bishop St. Nicholas is aiding me. I see him." Taking this for a convincing proof of his innocence, the crowd at once cut him down, and he hastened to the church of Bruweiler to give thanks for his miraculous escape.[1] It is curious to observe, however, that the pious contemporary narrator of this instance of the power of St. Nicholas is careful to let us understand that the man may have been guilty after all. St. Olaf of Norway once interfered in the same way to support, during nine hours of suspension, a man unjustly hanged on a false accusation of theft.[2]

Heaven could also be directly appealed to without the intervention of the hot iron or boiling water. A question of much importance to northern Italy was thus settled in the tenth century, when Uberto of Tuscany, driven into exile by Otho the Great, returned after a long absence, and found his wife Willa with a likely boy whose paternity he refused to acknowledge. After much parleying, the delicate question was thus settled. A large assembly, consisting principally of ecclesiastics, was convened, in which Uberto sat without anything to distinguish him. The boy, who had never seen him, was placed in the centre, and prayers were offered by all present that he should be led by divine instinct to his father. The prayers were promptly answered, for he rushed without hesitation to the arms of Uberto, who could no longer indulge in unworthy doubts, and in time Ugo became the most powerful prince of Italy.[3]

There would appear to have been a form of ordeal known as the judgment of the Holy Ghost, but its details are unknown.

---

[1] Cæsar. Heisterbach Dial. Mirac. Dist. VIII. c. lxxiii.
[2] Legendæ de S. Olavo (Langebek II. 551–2).
[3] Pet. Damian. Opusc. LVII. Diss. ii. c. 3, 4.

Pope Stephen VII. employed it for the condemnation of the body of his predecessor Pope Formosus, in 896. The corpse was dug up for the purpose, clad in papal vestments, and brought before a synod of bishops; after condemnation, the three fingers used in benediction were cut off, and it was cast into the Tiber. After the murder of Stephen in 898, John IX. assembled another council which annulled the condemnation and forbade such proceedings in the future, for the unanswerable reason that a dead body cannot vindicate itself, and the judgment was still further discredited when the corpse was fished out of the river, and on being brought into St. Peter's all the sacred images there bowed to it. Whatever may have been the judgment of the Holy Ghost it naturally became obsolete.[1]

Perhaps the simplest and at the same time one of the most barbarous of ordeals is prescribed in a MS. of the eleventh century for Jews unlucky enough to be involved in controversies with Christians. The Jew was made to stand up and his knees were closely bound together; a collar made of brambles was placed around his neck, and a switch of brambles, five cubits long and well furnished with thorns, was smartly dragged between his thighs. If he escaped without a scratch he was acquitted.[2]

In the crazied effort to detect the all-pervading and secret crime of witchcraft, a number of superstitious observances found currency among the people which practically assumed the position of ordeals. Thus in the latter half of the sixteenth century it was believed that a fragment of earth from a grave, when sanctified in the Mass and placed on the threshold of a church door, would prevent the egress of any witch who might be within; and a similar power was attributed to a splinter of oak from a gallows, sprinkled with holy water and hung up in the church porch.[3]

---

[1] Conc. Roman. ann. 904 (898) c. I (Harduin. VI. I. 487).—Liutprand. Antapodos. Lib. I. c. 30, 31.

[2] Patetta, Le Ordalie, p. 218.

[3] Wieri de Præstigiis Dæmonum, pp. 589–90.

CHAPTER XV.

CONDITIONS OF THE ORDEAL.

THE ordeal was thoroughly and completely a judicial process, ordained by the law for certain cases, and carried out by the tribunals as a regular form of ordinary procedure. From the earliest times, the accused who was ordered to undergo the trial was compelled to submit to it, as to any other decree of court. Thus, by the Salic law, a recusant was summoned to the royal court; and if still contumacious, he was outlawed and his property confiscated, as was customary in all cases of contempt.[1] The directions of the codes, as we have seen, are generally precise, and admit of no alternative.[2] Occasionally, however, a privilege of selection was afforded between this and other modes of compurgation, and also between the various forms of ordeal.[3]

There was, however, a remarkable exception to this enforcement of the ordeal in a provision existing in some codes by which a man condemned to it could buy himself off by compounding with his adversary. This mode of adjustment was not extensively introduced, but it nevertheless existed among

[1] That this was a settled practice is shown by its existence in the earliest text of the law (Tit. LVI.) as well as in the latest (L. Emend. Tit. LIX.).

[2] Si aufugerit et ordalium vitaverit, solvat plegius compellanti captale suum et regi weram suum.—L. Cnuti Sæc. cap. xxx.—See also cap. xli.

[3] Et eligat accusatus alterutrum quod velit, sive simplex ordalium, sive jusjurandum unius libre in tribus hundredis super xxx. den.—L. Henrici I. cap. LXV. § 3. By the municipal codes of Germany, a choice between the various forms of ordeal was sometimes allowed to the accused who was sentenced to undergo it.—Jur. Provin. Alaman. cap. xxxvii. §§ 15, 16. Jur. Provin. Saxon. Lib. I. Art. 39.

the Anglo-Saxons,[1] while among the Franks it was a settled
custom, permitted by all the texts of the Salic law, from the
earliest to the latest.[2]   By this a person condemned by the
court to undergo the ordeal could, by a transaction with the
aggrieved party, purchase the privilege of clearing himself by
canonical purgation, and thus escape the severer trial.   He
was bound to pay his accuser only a portion of the fine which
he would incur if proved guilty—a portion varying with different offences from one-fourth to one-sixth of the *wer-gild*.
The interests of the tribunal were guarded by a clause which
compelled him to pay to the *grafio*, or judge, the full *fredum*,
or public fine, if his conscience impelled him to submit to an
arrangement for more than the legal percentage.   Even as late
as 1229, by the Bohemian laws of Ottokar Premislas the accused could escape the ordeal by paying seven deniers to the
seigneur.[3]

The circumstances under which its employment was ordered
varied considerably with the varying legislations of races and
epochs ; and to enter minutely into the question of the power
of the court to decree it, or the right to demand it by the appellant or the defendant, would require too much space,
especially as this has already been discussed at some length
with regard to one of its forms, the wager of battle.   In
India, the accused was required to undergo the risk of a fine
if he desired to force his adversary to the ordeal ; but either
party could voluntarily undertake it, in which case the other
was subject to a mulct if defeated.[4]   The character of the defendant, however, had an important bearing upon its employment.   If he had already been convicted of a crime or of
perjury he was subject to it in all cases, however trifling ; if,
on the other hand, he was a man of unblemished reputation,
he was not to be exposed to it, however important was the

---

[1] Dooms of Ethelstan, I. cap. 21.
[2] First Text, Tit. LIII. and L. Emend. Tit. LV.
[3] Jura primæva Moraviæ, Brunæ, 1781, p. 27.
[4] Yajnavalkya, II. 96.

case.[1] In civil cases, however, it apparently was only employed to supplement deficient evidence.—"Evidence consists of writings, possession, and witnesses. If one of these is wanting, then one of the ordeals is valid."[2]

In Europe there appears at times to have been a custom under which, when the accused had escaped in the ordeal, the accuser was obliged to undergo it. Thus in the Frisian law, when a man accused of theft proved his innocence by the ordeal, the accuser was then obliged to clear himself of the charge of perjury by a similar trial,[3] but the law fails to define what are their respective positions if the second ordeal proves likewise innocuous. In the case of bier-right quoted above from Scott's Border Minstrelsy, this secondary ordeal seems to have been to prove whether the accuser herself was not the guilty person. In the heroic poems of the Elder Edda a similar trial appears to be resorted to, as in the Frisian laws, only for the purpose of showing the false witness borne by the accuser. When Gudrun the wife of Atli is defamed as an adulteress by the concubine Herkia, and is forced to the ordeal—

> She to the bottom plunged
> Her snow-white hand,
> And up she drew
> The precious stones.
> " See now, ye men,
> I am proved guiltless
> In holy wise,
> Boil the vessel as it may."
> Laughed then Atli's
> Heart within his breast
> When he unscathed beheld
> The hand of Gudrun.
>
> " Now must Herkia
> To the cauldron go,
> She who Gudrun
> Had hoped to injure."
> No one has misery seen
> Who saw not that,
> How the hand there
> Of Herkia was hurt.
> They then the woman led
> To a foul slough.
> So were Gudrun's
> Wrongs avenged.[4]

---

[1] Institutes of Vishnu, IX. 18–19.

[2] Yajnavalkya, II. 22.

[3] Leg. Frision. Tit. III. c. 8, 9.

[4] Guthrunarkvida Thridja, 9, 10 (Thorpe's Elder Edda, pp. 106-7).

Churchmen held that if the accused escaped in the ordeal the accuser was guilty of perjury and homicide and must atone for it by public penitence.[1]

The absence of satisfactory testimony, rendering the case one not to be solved by human means alone is frequently, as in India, alluded to as a necessary element;[2] and indeed we may almost assert that this was so, even when not specifically mentioned, as far as regards the discretion of the tribunal to order an appeal to the judgment of God. Yet there were some exceptions to this, as in the early Russian legislation, where the ordeal is prescribed for the accused in all cases in which the accusation is substantiated by testimony;[3] and a law of King Ethelred seems to indicate that the plaintiff might require his adversary to submit to it,[4] while numerous examples

[1] Roberti Pulli Sententt. Lib. VI. cap. liv. (Migne's Patrologia, T. CLXXXVI. p. 905).

[2] Si certa probatio non fuerit.—L. Sal. Tit. XIV. XVI. (MS. Guelferbyt). The same is found in the Pact. Childeberti et Chlotarii ¿ 5.—Decret. Chlotarii II. ann. 595, ¿ 6.—Capit. Carol. Calvi, ann. 873, cap. 3, 7.—Cnuti Constit. de Foresta ¿ 11: "Sed purgatio ignis nullatenus admittatur nisi ubi nuda veritas nequit aliter investigari."—In the customs of Tournay in 1187, when a man has been wounded and has no witnesses the accused can clear himself with six conjurators if the affair occurred in the daytime, but if at night he is forced to the cold-water ordeal (Consuet. Tornacens. ¿ ii. *ap.* D'Achery, Spicileg. III. 551). Horne's Myrror of Justice, cap. III. Sect. 23: "En case ou battaille ne se poit joindre ne nul tesmognage n'avoit lieu . . . . e le actor n'ad point de testmoignes a prover sa action, adonque estoit en le volunt del deffendant a purger sa fame per le miracle de Dieu." Yet in an English case of murder early in the thirteenth century, the accused was found with the murdered man's cap and the knife with which he had been slain, and the whole vicinage testified to it, yet he was allowed to purge himself with the water ordeal.—Maitland, Pleas, etc., p. 80.

[3] Ruskaia Prawda, art. 28. Even the evidence of a slave was sufficient to condemn the accused to the red-hot iron. If he escaped, the accuser paid him a small fine, which was not required if the witnesses had been freemen. In all cases of acquittal, however, there were fines payable to the sovereign and to the ministers of justice.

[4] Et omnis accusator vel qui alium impetit, habeat optionem quid velit,

among those cited above authorize the conclusion that an offer
on the part of the accused was rarely refused, even when there
was strong evidence against him,[1] though this laxity of practice was occasionally objected to stoutly.[2] When the custom
was declining, indeed, a disposition existed to require the assent of both parties before the tribunal would allow a case to
be thus decided.[3] In civil cases, we may assume that absence
of testimony, or the consent of both parties, was requisite to its
employment.[4]

---

sive judicium aque vel ferri . . . . et si fugiet (accusatus) ab ordalio, reddat
eum plegius wera sua.—Ethelr. Tit. III. c. vi. (Thorpe II. 516).

[1] Thus, in the Icelandic code—"Quodsi reus ferrum candens se gerere
velle obtulerit, hoc minime rejiciatur."—Grágás, Sect. VI. c. 33. So in
the laws of Bruges in 1190 (§ 31), we find the accused allowed to choose
between the red-hot iron and a regular inquest—" Qui de palingis inpeti-
tur, si ad judicium ardentis ferri venire noluerit, veritatem comitis qualem
melius super hoc inveniri poterit, accipiet" (Warnkönig, Hist. de la Fland.
IV. 372)—showing that it was considered the most absolute of testimony.
And in a constitution of Frederic Barbarossa "Si miles rusticum de violata
pace pulsaverit . . . . de duobus unum rusticus eligat, an divino aut hu-
mano judicio innocentiam suam ostendat."—Feudor. Lib. II. Tit. xxvii. § 3.

[2] Thus an anonymous ecclesiastic, in an epistle quoted by Juretus (Observat. in Ivon. Carnot. Epist. 74)—"Simoniaci non admittuntur ad judicium, si probabiles personæ, etiam laicorum, vel feminarum, pretium se ab
eis recipisse testantur; nec aliud est pro manifestis venire ad judicium nisi
tentare Dominum."

[3] Duellum vel judicium candentis ferri, vel aquæ ferventis, vel alia can-
onibus vel legibus improbata, nullomodo in curia Montispessulani rati sunt,
nisi utraque pars convenerit.—Statut: Montispess. ann. 1204 (Du Cange).

[4] Si accolis de neutrius jure constat, adeoque hac in re testimonium
dicere non queant, tum judicio aquæ res decidatur.—Jur. Provin. Alaman.
cap. cclxxviii. § 5.—Poterit enim alteruter eorum petere probationem per
aquam (wasser urteyll) nec Dominus nec adversarius detrectare possit;
sed non, nisi quum per testes probatio fieri nequit.—Jur. Feud. Alaman.
cap. lxxvii. § 2.

"Aut veritas reperiatur de hoc per aquaticum Dei judicium. Tamen
judicium Dei non est licitum adhiberi per ullam causam, nisi cujus veritas
per justitiam non potest aliter reperiri, hoc terminabitur judicio Dei."—Jur.
Feud. Saxon. § 100 (Senckenberg. Corp. Jur. Feud. German. p. 249).—So,

The comfort which the system must have afforded to indo-
lent judges in doubtful cases is well exhibited by a rule in
various ancient codes, by which a man suspected of crime,
even though no accuser came forward, was thrown into
prison and kept there until he could prove his innocence by
the ordeal of water.[1] No testimony was required save that
of evil repute. Thus in Hungary, in the eleventh century, a
man who was regarded as a thief by the whole village was
subjected to the ordeal: if he was cleared, he paid the fee to
the priest; if he was convicted, all his property was confiscated.[2] This, in fact, was virtually the process adopted and
systematized in England by the Assizes of Clarendon in 1166.
The grand jury was directed to present all persons suspected
of robbery, murder, theft, etc., when they were promptly sent
to the water ordeal to prove their innocence.[3] Thus it afforded an unfailing solution to all doubts and simplified
greatly the administration of criminal law, for it was equally
applicable to cases of individual prosecutions. In 1201, for
instance, a widow accuses a man of the murder of her husband and the court rejects her appeal because it does not state
that she saw the deed, but as the jurors when interrogated say

also, in a later text, " judicium Domini fervida aqua vel ferro non licet in
causa aliqua experiri, nisi in qua modis aliis non poterit veritas indagari."—
Cap. xxiv. § 19 (Ibid. p. 337).

[1] Établissements de Normandie, Tit. de Prison (Éd. Marnier). Precisely similar to this was a regulation in the early Bohemian laws.—Bracilai Leges. (Patrol. CLI., 1258-9). And an almost identical provision is
found in the Anglo-Saxon jurisprudence.—L. Cnuti Sæc. cap. xxxv.—L.
Henric. I. cap. lxi. § 5.—See, also, Assises de Jerusalem, Baisse Court,
cclix.

[2] Batthyany, Legg. Eccles. Hung. II. 105.

[3] Et qui inveniatur per sacramentum prædictorum rettatus vel publicatus
quod fuerit robator vel murdrator vel latro vel receptor eorum, postquam
dominus rex fuit rex, capiatur et eat ad juisiam aquæ.—Assisa de Claren-
duna § 2 (Stubbs, Select Charters, p. 137). For examples, see Maitland,
Pleas, pp. 3, 4, 5, etc.

that the accused is suspected of the crime, he is ordered at once to the ordeal.[1]

We have seen above occasional instances in which the accuser or plaintiff offered to substantiate his veracity by an appeal to the ordeal.   This was an established rule with regard to the wager of battle, but not as respects the other forms of the judgment of God, which were regarded rather as means of defence than of attack.   Still there are occasional instances of instructions for their employment by the accusing party.   In the primitive laws of Russia, an accuser who could not substantiate his case with witnesses was obliged to undergo the ordeal of red-hot iron.[2]   In England it seems to have been within the discretion of the court to order it for either the accuser or the accused.   A very singular case is recorded in 1202, in which Astin of Wispington accused Simon of Edlington of assaulting him and putting out an eye, when the court adjudged the red-hot iron ordeal and gave to the defendant the option whether he or the prosecutor should undergo it; Simon naturally preferred that his antagonist should try the dangerous experiment, and the result was that the case was settled without it.[3]   We have already seen (p. 385) that in some places where the accused succeeded in clearing himself by the ordeal the accuser was obliged to undergo it in order to determine the question of his perjury.

Sometimes the ordeal was employed in connection with compurgation, both for prosecution and defence, to supplement the notorious imperfections of that procedure.   Thus Archbishop Hincmar directs that cases of complaint against priests for dissolute life shall be supported by seven witnesses, of whom one must submit to the ordeal to prove the truth of his companions' oaths, as a wholesome check upon perjury and subornation.[4]   With a similar object, the same prelate likewise

---

[1] Maitland, Pleas, etc., I. 1.   P. 75 is a case of a youth detained in prison and sent to the ordeal apparently without a trial.

[2] Ruskaia Prawda, Art. 28.   [3] Maitland, Pleas, etc., I. 10.

[4] Hincmari Capit. Synod. ann. 852, II. xxi.

enjoins it on compurgators chosen by the accused, on his failing to obtain the support of those who had been selected for
him by his judge.[1]   Allied to this was a rule for its employment which was extensively adopted, allowing the accused the
privilege of compurgation with conjurators in certain cases,
only requiring him to submit to the ordeal on his failing to
procure the requisite number of sponsors.   Thus, in 794, a
certain Bishop Peter, who was condemned by the Synod of
Frankfort to clear himself, with two or three conjurators, of
the suspicion of complicity in a conspiracy against Charlemagne, being unable to obtain them, one of his vassals offered
to pass through the ordeal in his behalf, and on his success
the bishop was reinstated.[2]   That this was strictly in accordance with usage is shown by a very early text of the Salic
Law,[3] as well as by a similar provision in the Ripuarian code.[4]
Among the Anglo-Saxons it likewise obtained, from the time
of the earliest allusion to the ordeal occurring in their jurisprudence, down to the period of the Conquest.[5]   Somewhat
similar in tendency was a regulation of Frederic Barbarossa,
by which a slave suspected of theft was exposed to the red-hot
iron unless his master would release him by an oath.[6]   Occasionally it was also resorted to when the accused was outsworn
after having endeavored to defend himself by his oath or by
conjurators.   Thus a canon of the Council of Tribur in 895

[1] Hincmari Epist. xxxiv.

[2] Capit. Car. Mag. ann. 794, § 7.

[3] Se juratores non potuerit invenire, aut ad ineum ambulat aut, etc.—
MS. Guelferbyt. Tit. xiv.

[4] Quod si . . . . juratores invenire non potuerit, ad ignem seu ad sortem se excusare studeat.—L. Ripuar. Tit. xxxi. § 5.

[5] Dooms of Edward the Elder, cap. iii.   So also in the laws of William
the Conqueror, Tit. I. cap. xiv.—" Si sen escundira sei duzime main.   E
si il auer nes pot, si sen defende par juise."   The collection known by the
name of Henry I. has a similar provision, cap. lxvi. § 3.

[6] Radevic. de Reb. Frid. Lib. I. cap. xxvi.   This was an old feature of
the Barbarian codes which continued till late in the Middle Ages.   See
ante, p. 22.

declares that if a man is so generally suspected that he is out-sworn in compurgation, he must either confess or submit to the hot-iron ordeal.[1]   Popular belief evidently might give to the accuser a larger number of men willing to associate them-selves in the oath of accusation than the defendant could find to join him in rebutting it, and yet his guilt might not as yet be clear.   In such cases, the ordeal was a most convenient re-sort.

These regulations give to the ordeal decidedly the aspect of punishment, as it was thus inflicted on those whose guilt was so generally credited that they could not find comrades to stand up with them at the altar as partakers in their oath of denial ; and this is not the only circumstance which leads us to be-lieve that it was frequently so regarded.   This notion is visi-ble in the ancient Indian law, where, as we have seen, certain of the ordeals—those of red-hot iron, poison, and the balance —could not be employed unless the matter at stake were equivalent to the value of a thousand pieces of silver, or in-volved an offence against the king ;[2] and it reappears in Europe in the graduated scale of single and triple ordeals for offences of different magnitudes.   Such a scheme is so totally at vari-ance with the theory of miraculous interposition to protect innocence and punish guilt, that we can only look upon it as a mode of inflicting graduated punishments in doubtful cases, thus holding up a certain penalty *in terrorem* over those who would otherwise hope to escape by the secrecy of their crime —no doubt with a comforting conviction, like that of Legate Arnaud at the sack of Béziers, that God would know his own.   This same principle is visible in a provision of the charter of Loudun, granted by Louis le Gros in 1128, by which an assault committed outside of the liberties of the commune could be disproved by a simple sacramental oath ; but if within the limits of the commune, the accused was

[1] Concil. Tribur. ann. 895, can. xxii.
[2] Yajnavalkya, II. 99.

obliged to undergo the ordeal.[1]   In another shape we see it in
the customs of Tournay, granted by Philip Augustus in 1187,
where a person accused of assault with sharpened weapons, if
there were no witnesses, was allowed to purge himself with six
conjurators if the affair occurred in the daytime, but if at
night, was obliged to undergo the water ordeal.[2]   Further
illustration is afforded by the principle, interwoven in various
codes, by which a first crime was defensible by conjurators,
or other means, while the *tiht-bysig* man, the *homo infamatus*,
one of evil repute, whose character had been previously com-
promised, was denied this privilege, and was forced at once to
the hot iron or the water.   Thus, among the Anglo-Saxons,
in the earliest allusion to the ordeal, by Edward the Elder, it
is provided that perjured persons, or those who had once been
convicted, should not be deemed thereafter oath-worthy, but
should be hurried to the ordeal; a regulation repeated with
some variations in the laws of Ethelred, Cnut, and Henry I.[3]
The Carlovingian legislation establishes a similar principle,[4]
while the canons of Burckhardt show it to be still in force in
the eleventh century.[5]   A hundred and fifty years later, the
legislation of Flanders manifests the same tendency, the code
granted to Bruges in 1190 providing that a first accusation of
theft should be decided by witnesses, while a second was to
be met by the cold-water ordeal.[6]   In the German municipal
law of the thirteenth century, the same principle is observable.
A man who had forfeited his legal privileges by conviction for
theft or similar crimes was no longer admitted to the oath, but

---

1 Chart. Commun. Laudun. (Baluz. et Mansi IV. p. 39).

2 Consuetud. Tornacens. § iii. (D'Achery III. 551).   See above, p. 54.

3 Ut deinceps non sint digni juramento sed ordalio.—Legg. Edwardi
cap. iii.; Æthelredi cap. i. § 1; Cnuti Sæcul. cap. xxii. xxx.; Henrici I.
cap. lxv. § 3.

4 Capit. Car. Mag. I. ann. 809, cap. xxviii.—Capit Ludov. Pii. I. ann.
819.

5 Burchardi Decret. Lib. XVI. cap. 19.

6 Keure de la Châtellenie de Bruges, § 28 (Warnkönig, Hist. de la
Fland. IV. 371).

on subsequent accusations was compelled to choose between the hot iron, the cauldron, and a combat with a champion ; and similarly an officer of the mint issuing false money was permitted the first time to swear to his ignorance, but on a second offence he had to submit to the ordeal. In the codes in force throughout Germany, indeed, previous suspicion was sufficient to send the accused to the ordeal in place of the oath.[1] The contemporary jurisprudence of Spain has a somewhat similar provision, by which a woman accused of homicide could not be exposed to the ordeal unless she could be proved utterly abandoned, for which a curious standard was requisite ;[2] while for more serious crimes, such as sorcery or killing her husband, she was forced at once to the red-hot iron to prove her innocence. In the legislation of Charlemagne there is an elaborate provision, by which a man convicted seven times of theft was no longer allowed to escape on payment of a fine, but was required to undergo the ordeal of fire. If he succumbed, he was put to death ; if he escaped unhurt, he was not discharged as innocent, but his lord was allowed to enter bail for his future good behavior[3]—a mode at once of administering punishment and of ascertaining whether his death would be agreeable to Heaven. When we thus regard it as a penalty on those who by misconduct had forfeited the confidence of their fellow-men, the system loses part of its absurdity, in proportion as it departs from the principle under which it was established.

There is also another aspect in which it is probable that the ordeal was viewed by those whose common sense must have shrunk from it as a simple appeal to the judgment of God. There can be little doubt that it was frequently found of mate-

---

[1] Jur. Provin. Alaman. cap. clxxxvi. §§ 4, 6, 7 ; cap. ccclxxiv.—Jur. Provin. Saxon. Lib. I. Art. 39.—Sachsische Weichbild, Art. xcii. § 2.— Richstich Landrecht, cap. lii.

[2] Si non fuere provada por mala, que aya yazido con cinco omes.—Fuero de Baeça (Villadiego, Fuero Juzgo, fol. 317 a).

[3] Capit. Car. Mag. III. ann. 813, cap. 46.

rial use in extorting confession or unwilling testimony. By the early codes, as in the primitive Greek and Roman law, torture could be applied only to slaves, and the ordeal was a legalized torture, applied under circumstances peculiarly provocative of truth, and as such we occasionally find regulations which enable the freeman to escape by compurgation, while the slave is required to undergo the ordeal.[1] The elaborate nature of the ritual employed, with its impressive adjurations and exorcisms, was well fitted to excite the imagination and alarm the conscience; sometimes, indeed, to render it more effective, the mass celebrated was a mortuary one, which when sung for a living man was popularly believed to possess deadly powers of peculiar efficacy.[2] In those ages of faith, the professing Christian, conscious of guilt, must indeed have been hardened who could undergo these awful rites, pledging his salvation on his innocence, and knowing under such circumstances that the direct intervention of Heaven could alone save him from having his hand boiled to rags,[3] after which he was

[1] Concil. Mogunt. ann. 847, can. xxiv.—Burchardi Decret. Lib. XVI. cap. 19.—Keure de Gand, §§ 7, 8, 12 (Warnkönig, II. 228).

The law of William the Conqueror (Tit. II. c. 3.—Thorpe, I. 488) by which the duel was reserved for the Norman, and the vulgar ordeal for the Saxon, might be supposed to arise from a similar distinction. In reality, however, it was only preserving the ancestral customs of the races, giving to the defendant the privilege of his own law. The duel was unknown to the Anglo-Saxons, who habitually employed the ordeal, while the Normans, previous to the Conquest, according to Houard, who is good authority (Anc. Loix Franc. I. 221–222), only appealed to the sword.

[2] Martene de Antiq. Eccl. Ritibus Lib. III. c. vii. Ord. 6. For the beliefs connected with mortuary masses see Concil. Toletan XVII. ann. 694 c. 5; D'Argentré Collect. Judic. de novis Error. I. II. 344; Angeli de Clavasio Summa Angelica s. v. *Interrogationes ;* Diaz de Luco, Practica Criminalis Canonica cap. xxxv.; Grillandi de Sortilegiis q. xiv.

[3] The severity of the ordeal, when the sufferer had no friends among the operators to save him, may be deduced from the description of a hand when released from its three days' tying up after its plunge in hot water: " inflatam admodum et excoriatam sanieque jam carne putrida effluentem dexteram invitus ostendit" (Du Cange, s. v. *Aqua Ferv. Judicium*). In this

to meet the full punishment of his crime, and perhaps in addition lose a member for the perjury committed. With such a prospect, all motives would conspire to lead him to a prompt and frank acknowledgment in the early stages of the proceedings against him. These views are strengthened by the fact that when, in the thirteenth century, the judicial use of torture, as a means of obtaining testimony and confession, was becoming systematized and generally employed, the ordeal was falling into desuetude and rapidly disappearing. The latter had fulfilled its mission, and the former was a substitute better fitted for an age which reasoned more, believed less, and at the same time was quite as arbitrary and cruel as its predecessor. A further confirmation of this supposition is afforded by the coincidence that the only primitive jurisprudence which excluded the ordeal—that of the Wisigoths— was likewise the only one which habitually permitted the use of torture,[1] the only reference to the ordeal in their code being a provision which directs its employment as a preliminary to the more regular forms of torture.

In fact, the ordeal was practically looked upon as a torture by those whose enlightenment led them to regard as a superstition the faith popularly reposed in it. An epistle which is attributed both to Stephen V. and Sylvester II. condemns the whole system on the ground that the canons forbid the extortion of confessions by heated irons and boiling water; and that a credulous belief could not be allowed to sanction that which was not permitted by the fathers.[2] When, therefore, at the Council of St. Baseul, a priest named Adalger, in confessing the assistance he had rendered to Arnoul of Reims during Charles of Lorraine's resistance to the usurpation of

case, the sufferer was the adversary of an abbey, the monks of which perhaps had the boiling of the caldron.

[1] L Wisig. L. vi. Tit. i. § 3.

[2] Ivon. Carnot. Epist. 74; Ejusd. Decr. x. 27.—C. 20 Decr. Caus. ii. q.v.

This epistle is generally attributed to Stephen V., but two MSS. of Ivo of Chartres ascribe it to Sylvester II. (Migne's Patrologia CLXII. 96).

Hugh Capet, offered to substantiate his testimony by undergoing the ordeal, he did it in terms which show that he expected
it to be regarded as a torture giving additional weight to evidence—" If any of you doubt this and deem me unworthy of
belief, let him believe the fire, the boiling water, the glowing
iron. Let these tortures convince those who disbelieve my
words."[1] It is observable that he omits the cold-water as not
being a torture, just as in the ancient Indian law the limitation
referred to above as applicable to the red-hot iron, the poison,
and the balance, did not apply to the cold-water ordeal, or to
that in which was administered the water in which an idol
had been dipped.[2]

In the same way, some among the European ordeals, such
as that of the Eucharist, of bread and cheese, and bier-right,
do not come within the class of tortures, but they addressed
themselves powerfully to the conscience and imagination of
the accused, whose callous fortitude no doubt often gave way
under the trial. In our own country, and almost within our
own time, the latter ordeal was revived in one instance with
this object, and the result did not disappoint the expectations
of those who undertook it. In the case of People vs. Johnson,
tried in New York in 1824, the suspected murderer was led
from his cell to the hospital where lay the body of the victim,
which he was required to touch. Dissimulation which had
been before unshaken failed him at the awful moment; his
overstrung nerves gave way, and a confession was faltered
forth. The proceeding was sustained by court, and a subsequent attempt at retraction was overruled.[3] The powerful
influence of such feelings is shown in a custom which, as
recently as 1815, was still employed at Mandeure, near Mont-
belliard, and which is said to be even yet in use in some of

---

[1] Concil. Basol. cap. xi. Rainer, private secretary of Arnoul, offered to
prove his statement by giving up a slave to walk the burning ploughshares
in evidence of his truth (Ibid. cap. xxx.).

[2] Yajnavalkya, II. 99.

[3] Wharton and Stillé's Med. Jurisp., 2d Edit. 1860.

the remoter districts of the Ardennes. When a theft has been committed, the inhabitants are summoned to assemble after vespers on Sunday at the place of judgment. There the mayor calls upon the guilty person to make restitution and live in isolation for six months. If this appeal prove fruitless, recourse is had to the trial of the staff, in which two magistrates hold aloft a piece of wood, under which every one is bound to pass. No instance, it is said, is on record in which the culprit dares to do this, and he is always left alone.[1] Very similar to this is the use made of the Clog Oir or golden bell of St. Senan, the founder of the monastery of Inniscattery, at the mouth of the river Shannon, which was supposed to have peculiar virtue in revealing culprits. A case occurred as late as 1834, when a farmer, who had lost a sum of twenty pounds by a burglary, had the bell brought to his house with much ceremony, and the following Sunday was appointed for the whole parish to appear and clear themselves upon it. On Saturday night, however, the stolen bank notes were thrown through a window of his house.[2] The method described above (p. 334), as practised in Southern Russia to detect household thieves, affords another example of the power exercised over a guilty conscience. It is easy thus to imagine how the other forms of ordeal may have conduced to the discovery of crime in ages of lively superstition. A case occurring about the commencement of the twelfth century is a fair illustration of the manner in which it frequently worked on the imagination of those whose lives or fortunes were at stake. André de Trahent, a vassal of the convent of St. Mary of Saintes, claimed certain property belonging to the convent. On the final hearing it was decreed that he must abandon his claim unless he could prove it by oath and ordeal. This he agreed to do, and on the appointed day he appeared with his

---

[1] Michelet, Origines du Droit, p. 349.—Proost, Jugements de Dieu, p. 80. This seems to be derived from the *skirsla* of the Norsemen described above.

[2] London Athenæum, Aug. 20, 1881, p. 247.

men ready to undergo the trial. As there were two pieces of property in question, two ordeals were required. The caldrons of water were duly heated and André's men were prepared for the attempt, when his courage gave way; he abruptly abandoned his claim and submitted himself to the mercy of the abbess.[1]

This case illustrates the fact that in the vulgar ordeals as well as in the duel champions were sometimes allowed. To how great an extent this was permitted it would now be difficult to assert. It is not specially alluded to in any body of laws, but numerous examples of it have been incidentally given above, and in some of the *ordines* it is assumed as a matter of course. In one for the cold-water ordeal the substitutes are described as children who are made to fast for forty days in advance, and carefully watched and washed to prevent any illusions of the devil.[2] In the ordeal of the cross, however, it was a recognized privilege of the old or infirm to put forward a substitute, and when communities or churches were pleaders a champion was of course a necessity. A still greater relaxation, occasionally permitted but not approved by the Church, was the practice of writing the name of the accused on paper or some other substance and submitting this to the ordeal in place of the individual himself.[3] Perhaps the most illogical use of a champion in an ordeal is one suggested by Hincmar of Reims in 860, that a satisfactory person should undergo it in order to determine whether the secret motive alleged by another person for not living with his wife were true or not.[4]

---

1 Polyptichum Irminonis, App. No. 34 (Paris, 1836, p. 373).
2 Martene, De Antiq. Eccles. Ritibus Lib. III. cap. vii. Ordo 5.
3 Patetta, Le Ordalie, p. 192.
4 Hincmari Remens. Epist. XXII. (Migne's Patrol. CXXVI. 136).

CHAPTER XVI.

CONFIDENCE REPOSED IN THE ORDEAL.

THE degree of confidence really inspired by the results of the ordeal is a somewhat curious subject of speculation on which definite opinions are not easily reached. Judicially, the trial was, for the most part, conclusive; he who had duly sunk under water, walked unharmed among the burning shares, or withdrawn an unblistered hand from a caldron of legal temperature, stood forth among his fellows as innocent. So, even now, the verdict of a few fools or knaves in a jury-box may discharge a criminal, against the plainest dictates of common sense, but in neither case would the sentiments of the community be probably changed by the result. The reverential feelings which alone could impart faith in the system seem scarcely compatible with the practice of compounding for ordeals, which, as we have seen above (p. 384), was occasionally permitted.

Charlemagne, at the commencement of his reign, does not seem to have entertained much respect for the judgment of God when he prescribed the administration of the ordeal for trifling affairs only, cases of magnitude being reserved for the regular investigation of the law.[1] Thirty years later, the public mind appears afflicted with the same doubts, for we

---

[1] Quod si accusatus contendere voluerit de ipso perjurio stent ad crucem. . . . Hoc vero de minoribus rebus. De majoribus vero, aut de statu ingenuitatis, secundum legem custodiant.—Capit. Car. Mag. ann. 779, § 10. That this was respected as law in force, nearly a hundred years later, is shown by its being included in the collection of Capitularies by Benedict the Levite (Lib. v. cap. 196).

find the monarch endeavoring to enforce confidence in the system by his commands.[1] The repeated use of the ordeal in the affair of the divorce of Teutberga shows that it was expected to have no little effect on public opinion, and the same is seen when in 876 Charlemagne's grandson, Louis of Saxony, forced to defend his dominions against his uncle Charles le Chauve, commenced by proving the justness of his title by the judgment of God. After fasting and prayer ten of his followers were exposed to the ordeal of red-hot iron and ten each to those of cold and boiling water; all escaped without injury, and the righteousness of the verdict was shown soon after by the victory of Andernach, which sent the invader flying back to France.[2] Yet a rule of English law, nearly four hundred years later, during the expiring struggles of the practice, would show that the result was regarded as by no means conclusive. By the assizes of Clarendon in 1166, which directed that all malefactors defamed for murder, robbery, and other felonies should be at once tried by the water ordeal, it was provided that those who had confessed or who had been found in possession of stolen property should not be allowed the privilege of clearing themselves in this manner; and a still more irreverential rule decreed that those who were pronounced innocent by the judgment of God, if regarded as guilty by common report, should have eight days to quit the kingdom, under pain of outlawry.[3] In the revision of these laws, made at Northampton ten years later, it was provided that in all cases those who passed safely through the ordeal should give bail for their future good conduct, except in charges of murder or aggravated felony, when they were

[1] Ut omnes judicio Dei credant absque dubitatione.—Capit. Car. Mag. 1. ann. 809, § 20.

[2] Aimoini Chron. Continuat. Lib. v. c. 34.

[3] Assisa facta apud Clarendune §§ 12, 13, 14 (Gesta Henrici II. T. II. p. clii.—M. R. Series). A case in accordance with this occurs in 1212 (Maitland, Pleas, I. 63).

banished within forty days, under penalty of outlawry as before.[1]

St. Ivo of Chartres, though he had no scruple in recommending and enjoining the ordeal for laymen, and, on one occasion at least, pronounced its decisions as beyond appeal, yet has placed on record his conviction of its insufficiency, and his experience that the mysterious judgment of God not infrequently allowed in this manner the guilty to escape and the innocent to be punished.[2] A case related by Peter Cantor in the twelfth century shows how recklessly it often was abused as a relief to careless judges in doubtful cases. Two Englishmen were returning in company from a pilgrimage to the Holy Land, when one of them wandered off to the shrine of St. Jago de Compostella, and the other went directly home. The kindred of the absent one accused the latter of murdering his companion ; as no evidence was procurable on either side, he was hurried to the ordeal, convicted, and executed, shortly after which the missing man came back in safety.[3]

The manifest injustice of the decisions thus rendered by the ordeal put a severe strain on the faith of believers, and led them to the most ingenious sophistry for an explanation. When, in 1127, the sacrilegious murder of Charles the Good, Count of Flanders, sent a thrill of horror throughout Europe, Lambert of Redenberg, whose participation in the crime was notorious, succeeded in clearing himself by the hot iron. Shortly afterwards he undertook the siege of Ostbourg, which he prosecuted with great cruelty, when he was killed in a sally of the besieged. The pious Galbert assumes that Lambert, notwithstanding his guilt, escaped at the ordeal in consequence

---

[1] Gesta Henrici II. T. I. p. 108.—Cf. Bracton, Lib. III. Tract. ii. cap. 16 § 3.

[2] Simili modo, cauterium militis nullum tibi certum præbet argumentum, cum per examinationem ferri candentis occulto Dei judicio multos videamus nocentes liberatos, multos innocentes sæpe damnatos,—Ivon, Carnot. Epist. cccv.

[3] Pet. Cantor. Verb. Abbreviat. c. lxxviii.

of his humility and repentance, and philosophically adds: "Thus it is that in battle the unjust man is killed, although in the ordeal of water or of fire he may escape, if truly repentant."[1] The same doctrine was enunciated under John Cantacuzenes, in the middle of the fourteenth century, by a bishop of Didymoteichos in Thrace. A frail fair one being violently suspected by her husband, the ordeal of hot iron was demanded by him. In this strait she applied to the good bishop, and he, being convinced of her repentance and intention to sin no more, assured her that in such a frame of mind she might safely venture on the trial, and she accordingly carried the glowing bar triumphantly twice around the bishop's chair, to the entire satisfaction of her lord and master.[2]

In fact it was a recognized doctrine of the Church that confession, contrition, and absolution so thoroughly washed away a sin that a culprit thus prepared could safely tempt the justice of God. A case related by Cæsarius of Heisterbach as a most edifying example illustrates the curious nature of the superstition thus inculcated by the religious teachers of the period. In the diocese of Utrecht a fisherman notoriously maintained illicit relations with a woman, and fearing to be called to account for it by an approaching synod, where he would be convicted by the red-hot iron, and be forced to marry her, he consulted a priest. This ghostly counsellor advised him that, if he was firmly resolved to sin no more, he could safely deny the fact and endure the ordeal, after receiving absolution. The event verified the prediction; he carried the burning iron unhurt, and to the surprise of all the country round he was acquitted. Shortly afterwards, while in his boat, a companion expressed his wonder, when the fisherman, whose short-lived repentance was already over, boastingly struck his hand on the water, exclaiming, "It hurt me no more than that!" By the marvellous justice of God, the water was to

---

[1] Vit. Carol. Comit. Flandren. cap. xx.
[2] Collin de Plancy, *op. cit.* s. v. *Fer Chaud.*

him as red-hot iron, and as he hastily withdrew his hand the skin peeled off in strips.[1] Even as late as 1539, the learned Ciruelo reproves the use of ordeals because the accused, though innocent of the special crime at issue, may succumb in consequence of other offences; or though guilty may escape because he has confessed and received absolution; and he states that he had personally known more than one case in which women, rightly accused of adultery by their husbands and forced to undergo the ordeal, had thus succeeded in being acquitted.[2]

This doctrine of Ciruelo's that the innocent were sometimes liable to conviction on account of previous misdeeds was likewise a belief of old standing. We have already seen (p. 137) that there was papal authority for it in the wager of battle. A striking instance of the vague notions current is afforded in the middle of the eleventh century by a case related by Othlonus, in which a man accused of horse-stealing was tried by the cold-water ordeal and found guilty. Knowing his own innocence, he appealed to the surrounding monks, and was told that it must be in consequence of some other sin not properly redeemed by penance. As he had confessed and received absolution before the trial, he denied this, till one of them pointed out that in place of allowing his beard to grow, as was meet for a layman, he had impiously carried the smooth chin reserved for ecclesiastics. Confessing his guilt, promising due penance, and vowing never to touch his beard with a razor again, he was conducted a second time to the water, and being now free from all unrepented sin, he was triumphantly acquitted. It is added that, taking advantage of a quibble as to the kind of instrument employed, he lapsed again into the sin of shaving, when the anger of Heaven manifested itself by allowing him to fall into the hands of an enemy, who put out his eyes.[3]

---

[1] Cæsar. Heisterbach. Dial. Mirac. Dist. X. c. xxxv.

[2] Ciruelo, Reprovacion de las Supersticiones, P. II. c. vii.

[3] Othlon. Narrat. de Mirac. quod nuper accidit, &c. (Migne's Patrol. CXLVI. 243–4).

Yet, on the other hand, the ordeal sometimes was regarded as the most satisfactory kind of proof, entitled to respect beyond any other species of evidence. The age was not logical, men acted more from impulse than from reason, and the forms of jurisprudence were still in a state too chaotic for regular and invariable rules to be laid down. The confusion existing in the popular mind is well illustrated by a case occurring in the twelfth century. A serf of the Abbey of Marmoutiers married a serf who had been given by the Viscount of Blois to one of his retainers named Erbald. The husband purchased his wife's liberty, and by paying an additional sum had the deed of manumission confirmed by the viscount and viscountess. Years passed away, the serf and wife died, and then also their son, when their property fell to the abbey, which enjoyed it until the heirs of Erbald and the viscount claimed it. The monks produced the deeds of manumission, and the viscountess, then the only surviving witness to the transaction, testified to its authenticity, but to no purpose. The claimants demanded the wager of battle, and the monks, in refusing this as unsuited to their calling, were obliged to produce a man who offered to undergo the ordeal of red-hot iron to prove the validity of the deed. Then the claimants at last desisted, but still succeeded in extorting sixteen livres from the abbey as the price of appending their signatures to the controverted deed.[1]

In general, however, as the result depended mostly upon those who administered the ordeal, it conferred an irresponsible power to release or to condemn, and it would be expecting too much of human nature to suppose that men did not yield frequently to the temptation to abuse that power. When Sigurd Thorlaksson was accused by Saint Olaf the King of the murder of his foster-brother Thoralf, and offered to clear himself by the red-hot iron, King Olaf accepted his offer, and appointed the next day for the trial at Lygra, where the bishop

---

[1] Polyptichum Irminonis, App. No. 20 (Paris, 1836, p. 354).

was to preside over it. When Sigurd went back at night to his ship, he said to his comrades that their prospects were gloomy, for the king had probably caused himself the death of Thoralf, and then brought the accusation against them, adding, "For him, it is an easy matter to manage the iron ordeal so that I doubt he will come ill off who tries it against him;" whereupon they hoisted sail in the darkness and escaped to their home in the Faroe Islands.[1] The collusion thus hinted at must often have been practised, and must have shaken the most robust faith, and this cause of disbelief would receive additional strength from the fact that the result itself was not seldom in doubt, victory being equally claimed by both parties. Of this we have already seen examples in the affairs of the lance of St. Andrew and of the Archbishop of Milan, and somewhat similar is an incident recorded by the Bollandists in the life of St. Swithin, in which, by miraculous interposition, the opposing parties beheld entirely different results from an appeal to the red-hot iron.[2]

Efforts of course were made from time to time to preserve the purity of the appeal, and to secure impartiality in its application. Clotair II., in 595, directs that three chosen persons shall attend on each side to prevent collusion;[3] and among the Anglo-Saxons, some four hundred years later, Ethelred enjoins the presence of the prosecutor under penalty of loss of suit and fine of twenty *ores*, apparently for the same object, as well as to give authenticity to the decision.[4] So in Hungary, the laws of St. Ladislas, in 1092, direct that three sworn witnesses shall be present to attest the innocence or guilt of the

---

[1] Olaf Haraldssons Saga, cxlv. (Laing's Heimskringla, II. 210).

[2] Enimvero mirum fuit ultra modum, quod fautores arsuram et inflationem conspiciebant; criminatores ita sanam ejus videbant palmam, quasi penitus fulvum non tetigisset ferrum.—Mirac. S. Swithuni c. ii. ¿ 37. In this case the patient was a slave, whose master had vowed to give him to the Church in case he escaped.

[3] Ad utramque partem sint ternas personas electas, ne conludius fieri possit.—Decret. Chlotharii II. cap. VII.

[4] Ethelred, III. ¿ 4.

accused as demonstrated by the result.[1]   A rule announced by
the Council of Grateley in 928, that if the accused is accompanied by more than twelve comrades he shall be adjudged as
though he had failed in the ordeal, points to an obvious source
of miscarriage of justice by which a crowd of partisans could
interfere with the proceedings and then proclaim that the
result had been successful.[2]   A law adopted by the Scottish
Parliament under William the Lion, in the second half of the
twelfth century, shows that corruption was not uncommon, by
forbidding those concerned in the administration of ordeals
from receiving bribes to divert the course of justice,[3] and a
further precaution was taken by prohibiting the Barons from
adjudging the ordeal without the intervention of the sheriff to
see that law and justice were observed.[4]

In spite of all that we have seen, the ordeal, with its undoubted cruelty, was not as cruel as it appears to us, and in
its practical results it probably acquitted the guilty far more
often than it convicted the innocent.   Mr. Maitland tells us
that in his researches in the English records from 1201 till the
abolition of the ordeal in 1219—a period in which, as stated
above (p. 387), it was in constant use—he has found but one
instance in which it failed to clear the accused.[5]   It is true that
the cold-water ordeal was the one most freely resorted to, but
the red-hot iron was also freely employed, and the one case of
failure occurred in the water ordeal.   At this distance of time
it would be useless to frame a positive explanation of this,
although bribery and collusion of course naturally suggest
themselves in the notorious and almost universal corruption of
the period.   Contemporaries reconciled themselves to this as
best they could, but while relying comfortably upon the inscrutable judgment of God, and the preservative power of

---

[1] Synod. Zabolcs can. 27 (Batthyani, Legg. Eccles. Hung. T. I. p. 439).
[2] Martene de Antiq Eccl. Ritibus Lib. III. c. vii. Ordo I.
[3] Statut. Wilhelmi Regis cap. 7 § 3 (Skene II. 4).
[4] Ibid. cap. 16.
[5] Maitland, Pleas of the Crown, I. 75.

contrition and confession, they were not without other solutions of the problem.

We have seen that in the judicial duel magic arts were popularly supposed to have power to control the interposition of God. This was likewise the case with the vulgar ordeals, and in addition a special power was attributed to the use or abuse of the holy chrism. The Council of Tours, in 813, informs us that it was generally believed that a criminal who drank the chrism or anointed himself with it could not be convicted by any ordeal.[1] So serious indeed was this considered that Charlemagne in 809 decreed that a priest giving out the chrism for this purpose should not only be degraded but should lose a hand—a law which long continued in force, nominally at least.[2] The belief was not ephemeral, for until the early part of the twelfth century a canon was carried through all the collections which speaks of the matter as a fact proved by experience.[3] The superstition probably died out towards the middle of the century when the number of sacraments was increased from three to seven, and the comparative importance of the chrism was thus diminished in the popular eyes. The belief that the judgment of God could be perverted or eluded by magic arts still continued, however, and precautions were commonly taken to prevent their use.[4] Holy water, moreover, was lavishly sprinkled on the materials employed in the ordeal and on the patient, and was given to him

[1] Nam criminosos eodem chrismate unctos aut potatos nequaquam ullo examine deprehendi posse a multis putatur.—C. Turonens. III. ann. 813 c. 20 (Harduin. IV. 1026).

[2] Capit. Car. Mag. II. ann. 809.—Capitul. Lib. III. c. 55.—Reginon. de Discip. Ecclesiæ I. 73.

[3] Reginon. *op. cit.* I. 72.— Burchardi Decret. IV. 80.— Ivon. Carnot. Decret. I. 274.

[4] Martene de Antiq. Ritibus Ecclesiæ Lib. III. c. vii. Ordo 8. So in a ninth century exorcism of the hot water—" et si culpabilis de hac causa est et aliqua maleficia aut per herbas peccatum suum tegere voluerit tua dextera evacuare dignetur."—Patetta, Archivio Giuridico, Vol. XLV.

to drink to prevent diabolic illusions by which it was imagined that the purposes of God could be defeated.[1]

Precautions also were taken to guard against processes by which, in the fire ordeals, it was believed that the human frame could be rendered incombustible, and for this object a widely prevailing custom required that for three days previous the hand should be wrapped up to guard against its being thus fortified.[2] The nature of these unguents may be guessed from a prescription given by Albertus Magnus, consisting of mallow and radish juice, white of egg, lime, and "psillus" seeds, the use of which he assures us will enable a man with impunity to enter the flames or to carry red-hot iron.[3]   Doubtless reliance on some such expedients may partially explain the readiness with which the ordeal was undertaken.

CHAPTER XVII.

THE CHURCH AND THE ORDEAL.

THE relation of the Church to the vulgar ordeals presents even a more complex question than that which has already been discussed of its connection with the judicial combat. The ordeals were less repugnant to its teachings and more completely dependent upon its ministrations, for while a duel might be fought without the aid of a priest the efficacy of an

----

[1] Martene, *loc. cit.* Ord. 10, 18.

[2] Du Cange, s. v. *Ferrum candens.*

[3] Experimentum mirabile quod facit homines ire in ignem sine læsione, vel portare ignem vel ferrum ignitum sine læsione in manu.   Recipe succum bismalvæ et albumen ovi et semen psilli et calcem et pulveriza et confice; cum illo albumine ovi succum raphani commisce et ex hac confectione illinas corpus tuum et manum et dimitte siccari; et postea iterum illinas et post hoc poteris audacter sustinere ignem sine nocumento.—Alb. Mag. de Miraculis Mundi (Binterim, Denkwürdigkeiten der Christ-Katholischen Kirche, Bd. V. Th. iii. p. 70).

ordeal depended wholly upon the religious rites which gave it the sanction of a direct invocation of the Almighty.

We have seen above that the Church readily accepted the pagan practices of its Barbarian converts, and gave them fresh claim to confidence by surrounding them with the most impressive solemnities of the faith. Notwithstanding the worldly advantage derivable from this policy, there were some minds superior to the superstition or the cunning of their fellows. Even as early as the commencement of the sixth century, Avitus, Bishop of Vienne, remonstrated freely with Gundobald on account of the prominence given to the battle ordeal in the Burgundian code ; and some three centuries later, St. Agobard, Archbishop of Lyons, attacked the whole system in two powerful treatises, which in many points display a breadth of view and clearness of reasoning far in advance of his age.[1] Shortly after this we find an echo of these arguments in some utterances of the papacy, such as the disapproval of the lot by Leo IV. (p. 353), of the duel by Nicholas I. (p. 207), and the more general condemnation by Stephen V. (p. 395), while on the other hand we have seen (p. 382) the ordeal adopted by Stephen VII. in the trial of his predecessor Formosus.

Whether the Holy See condemned or approved the judgment of God was a matter of the utmost indifference to the Church at large. The universal use of the ordeal, involving as it did the indispensable employment of priestly ministrations, shows sufficiently that no ecclesiastic hesitated to sanction it, and that practically it had the universal sympathy and support of the Church. Nor was this left to be merely a matter of inference, for the local churches had no scruple in advocating and prescribing it in the most authoritative manner. In 799 the Council of Salzburg ordered the ret-hot iron for the trial of witches and necromancers.[2] In 810, Ahyto, Bishop

---

[1] The " Liber adversus Legem Gundobadi" and " Liber contra Judicium Dei."

[2] Concil. Salisburg. I. can. ix. (Dalham Concil. Salisburg. p. 35).

of Basle, could suggest no other mode of determining doubtful cases of consanguinity between husband and wife.[1] In 853, the Synod of Soissons ordered Burchard, Bishop of Chartres, to prove his fitness for the episcopal office by undergoing the ordeal.[2] Hincmar, Archbishop of Reims, lent to it all the influence of his commanding talents and position; the Council of Mainz in 888, and that of Tribur near Mainz in 895, recommended it; that of Tours in 925 ordered it for the decision of a quarrel between two priests respecting certain tithes;[3] the synod of the province of Mainz in 1028 authorized the hot iron in a case of murder;[4] that of Elne in 1065 recognized it; that of Auch in 1068 confirmed its use; a penitential of the same period in Bohemia ordered the ordeal for those who pleaded ignorance when accused of marrying within the prohibited degrees;[5] Burckhardt, Bishop of Worms, whose collection of canons enjoyed high authority, in 1023 assisted at the Council of Selingenstadt, which directed its employment, and in his penitential he prescribes five years' penance for endeavoring by magic arts to escape conviction by it—a practice which, as we have seen, was not uncommon.[6] The synod of Gran, in 1099, decided that the ordeal of hot iron might be administered during Lent, except in cases involving the shedding of blood.[7] Moreover, we find St. Bernard alluding approvingly to the conviction and martyrdom of heretics by the cold-water process,[8] of which Guibert de Nogent gives us an instance wherein he aided the Bishop of Soissons in admin-

---

[1] Ahytonis Capitular. cap. xxi. (D'Achery I. 585).

[2] Capit. Carol. Calvi Tit. XI. c. iii. (Baluze).

[3] Concil. Turon. ann. 925 (Martene et Durand Thes. T. IV. pp. 72-3).

[4] Annalist. Saxo. ann. 1028.

[5] Höfler, Concilia Pragensia, p. xiv. Prag, 1862.

[6] Burchardi Decret. Lib. XIX. c. 5 (Migne's Patrologia CXL. p. 973).— Corrector Burchardi cap. 155 (Wasserschleben, Bussordnungen der abenländischen Kirche, p. 660).

[7] Batthyani, Legg. Eccles. Hung. II. 126.

[8] Examinati judicio aquæ mendaces inventi sunt . . . . aqua eos non suscipiente.—In Cantica, Sermon. 66 cap. 12.

istering it to two backsliders with complete success.[1] In 1157 the red-hot iron ordeal was prescribed by the Council of Reims for all persons accused of belonging to the fast-growing sect of the Cathari or Manichæans, whose progress was alarming the Church;[2] and in 1167 two heretics at Vezelai were tried by cold water in the presence of the Archbishop of Lyons and two bishops, when, singularly enough, they escaped.[3] In 1172 a learned clerk named Robert was involved in a debate with a knight on the delicate question whether the Eucharist became corrupted when voided from the body : he was accused as a heretic to the Bishop of Arras, who called in the Archbishop of Reims and numerous clerks to try him. Robert was so confident of his innocence that he offered to undergo the hot-iron ordeal, but his guilt was miraculously shown when burns appeared not only on the right hand that carried the iron, but also on the left hand, on both feet, both sides and on his chest and belly, wherefore he was promptly burned alive as a heretic.[4] Other cases, moreover, are related by Peter Cantor, in which good Catholics were successfully convicted of heresy in this manner, and one instance presents a curious view of the singular confusion which existed in judicial logic at the time. A poor fellow who professed the most entire orthodoxy, and against whom there was no proof, was ordered to carry the red-hot iron. This he refused unless the assembled bishops would prove that he could do so without incurring mortal sin by tempting God. This they were unable to accomplish, so all unpleasant doubts were settled by promptly having him burnt.[5] Even after the Lateran Council of 1215, some miracles related by Cæsarius of Heisterbach show that the conviction

---

[1] De Vita Sua Lib. III. cap. 18.

[2] Concil. Remens. ann. 1157, can. 1 (Martene Ampl. Coll. VII. 75).

[3] Hist. Vizeliacens. Lib. IV. (D'Achery Spicileg. II. 560).

[4] Godefridi S. Pantaleon. Annal. ann. 1172 (Freher et Struv. Rer. German. Scriptt. I. 340).

[5] Pet. Cantor. Verb. Abbreviat. cap. lxxviii. (Patrol. CCV. 230).

of heretics by the hot iron was regarded as a matter of course,[1] and a penitential of a somewhat later period complains that suspected heretics on trial had no other means of proving their orthodoxy or their conversion to the true faith. It also mentions a curious custom prevalent in some places that where there was doubt as to a man having died in grace, his friends had to prove his penitence by undergoing the cold-water ordeal before he was admitted to Christian sepulture.[2]

Prelates, moreover, were everywhere found granting charters containing the privilege of conducting trials in this manner. It was sometimes specially appropriated to members of the Church, who claimed it, under the name of *Lex Monachorum*, as a class privilege exempting them from being parties to the more barbarous and uncanonical wager of battle,[3] and in 1061 a charter of John, Bishop of Avranches, to the Abbot of Mont S. Michel, alludes to hot water and iron as the only mode of trying priests charged with offences of magnitude.[4] St. Ivo of Chartres, who denied the liability of churchmen to the ordeal, admitted that it could be properly used on laymen, and even pronounces its result to be beyond appeal.[5] Pope Calixtus II. in 1119 gave his sanction to it at the Council of Reims, and soon afterwards at the Council of Chartres he admitted the red-hot iron to decide a case of alleged violation of the right of asylum in a church.[6] About the same time

[1] Cæsar. Heisterbach. Dial. Mirac. Dist. III. c. xvi. xvii.

[2] Döllinger, Beiträge zur Sektengeschichte des Mittelalters, München, 1890, II. 621, 622.

[3] Theodericus Abbas Vice-Comitem adiit paratus aut calidi ferri judicio secundum legem monachorum per suum hominem probare, aut scuto et baculo secundum legem secularium deffendere.—Annal. Benedict. L. 57, No. 74, ann. 1036 (*ap.* Houard, Loix Anc. Franç. I. 267).

[4] Judicium ferri igniti et aquæ ferventis Abrincis portaretur, si clerici lapsi in culpam degradationis forte invenirentur.—Chart. Joan. Abrinc. (Patrolog. CXLVII. 266).

[5] Ivon. Carnot. Epist. ccxxxii. ccxlix. cclii.

[6] C. Remens. ann. 1119 (Harduin. VI. 1986).—Hildeberti Cenomanens. Epist. (D'Achery Spicileg. III. 456).

the learned priest, Honorius of Autun, specifies the benediction of the iron and water of the ordeal as part of the legitimate functions of his order;[1] and even Gratian, in 1151, hesitates to condemn the whole system, preferring to consider the canon of Stephen V. as prohibiting only the ordeals of hot water and iron.[2]

The Church, in fact, lent its most impressive ceremonies to enhance the effect on the popular mind of these trials. An *Ordo* or Ritual, of about the year 1100, informs us that when any one accused of theft or adultery or other crime refused to confess, the priest was to go to the church, put on his sacred vestments, except the chasuble, and then, holding the gospels and chrismatory, the chalice and paten and relics of saints, he from the vestibule summoned the people, while forbidding the accused, if guilty, and any of his accomplices to enter. At the same time he designated the spot in the vestibule where the fire was to be built to heat the caldron or the ploughshares, and sprinkled them all with holy water to prevent diabolical illusions. Then the accused entered. He was first required to forgive all offences as he hoped for pardon; he made confession of his sins and accepted penance, while the penitential psalms were sung customary for penitents on Ash Wednesday; if there was suspicion as to his faith he was made to swear on the altar his reliance on God rather than on the devil to manifest his innocence in the ordeal. Mass was then celebrated and communion was administered to him under the tremendous adjuration, " May the body and blood of our Lord Jesus Christ be unto thee a proof !" After this the priest led the

---

[1] Gemma Animæ, Lib. I. cap. 181. At least this is the only reading which will make the passage intelligible—" Horum officium est . . . vel nuptias vel arma, vel peras, vel baculos vel judicia ferre et aquas vel candelas . . . benedicere," where " ferre et aquas" is evidently corrupt for " ferri et aquæ."

[2] Hoc autem utrum ad omnia genera purgationis, an ad hæc duo tantum, quæ hic prohibita esse videntur, pertineat, non immerito dubitatur propter sacrificium zelotypiæ, et illud Gregorii.—C. 20, caus. II. q. V.

people to the spot where the trial was to take place. Prayers were uttered to God to render judgment, litanies and psalms were sung, the material of the ordeal, whether iron or hot or cold water, was blessed with an adjuration that it would be the means of rendering a just verdict, and the accused was exorcised with an adjuration to abandon the trial if he was conscious of guilt. Then the oath was administered to him, and he took hold of the glowing iron, or plunged his hand into the seething caldron, or was bound and cast into the water. Nothing was omitted that would add to the effectiveness of the prolonged ritual, and throughout it was in the hands of the priest; the secular tribunal effaced itself and abandoned the whole conduct of the affair to the Church.[1]

Gradually, however, the papacy ranged itself in opposition to the ordeal. After a silence of nearly two centuries, Alexander II., about 1070, denounced it as a popular invention, destitute of canonical authority, and forbade its use for ecclesiastics.[2] This was a claim which had already in the eighth century been advanced in England by Ecgbehrt, Archbishop of York, who piously declared that their oath on the cross was sufficient for acquittal, and that if guilty their punishment must be left to God.[3] About the year 1000, St. Abbo of Fleury revived this assertion of exemption,[4] and a century later St. Ivo of Chartres insisted on it.[5] As we have seen, these demands for clerical immunity were wholly disregarded, but they serve as a key to the motive of the papal opposition to the ordeal which developed itself so rapidly in the second half of the twelfth century. The Church had long sought, with little practical result, to emancipate the clergy from subjection to the secular law. This was one of the leading objects of the forgers of the Pseudo-Isidorian decretals; it had

[1] Ordo ad Frigidam Aquam, etc. (Pez, Thesaur. Anecd. T. II. P. II. p. 635).

[2] Ivon. Decret. x. 15.

[3] Dialog. Ecbert. Ebor. Interrog. III. (Thorpe, II. 88).

[4] Abbon. Floriac. Epist. viii.   [5] Ivon. Carnotens. Epist. lxxiv.

met with promising success at the time;[1] in the confusion of
the tenth and eleventh centuries it had well-nigh been forgotten, but now it was revived and insisted on with a persistent
energy which won the victory in the thirteenth century. When
this point was gained and ecclesiastics were relieved from ordeals and duels, the next step was inevitably to extend the
prohibition to the laity. The papal battle was really fought
for the advantage of the clergy, but the clergy was ranged in
opposition because the prospective benefit seemed inadequate
to compensate for present loss. The local churches found in
the administration of the ordeal a source of power and profit
which naturally rendered them unwilling to abandon it at the
papal mandate. Chartered privileges had accumulated around
it, such as we have already seen in the case of the judicial
duel, and these privileges were shared or held by prelates and
churches and monasteries. Thus in 1148 we find Thibaut the
Great of Champagne making over to the church of St. Mary
Magdalen the exclusive right of administering the oaths required on such occasions in the town of Chateaudun;[2] and
in 1182 the Vicomte de Béarn conferred on the Abbey de la
Seauve the revenue arising from the marble basin used for the
trial by boiling water at Gavarret.[3] In the statutes of King
Coloman of Hungary, collected in 1099, there is a provision
prohibiting the administration of the ordeal in the smaller
churches, and reserving the privilege to the cathedral seats
and other important establishments.[4]

According to a grant from Péregrin de Lavedan to the monastery of Saint-Pé, in Bigorre, the fee for administering the hot-
water ordeal was five crowns, of which two were paid to the
monastery, two to the cathedral at Tarbes, and one to the
priest who blessed the water and stone.[5] By the laws of St.

---

[1] I have treated this matter in some detail in "Studies in Church History," pp. 69–74, 190 sqq.

[2] Du Cange, s. v. *Adramire.*   [3] Revue Hist. de Droit, 1861, p. 478.

[4] Decret. Coloman. c. 11 (Batthyani T. I. p. 454).

[5] Lagrèze, Hist. du Droit dans les Pyrénées, p. 246.

Ladislas of Hungary, in 1092, the stipend of the officiating priest for the red-hot iron was double that which he received for the water ordeal;[1] in Bohemia the laws of Otto Premizlas in 1229 give the priest a fee of fourteen deniers for the latter.[2] How rigidly these rights were enforced is shown in a case related by Peter Cantor in the twelfth century. A man accused of crime was sentenced to undergo the ordeal of cold water. When stripped and bound and seated on the edge of the tank, the prosecutor withdrew the suit, but the official of the court refused to release the accused until he should pay fees amounting to nine livres and a half. A long wrangle ensued, until the defendant declared that he would pay nothing, but would rather undergo the ordeal, and, after establishing his innocence, would give fifty sols to the poor. He was accordingly thrown in and sank satisfactorily, but on being drawn out was met with a fresh claim from the officiating priest, of five sols, for blessing the water.[3]

As these fees were paid, sometimes on conviction and sometimes on acquittal, there was danger that, even without direct bribery, self-interest might affect the result. Thus by the acts of the Synod of Lillebonne, in 1080, a conviction by the hot-iron ordeal entailed a fine for the benefit of the bishop;[4] and it was apparently to prevent such influences that the Swedish code, compiled by Andreas Archbishop of Lunden early in the thirteenth century, made the successful party, whether the prosecutor or defendant, pay the fee to the officiating priest—a regulation sufficiently degrading to the sacerdotal character.[5]   But besides these pecuniary advan-

---

[1] "Presbyter de ferro duas pensas et de aqua unam pensam accipiat." Synod. Zabolcs. ann. 1092 can. 27 (Batthyani I. 439). Another reading makes the fee equal for both (Ib. II. 101).

[2] Jura Primæva Moraviæ, Brunæ, 1781, p. 26.

[3] Pet. Cantor. Verb. Abbreviat. cap. xxiv.

[4] Orderic. Vital. Lib. v. cap. v.

[5] Leg. Scanicar. Lib. VII. cap. 99 (Ed. Thorsen, p. 171). There is another provision that in certain cases of murder the accused could not be

tages, the ordeal had a natural attraction to the clergy, as it afforded the means of awing the laity, by rendering the priest a special instrument of Divine justice, into whose hands every man felt that he was at any moment liable to fall ; while, to the unworthy, its attractions were enhanced by the opportunities which it gave for the worst abuses. From the decretals of Alexander III. we learn authoritatively that the extortion of money from innocent persons by its instrumentality was a notorious fact[1]—a testimony confirmed by Ekkehardus Junior, who, a century earlier, makes the same accusation, and moreover inveighs bitterly against the priests who were wont to gratify the vilest instincts in stripping women for the purpose of exposing them to the ordeal of cold water.[2]

With all these influences, moral and material, to give to the local clergy a direct interest in the maintenance of the ordeal, it is no wonder that they battled resolutely for its preservation. In this, however, as in so many other details of ecclesiastical policy, centralization triumphed. When the papal authority reached its culminating point, a vigorous and sustained effort to abolish the whole system was made by the popes who occupied the pontifical throne from 1159 to 1227. Nothing can be more peremptory than the prohibition uttered by Alexander III.,[3] who sought moreover to enlist on his side the local churches by stigmatizing as an intolerable abuse the liability which in Sweden forced the highest prelates to sub-

compelled to undergo the ordeal of the red-hot ploughshares unless the accuser was supported by twelve conjurators, when, if the accused was successful each of the twelve was obliged to pay him three marks, and the same sum to the priest.—Ib. L. v. c. 58 (p. 140). It was scarcely intelligible why these ordeals were not allowed to be performed in any week in which there was a church-feast (Ibid. p. 170–1).

[1] Post. Concil. Lateran. P. II. cap. 3, 11.

[2] Holophernicos . . . . Presbyteros, qui animas hominum carissime appreciatas vendant; fœminas nudatas aquis immergi impudicis oculis curiose perspiciant, aut grandi se pretio redimere cogant.—De Casibus S. Galli cap. xiv.

[3] Alex. PP. III. Epist. 74.

mit to the red-hot iron ordeal.[1]   About the same time we find
the celebrated Peter Cantor earnestly urging that it was a sinful tempting of God and a most uncertain means of administering justice, which he enforces by numerous instances of
innocent persons who, within his own knowledge, had been
condemned by its means and put to death ; and he declares
that any priest exorcising the iron or water, or administering
the oaths preliminary to the judicial duel, is guilty of mortal
sin.[2]   Somewhat earlier than this, Ekkehard Bishop of Munster
took the same ground when he refused to his steward Richmar
permission to undergo the red-hot iron ordeal in order to convert the Jew, Hermann of Cologne ; it would be, he said, a
tempting of God.[3]   A different reason was given when Albero,
a priest of Mercke near Cologne, offered to pass through fire
to prove the orthodoxy of his teaching that the sacraments
were vitiated in the hands of sinful priests, and his request
was refused on the ground that skilful sorcery might thus lead
to the success of a flagrant heresy.[4]   In 1181, Lucius III.
pronounced null and void the acquittal of a priest charged
with homicide, who had undergone the water ordeal, and
ordered him to prove his innocence with compurgators, giving
as a reason that all such "peregrina judicia" were prohibited.[5]
Even more severe was the blow administered by Innocent III.
early in the thirteenth century.   At Albenga, near Genoa, a
man suspected of theft offered to prove his innocence by the
red-hot iron, and agreed to be hanged if he should fail.   The
ordeal took place in the presence of the bishop and judge ;
the man's hand was burnt and after some consultation the
bishop ordered him to be hanged.   When Innocent heard of
this he promptly had the bishop deprived of his see and a

---

[1] Alex. PP. III. Epist. (Harduin. VI. II. 1439).

[2] Pet. Cantor. Verb. Abbreviat. cap. lxxviii.

[3] Hermanni Opusc. de sua Conversione c. 5 (Migne, CLXX. 814).

[4] Anon. Libell. adversus Errores Alberonis (Martene Ampl. Coll. IX.
1265).

[5] C. 8 Extra v. xxxiv.

successor elected; his decision in this case was carried into the
canon law as a precedent to be followed.[1]   In 1210, moreover,
when Bishop Henry of Strassburg was vigorously persecuting
heresy and convicting heretics by the ordeal, one of them
named Reinhold hurried to Rome and returned with a letter
from Innocent forbidding it for the future; ordeals might be
adjudged, he said, by the secular tribunals, but they were not
admissible in ecclesiastical judgments.[2]   Still more effective
was his action when, under his impulsion, the Fourth Council
of Lateran, in 1215, formally forbade the employment of any
ecclesiastical ceremonies in such trials.[3]   As the moral influence
of the ordeal depended entirely upon its religious associations,
a strict observance of this canon must speedily have swept the
whole system into oblivion.   Yet shortly after this we find the
inquisitor Conrad of Marburg employing in Germany the red-
hot iron as a means of condemning his unfortunate victims by
wholesale, and the chronicler relates that, whether innocent or
guilty, few escaped the test.[4]   The canon of Lateran, however, was actively followed up by the papal legates, and the
system may consequently be considered to have fairly entered
on its decline.

So far as the Church was concerned its condemnation was
irrevocable.   By this time the papacy had become the supreme
and unquestioned legislator.   The compilation of papal decrees known as the Decretals of Gregory IX., issued in 1234,
was everywhere accepted as the "new law" of binding force,
and in it the compiler, St. Ramon de Peñafort, had sedulously

---

[1] Can. 10 Extra V. 31.

[2] Innoc. PP. III. Regest. XIV. 138.—Yet abundant miracles in Strassburg testified to the divine favor in these trials.—Cæsar. Hiesterbac. Dist.
III. c. 16, 17.

[3] Nec . . . . quisquam purgationi aquæ ferventis vel frigidæ, seu ferri
candentis ritum cujuslibet benedictionis seu consecrationis impendat.—Concil Lateran. can. 18.   In 1227, the Council of Trèves repeated the prohibition, but only applied it to the red-hot iron ordeal.   "Item. nullus
sacerdos candens ferrum benedicat."—Concil. Trevirens. ann. 1227, cap. ix.

[4] Trithem. Chron. Hirsaug. ann. 1215.

inserted the prohibitions so repeatedly issued during the preceding three-quarters of a century. These prohibitions were no longer construed as limited to ecclesiastics; the whole system was condemned. St. Ramon himself in his *Summa*, which had immense and lasting authority, had no hesitation in denouncing all ordeals as an accursed invention of the devil.[1] His contemporary, Alexander Hales, whose reputation as a theologian stood unrivalled, after presenting the arguments on both sides, concludes that they are wholly to be rejected.[2] Soon afterwards Cardinal Henry of Susa, the leading canonist of his day, gave a severer blow by proving that as ordeals are illegal all sentences rendered by their means are null and void.[3] Still the practice was hard to suppress, for at the end of the century we find John of Freiburg denouncing it as forbidden and accursed; bishops and abbots permitting ordeals in their courts are guilty of mortal sin, and preachers should denounce them from their pulpits with all due modesty.[4] This shows that the spiritual lords were still deaf to the voice of the papacy, but the principle was settled and in 1317 Astesanus, whose authority was of the highest, treats the whole system of duels and ordeals as mere appeals to chance, having no warrant in divine law and forbidden by the Church.[5] This attitude was consistently preserved, and Gregory XI. in 1374, when condemning the Sachsenspiegel, enumerated, among other objectionable features, its provisions of this nature as contrary to the canon law and a tempting of God.[6]

---

[1] Vulgaris purgatio est quæ a vulgo est inventa, ut ferri candentis, aquæ ferventis vel frigidæ, panis vel casei, monomachiæ id est duelli et ceteræ hujusmodi: sed ista hodie in totum reprobata est et maledicta, tum quia inventa est a diabolo fabricante.—S. Raymundi Summæ Lib. III. Tit. xxxi. § 1.

[2] Ergo hujusmodi judicia sunt penitus reprobanda et purgatio per talia.— Alex. de Ales Summæ P. III. Q. xlvi. Membr. 3.

[3] Hostiensis Aureæ Summæ Lib. V. *De Purg. Vulg.* § 3.

[4] Joh. Friburgens. Summæ Confessorum Lib. III. Tit. xxxi. Q. 2, 3.

[5] Astesani de Ast Summæ de Casibus Conscientiæ, P. I. Lib. I. Tit. xiv.

[6] Sachsenspiegel, ed. Ludovici, 1720, p. 619.

CHAPTER XVIII.

REPRESSIVE SECULAR LEGISLATION.

ENLIGHTENED legislators were not slow in seconding the efforts of the papacy. Perhaps the earliest instance of secular legislation directed against the ordeal, except some charters granted to communes, is an edict of Philip Augustus in 1200, bestowing certain privileges on the scholars of the University of Paris, by which he ordered that a citizen accused of assaulting a student shall not be allowed to defend himself either by the duel or the water ordeal.[1] In England, a rescript of Henry III., dated January 27, 1219, directs the judges then starting on their circuits to employ other modes of proof— "seeing that the judgment of fire and water is forbidden by the Church of Rome."[2] A few charters and confirmations, dated some years subsequently, allude to the privilege of administering it; but Matthew of Westminster, when enumerating, under date of 1250, the remarkable events of the half century, specifies its abrogation as one of the occurrences to be noted,[3] and we may conclude that thenceforth it was practically abandoned throughout the kingdom. This is confirmed by the fact that Bracton, whose treatise was written a few years later, refers only to the wager of battle as a legal procedure, and, when alluding to other forms, speaks of them as things of the past. About the same time, Alexander II. of Scotland forbade its use in cases of theft.[4] Nearly con-

---

[1] Fontanon, IV. 942. [2] Rymer, Fœd. I. 228.

[3] Prohibitum est judicium quod fieri consuevit per ignem et per aquam.— Mat. Westmon. ann. 1250.

[4] De cetero non fiat judicium per aquam vel ferrum, ut consuetum fuit antiquis temporibus.—Statut. Alex. II. cap. 7 § 3. There is some obscurity

temporary was the Neapolitan Code, promulgated in 1231, by authority of the Emperor Frederic II., in which he not only prohibits the use of the ordeal in all cases, but ridicules, in a very curious passage, the folly of those who could place confidence in it.[1] We may conclude, however, that this was not effectual in eradicating it, for, fifty years later, Charles of Anjou found it necessary to repeat the injunction.[2] About the same time, Waldemar II. of Denmark, Hako Hakonsen of Iceland and Norway, and soon afterwards Birger Jarl of Sweden, followed the example.[3] In Frisia we learn that the inhabitants still refused to obey the papal mandates, and insisted on retaining the red-hot iron, a contumacy which Emo, the contemporary Abbot of Wittewerum, cites as one of the causes of the terrible inundation of 1219;[4] though a century later the Laws of Upstallesboom show that ordeals of all

about this provision owing to variants in the MSS., but Mr. Neilson holds (Trial by Combat, p. 113) that there can be little doubt that it abolished the ordeal wholly.

[1] Leges quæ a quibusdam simplicibus sunt dictæ paribiles .... præsentis nostri nominis sanctionis edicto in perpetuum inhibentes omnibus regni nostri judicibus, ut nullus ipsas leges paribiles, quæ abscensæ a veritate deberent potius nuncupari, aliquibus fidelibus nostris indicet .... Eorum etinim sensum non tam corrigendum duximus quam ridendum, qui naturalem candentis ferri calorem tepescere, imo (quod est stultius) frigescere, nulla justa causa superveniente, confidunt; aut qui reum criminis constitutum, ob conscientiam læsam tantum asserunt ab aquæ frigidæ elemento non recipi, quem submergi potius aeris competentis retentio non permittit.— Constit. Sicular. Lib. II. Tit. 31. This last clause would seem to allude to some artifice of the operators by which the accused was prevented from sinking in the cold-water ordeal when a conviction was desired.

This common sense view of the miracles so generally believed is the more significant as coming from Frederic, who, a few years previously, was ferociously vindicating with fire and sword the sanctity of the Holy Seamless Coat against the aspersions of unbelieving heretics. See his Constitutions of 1221 in Goldastus, Const. Imp. I. 293-4.

[2] Statut. MSS. Caroli I. cap. xxii. (Du Cange, s. v. Lex Parib.).

[3] Königswarter, op. cit. p. 176.

[4] Emon. Chron. ann. 1219 (Matthæi Analect. III. 72).

kinds had fallen into desuetude.[1] In France, we find no formal abrogation promulgated; but the contempt into which the system had fallen is abundantly proved by the fact that in the ordinances and books of practice issued during the latter half of the century, such as the *Établissements* of St. Louis, the *Conseil* of Pierre de Fontaines, the *Coutumes du Beau-voisis* of Beaumanoir, and the *Livres de Justice et de Plet*, its existence is not recognized even by a prohibitory allusion, the judicial duel thenceforward monopolizing the province of irregular evidence. Indeed, a Latin version of the Coutumier of Normandy, dating about the middle of the thirteenth century, or a little earlier, speaks of it as a mode of proof formerly employed in cases where one of the parties was a woman who could find no champion to undergo the wager of battle, adding that it had been forbidden by the Church, and that such cases were then determined by inquests.[2]

Germany was more tardy in yielding to the mandates of the Church. The Teutonic knights who wielded their proselyting swords in the Marches of Prussia introduced the ordeal among other Christian observances, and in 1222 Honorius III., at the prayer of the Livonian converts, promulgated a decree by which he strictly interdicted its use for the future.[3] Even in 1279 we find the Council of Buda, and in 1298 that of Wurzburg, obliged to repeat the prohibition uttered by that of Lateran.[4] These commands enjoyed little respect, and the

1222

1279
1298

---

[1] Issued in 1323.

[2] Cod. Leg. Norman. P. II. c. x. §§ 2, 3 (Ludewig, Reliq. Mictorum. VII. 292). It is a little singular that the same phrase is retained in the authentic copy of the Coutumier, in force until the close of the sixteenth century.—Anc. Cout. de Normandie, c. 77 (Bourdot de Richebourg. IV. 32).

[3] C. iii. Extra, Lib. v. Tit. xxxv.—As embodied in the Decretals of Gregory IX. this canon omits a clause indicating how great was the detestation of the people for the ordeal thus imposed on them—"quare conversis et convertendis scandalum incutiunt et terrorem."—Quint. Compilat. Honorii III. Lib. iv. Tit. xiv.

[4] Batthyani, Legg. Eccles. Hung. T. II. p. 436.—Hartzheim, IV. 27.

independent spirit of the Empire still refused obedience to the commands of the Church. It may probably be to Germany that Roger Bacon refers, about this time, when he speaks of the ordeals of red-hot iron and cold water being still in use by authority of the Church, and admits that the exorcisms employed in them by the priests may have virtue in the detection of guilt and acquittal of innocence.[1] Even in the fourteenth century the ancestral customs were preserved in full vigor as regular modes of procedure in a manual of legal practice still extant. An accusation of homicide could be disproved only by the judicial combat, while in other felonies a man of bad repute had no other means of escape than by undergoing the trial by hot water or iron.[2]

In Aragon, Don Jayme I. included the ordeal in his prohibition of the duel when framing laws for his Minorcan conquest in 1230, and that this was his settled policy is seen by a similar clause of the fuero of Huesca in 1247.[3] In Castile and Leon, the charter of Medina de Pomar, granted in 1219 by Fernando III., provides that there shall be no trial by the hot-water ordeal,[4] and that of Treviño in 1254, by Alfonso X., forbids all ordeals.[5] Still the Council of Palencia, in 1322, was obliged to threaten with excommunication all concerned in administering the ordeal of fire or of water,[6] which proves how little had been accomplished by the enlightened code of the "Partidas," issued about 1260 by Alfonso the Wise. In this the burden of proof is expressly thrown upon the com-

[1] Rogeri Bacon Epist. de Secretis Operibus Artis c. ii. (M. R. Series I. 526).

[2] Richstich Landrecht, cap. LII. The same provisions are to be found in a French version of the Speculum Suevicum, probably made towards the close of the fourteenth century for the use of the western provinces of the Empire.—Miroir de Souabe, P. I. c. xlviii. (Éd. Matile, Neufchatel, 1843).

[3] Villaneuva, Viage Literario, XXII. 288.— Du Cange, s. vv. *Ferrum candens, Batalia.*

[4] Coleccion de Cédulas, etc., Madrid, 1830, Tom. V. p. 142.

[5] Memorial Histórico Español, Madrid, 1850, Tom. I. p. 47.

[6] Concil. Palentin. ann. 1322, can. xxvi.

plainant, and no negative evidence is demanded of the defendant, who is specially exempted from the necessity of producing it;[1] and although in obedience to the chivalrous spirit of the age, the battle ordeal is not abolished, yet it is so limited as to be practically a dead letter, while no other form of negative proof is even alluded to.

In Italy, even in the middle of the fifteenth century St. Antonino of Florence considers it necessary, in his instructions to confessors, to tell them that a judge who prescribes the combat or the red-hot iron commits mortal sin;[2] and Angelo da Chiavasco, who died in 1485, requires confessors to inquire of penitents whether they have ordered or accepted the hot-iron ordeal.[3] Even as late as 1599 G. Ferretti tells us that in some districts of Naples, inhabited by Epirotes, husbands who suspect their wives of adultery force them to prove their innocence by the ordeal of red-hot iron or boiling water.[4]

Although the ordeal was thus removed from the admitted jurisprudence of Europe, the principles of faith which had given it vitality were too deeply implanted in the popular mind to be at once eradicated, and accordingly, as we have seen above, instances of its employment continued occasionally for several centuries to disgrace the tribunals. The ordeal of battle, indeed, as shown in the preceding essay, was not legally abrogated until long afterward; and the longevity of the popular belief, upon which the whole system was founded, may be gathered from a remark of Sir William Staundford, a learned judge and respectable legal authority, who, in 1557, expresses the same confident expectation of Divine interference

---

[1] Non es tenuda la parte de probar lo que niega porque non lo podrie facer.—Las Siete Partidas, P. III. Tit. xiv. l. 1.

[2] S. Antonini Confessionale.

[3] Angeli de Clavasio Summa Angelica s. v. *Interrogationes*. The contemporary Baptista de Saulis speaks of ordeals in the present tense when saying that all concerned in them are guilty of mortal sin.—Summa Rosella, s. v. *Purgatio.*

[4] Patetta, Le Ordalie, p. 450.

which had animated Hincmar or Poppo.   After stating that
in an accusation of felony, unsupported by evidence, the defendant had a right to wager his battle, he proceeds : "Because in that the appellant demands judgment of death against
the appellee, it is more reasonable that he should hazard his
life with the defendant for the trial of it, than to put it on the
country . . . . and to leave it to God, to whom all things are
open, to give the verdict in such case, *scilicet*, by attributing
the victory or vanquishment to the one party or the other, as
it pleaseth Him."[1]   Nearly about the same time, Ciruelo, who
for thirty years was Inquisitor at Saragossa, alludes to cases in
which he had personally known of its employment, thus showing that it was in popular use, even though not prescribed by
the law, in Spain during the middle of the sixteenth century.[2]
In Germany not long before the learned Aventinus showed
plainly that the existing incredulity which treated all such
reliance on God as insanity was much less to his taste than the
pious trust which through ages of faith had led princes and
prelates to place their hope in God and invoke him with all
the solemnities of religion to decide where human wisdom was
at fault.[3]

While the prohibitions uttered by the papacy had undoubtedly much to do in influencing monarchs to abolish the ordeal,
there were other causes of scarcely less weight working to the
same end.   The revival of the Roman law in the twelfth and
thirteenth centuries and the introduction of torture as an unfailing expedient in doubtful cases did much to influence the
secular tribunals against all ordeals.   So, also, a powerful
assistant must be recognized in the rise of the communes,
whose sturdy common sense not infrequently rejected its absurdity.   These influences, however, have been discussed at

[1] Plees del Corone, chap. XV. (quoted in I Barnewall & Alderson, 433).
[2] Ciruelo, Reprovacion de las Supersticiones. P. II. cap. vii.   Salamanca,
1539.
[3] Aventini Annal. Boior. Lib. IV. c. xiv. n. 31.

some length in the previous essay, and it is scarce worth while
to repeat what has there been said, except to add that, as a
recognized legal procedure, the ordeal succumbed with a less
prolonged struggle than the single combat.

Yet no definite period can be assigned to the disappearance
in any country of the appeals to Heaven handed down from
our ancestors in the illimitable past. We have seen above
how certain forms of the ordeal, such as bier-right and the trial
by cold water, have lingered virtually to our own times, though
long since displaced from the statute-book; and we should err
if we deemed the prohibition of the system by law-givers to
be either the effect or the cause of a change in the constitution
of the human mind. The mysterious attraction of the unknown, the striving for the unattainable, the yearning to con-
nect our mortal nature with some supernal power—all these
mixed motives assist in maintaining the superstitions which
we have thus passed in review. Even though the external
manifestations may have been swept away, the potent agencies
which vivified them have remained, not perhaps less active
because they work more secretly. One generation of follies
after another, strangely affiliated, waits on the successive
descendants of man, and perpetuates in another shape the
superstition which seemed to be eradicated. In its most
vulgar and abhorrent form, we recognize it in the fearful epidemic of sorcery and witchcraft which afflicted the sixteenth
and seventeenth centuries; sublimed to the verge of heaven,
we see it reappear in the seraphic theories of Quietism; de-
scending again towards earth, it stimulates the mad vagaries
of the Convulsionnaires. In a different guise, it leads the
refined scepticism of the eighteenth century to a belief in the
supernatural powers of the divining rod, which could not only
trace out hidden springs and deep-buried mines, but could
also discover crime, and follow the malefactor through all the
doublings of his cunning flight.[1] Even at the present day, as

---

[1] When, in 1692, Jacques Aymar attracted public attention to the miracles of the diving-rod, he was called to Lyons to assist the police in dis-

various references in the preceding pages sufficiently attest, there is a lurking undercurrent of superstition which occasionally rises into view and shows that we are not yet exempt from the weakness of the past. Each age has its own sins and follies to answer for—happiest that which best succeeds in hiding them, for it can scarce do more. Here, at the close of the nineteenth century, when the triumph of human intelligence over the forces of nature, stimulating the progress of material prosperity, has deluded us into sacrificing our psychical to our intellectual being—even here the duality of our nature reasserts itself, and in the crudity of Mormonism and in the fantastic mysteries of spiritism we see a protest against the despotism of mere reason. If we wonder at these perversions of our noblest attributes, we must remember that the intensity of the reaction measures the original strain, and in the insanities of the day we thus may learn how utterly we have forgotten the Divine warning, "Man shall not live by bread alone!"

covering the perpetrators of a mysterious murder, which had completely baffled the agents of justice. Aided by his rod, he traced the criminals, by land and water, from Lyons to Beaucaire, where he found in prison a man whom he declared to be a participant, and who finally confessed the crime. In 1703 Marshal Montrevel and the intendant Baville made use of Aymar to discover Calvinists, of whom numbers were condemned on the strength of his revelations (Patetta, Le Ordalie, p. 33). Aymar was at length proved to be merely a clever charlatan, but the mania to which he gave rise lasted through the eighteenth century, and nearly at its close his wonders were rivalled by a brother sharper, Campetti. The belief in the powers of the divining-rod has not yet died out, and it is frequently used to discover oil wells, springs, mines, etc.

A good account of Aymar's career and the discussion to which it gave rise may be found in Prof. Rubio y Diaz's "Estudios sobre la Evocacion de los Espiritus," Cadiz, 1860, pp. 116–28.

APPENDIX.

THE ORDEAL: ORIGINAL
SOURCES IN TRANSLATION.

Volume IV, Part 4 of the publication series *Translations and Reprints from the Original Sources of European History* consisted of a pamphlet by Arthur E. Howland entitled *Ordeals, Compurgation, Excommunication, and Interdict.* The materials translated by Howland are still valuable to the reader of history, but the pamphlet has long since gone out of print. The following documents in translation are all those that Howland included in that pamphlet touching on the subject of the ordeal and, together with Lea's text, they constitute the only readily available source in English for the history of the ordeal. It is the Editor's hope that by joining these two works, which were closely related when Howland published his translations using materials from Lea's own library, of which he was the curator, the reader will have easy access to both an excellent historical account of the ordeal and illustrative documents in translation.

1. FORMULA FOR CONDUCTING THE ORDEAL OF BOILING WATER. Source: The breviary of Eberhard of Bamberg, ed. K. Zeumer, *Monumenta Germaniae Historica, Legum, Sectio V,* p. 650. The breviary dates from the late twelfth or early thirteenth century.

Let the priest go to the church with the prosecutors and with him who is about to be tried. And while the rest wait in the vestibule of the church let the priest enter and put on the sacred garments except the chasuble and, taking the Gospel and the chrismarium and the relics of the saints and the chalice, let him go to the altar and speak thus to all the people standing near: Behold, brethren, the offices of the Christian religion. Behold the law in which is hope and remission of sins, the holy oil of the chrisma, the consecration of the body and blood of our Lord. Look that ye be not deprived of the heritage of such great blessing and of participation in it by implicating yourselves in the crime of another, for it is written, not only are they worthy of death who do these things, but they that have pleasure in them that do them.

Then let him thus address the one who is to undertake the ordeal: I command thee, N., in the presence of all, by the Father, the Son, and the Holy Ghost, by the tremendous day of judgment, by the ministry of baptism, by thy veneration for the saints, that, if thou art guilty of this matter charged against thee, if thou hast done it, or consented to it, or hast knowingly seen the perpetrators of this crime, thou enter not into the church nor mingle in the company of Christians unless thou wilt confess and admit thy guilt before thou art examined in public judgment.

Then he shall designate a spot in the vestibule where the fire is to be made for the water, and shall first sprinkle the place with holy water, and shall also sprinkle the kettle when it is ready to be hung and the water in it, to guard against the illusions of the devil. Then, entering the church with the others, he shall celebrate the ordeal mass. After the celebration let the priest go with the people to the place of the ordeal, the Gospel in his left hand, the cross, censer and relics of the saints being carried ahead, and let him chant seven penitential psalms with a litany.

Prayer over the boiling water: O God, just Judge, firm and patient, who art the Author of peace, and judgest truly, determine what is right, O Lord, and make known Thy righteous judgment. O Omnipotent God, Thou that lookest upon the earth and makest it to tremble, Thou that by the gift of Thy Son, our Lord Jesus Christ, didst save the world and by His most holy passion didst redeem the human race, sanctify, O Lord, this water being heated by fire. Thou that didst save the three youths, Sidrac, Misac, and Abednago, cast into the fiery furnace at the command of Nebuchadnezzar, and didst lead them forth unharmed by the hand of Thy angel, do Thou O clement and most holy Ruler, give aid if he shall plunge his hand into the boiling water, being innocent, and, as Thou didst liberate the three youths from the fiery furnace and didst free

Susanna from the false charge, so, O Lord, bring forth his hand safe and unharmed from this water. But if he be guilty and presume to plunge in his hand, the devil hardening his heart, let Thy holy justice deign to declare it, that Thy virtue may be manifest in his body and his soul be saved by penitence and confession. And if the guilty man shall try to hide his sins by the use of herbs or any magic, let Thy right hand deign to bring it to no account. Through Thy only begotten Son, our Lord Jesus Christ, who dwelleth with Thee.

Benediction of the water: I bless thee, O creature of water, boiling above the fire, in the name of the Father, and of the Son, and of the Holy Ghost, from whom all things proceed; I adjure thee by Him who ordered thee to water the whole earth from the four rivers, and who summoned thee forth from the rock, and who changed thee into wine, that no wiles of the devil or magic of men be able to separate thee from thy virtues as a medium of judgment; but mayest thou punish the vile and the wicked, and purify the innocent. Through Him whom hidden things do not escape and who sent thee in the flood over the whole earth to destroy the wicked and who will yet come to judge the quick and the dead and the world by fire. Amen.

Prayer: Omnipotent, Eternal God, we humbly beseech Thee in behalf of this investigation which we are about to undertake here amongst us that iniquity may not overcome justice but that falsehood may be subjected to truth. And if any one seek to hinder or obscure this examination by any magic or by herbs of the earth, deign to bring it to naught by Thy right hand, O upright Judge.

Then let the man who is to be tried, as well as the kettle or pot in which is the boiling water, be fumed with the incense of myrrh, and let this prayer be spoken: O God, Thou who within this substance of water hast hidden Thy most solemn sacraments, be graciously present with us who invoke Thee, and upon this element made ready by much purification pour down the virtue of Thy benediction that this creature, obedient to Thy mysteries, may be endued with Thy grace to detect diabolical and human fallacies, to confute their inventions and arguments, and to overcome their mulitform arts. May all the wiles of the hidden enemy be brought to naught that we may clearly perceive the truth regarding those things which we with finite senses and simple hearts are seeking from Thy judgment through invocation of Thy holy name. Let not the innocent, we beseech Thee, be unjustly condemned, or the guilty be able to delude with safety those who seek the truth from Thee, who art the true Light, who seest in the shadowy darkness, and who makest our darkness light. O Thou who perceivest hidden things and knowest what is secret, show and declare this by Thy grace and make the knowledge of the truth manifest to us who believe in Thee.

Then let the hand that is to be placed in the water be washed with soap and let it be carefully examined whether it be sound; and before it is thrust in let the priest say: I adjure thee, O vessel, by the Father, and the Son, and the Holy Ghost, and by the holy resurrection, and by the tremendous day of judgment, and by the four Evangelists, that if this man be guilty of this crime either by deed or by consent, let the water boil violently, and do thou, O vessel, turn and swing.

After this let the man who is to be tried plunge in his hand, and afterwards let it be immediately sealed up. After the ordeal let him take a drink of holy water. Up to the time of the decision regarding the ordeal* it is a good thing to mix salt and holy water with all his food and drink.

2. The Ordeal of Hot Water Undertaken by a Priest To Confute a Heretic. Source: Gregory of Tours, *Liber in Gloria Martyrum Beatorum,* c. 80, *Monumenta Germaniae Historica, Scriptores Rerum Merovingicarum,* Vol. I, p. 542. The text dates from the sixth century.

An Arian presbyter disputing with a deacon of our religion made venemous assertions against the Son of God and the Holy Ghost, as is the habit of that sect. But when the deacon had discoursed a long time concerning the reasonableness of our faith, and the heretic blinded by the fog of unbelief continued to reject the truth, according as it is written, "Wisdom

---

* A period of three days was allowed to elapse before the hand was examined.

shall not enter the mind of the wicked," the former said: "Why weary ourselves with long discussions? Let acts approve the truth; let a kettle be heated over the fire and some one's ring be thrown into the boiling water. Let him who shall take it from the heated liquid be approved as a follower of the truth, and afterwards let the other party be converted to the knowledge of this truth. And do thou also understand, O heretic, that this our party will fulfil the conditions with the aid of the Holy Ghost; thou shalt confess that there is no discordance, no dissimilarity in the Holy Trinity." The heretic consented to the proposition and they separated after appointing the next morning for the trial. But the fervor of faith in which the deacon had first made this suggestion began to cool through the instigation of the enemy. Rising with the dawn he bathed his arm in oil and smeared it with ointment. But nevertheless he made the round of the sacred places and called in prayer on the Lord. What more shall I say? About the third hour they met in the market place. The people came together to see the show. A fire was lighted, the kettle was placed upon it, and when it grew very hot the ring was thrown into the boiling water. The deacon invited the heretic to take it out of the water first. But he promptly refused, saying, "Thou who didst propose this trial art the one to take it out." The deacon all of a tremble bared his arm. And when the heretic presbyter saw it besmeared with ointment he cried out: "With magic arts thou hast thought to protect thyself, that thou hast made use of these salves, but what thou hast done will not avail." While they were thus quarreling there came up a deacon from Ravenna named Iacinthus and inquired what the trouble was about. When he learned the truth he drew his arm out from under his robe at once and plunged his right hand into the kettle. Now the ring that had been thrown in was a little thing and very light so that it was thrown about by the water as chaff would be blown about by the wind; and searching for it a long time he found it after about an hour. Meanwhile the flame beneath the kettle blazed up mightily so that the greater heat might make it difficult for the ring to be followed by the hand; but the deacon extracted it at length and suffered no harm, protesting rather that at the bottom the kettle was cold while at the top it was just pleasantly warm. When the heretic beheld this he was greatly confused and audaciously thrust his hand into the kettle saying, "My faith will aid me." As soon as his hand had been thrust in all the flesh was boiled off the bones clear up to the elbow. And so the dispute ended.

3. HINCMAR OF REIMS' DESCRIPTION OF THE COLD WATER ORDEAL. Source: Hincmar of Reims, *De Divortio Lotharii,* c. 6, *Patrologia Latina,* Vol. 125, cols. 668-69. This famous work was written in the ninth century as part of the material concerning the particularly troublesome divorce proceedings between the Emperor Lothar II and his wife Theutberga. In it, Hincmar has much to say concerning legal proofs, of which this text is a good example.

Now the one about to be examined is bound by a rope and cast into the water because, as it is written, each one shall be holden with the cords of his iniquity. And it is evident that he is bound for two reasons; to wit, that he may not be able to practice any fraud in connection with the judgment, and that he may be drawn out at the right time if the water should receive him as innocent, so that he perish not. For as we read that Lazarus, who had been dead four days (by whom is signified each one buried under a load of crimes), was buried wrapped in bandages and, bound by the same bands, came forth from the sepulchre at the word of the Lord and was loosed by the disciples at his command; so he who is to be examined by this judgment is cast into the water bound, and is drawn forth again bound, and is either immediately set free by the judgment of the judges, being purged, or remains bound till the time of his purgation and is then examined by the court. . . . And in this ordeal of cold water whoever, after the invocation of God, who is the Truth, seeks to hide the truth by a lie, cannot be submerged in the waters above which the voice of the Lord God has thundered; for the pure nature of the water recognizes as impure and therefore rejects as inconsistent with itself such human nature as has once been regenerated by the waters of baptism and is again infected by falsehood.

4. The Doom of King Aethelstan Regarding the Ordeal of Red-Hot Iron and Water. Source; B. Thorpe, *Ancient Laws and Institutes of England* (London, 1840), Vol. I, pp. 210-213; 226-229; Vol. II, pp. 495-496. The editor has included the full texts and has indicated the different locations of materials which Howland included as one selection.

A.

Aethelstanes Domas, I, c. 23: Of Him Who Gives Pledge for an Ordeal.

If anyone gives pledge for an ordeal, then let him come three days before to the mass-priest who is to hallow it; and let him feed himself with bread and water, and salt, and herbs, before he shall go to it; and let him attend mass each of the three days, and make an oblation, and go to communion on the day that he shall go to the ordeal: and then swear the oath that he is, according to folk-right, guiltless of the charge, before he goes to the ordeal. And if it be water, that he dive an ell and a half by the rope; if it be iron ordeal, let it be three days before the hand be undone. And let every man begin his charge with a fore-oath, as we before ordained: and be each of those fasting, on either hand, who may be there together, by God's command and the archbishop's; and let there not be on either side more than twelve men. If the accused man be with a larger company than some twelve, then be the ordeal void, unless they will go from him.

B.

Aethelstanes Domas, IV, c. 7: Doom Concerning Hot Iron and Water.

Concerning the ordeal we enjoin by command of God, and of the archbishop, and of all bishops: that no man come within the church after the fire is borne in with which the ordeal is to be heated except the priest and him who is to undergo judgement. And let nine feet be measured from the stake to the mark, by the feet of him who is to be tried. But if [the ordeal] be water, let it be heated till it comes to boiling. And

be the kettle of iron or of brass, of lead, or of clay. And if it be
a single accusation, let the hand dive for the stone up to the
wrist; and if it be threefold, up to the elbow. And when the
ordeal is ready let two men from each side go in and certify
that it is as hot as we have directed it to be. Then let an equal
number from both sides enter and stand on either side of the
judgment place along the church, and let them all be fasting
and abstinent from their wives on the preceding night. And let
the priest sprinkle them all with water and let them bow themselves every one to the holy water and let the holy Gospel and
the cross be given them all to kiss. And no one shall mend the
fire any longer than the beginning of the hallowing, but let the
iron lie on the coals until the last collect. Afterwards let it be
placed on a frame, and let no one speak except to pray dili-
gently to God, the Father Omnipotent, to deign to manifest
His truth in the matter. And let the accused drink of the holy
water and then let the hand with which he is about to carry
the iron be sprinkled, and so let him go [to the ordeal]. Let
the nine feet that were measured off be divided into three sections. In the first division let him hold his right foot, close to
the stake. Then let him move his right foot across the second
into the third division, where he shall cast the iron in front of
him and hasten to the holy altar. Then let his hand be sealed
up, and on the third day let examination be made whether it is
clean or foul within the wrapper. And whoever shall trans-
gress these laws, be the ordeal of no worth in his case, but let
him pay the king a fine of twenty shillings.

5. THE ORDEAL OF GLOWING PLOWSHARES UNDERGONE BY
QUEEN EMMA. Source: H. R. Luard, ed., *Annales Monastici,*
Rerum Britannicarum medii aevi scriptores (Rolls Series), No.
36, Vol. II (London, 1864), pp. 23-4. This selection is taken
from the Annals of Winchester, which themselves are attributed
to Richard of Devizes, for the early period up to the Norman
Conquest. The ordeal of Queen Emma, under the entry for the
year 1043, is probably apocryphal, but illustrates the twelfth-
century writer's conception of the ceremony.

The queen was brought at the king's command from Whew-
ell to Winchester and throughout all the night preceding her

trial she kept her vigil at the shrine of St. Swithin. . . . On the appointed day the clergy and the people came to the church and the king himself sat on the tribunal. The queen was brought before her son and questioned whether she was willing to go through with what she had undertaken. . . . Nine glowing ploughshares were placed on the carefully swept pavement of the church. After these had been consecrated by a short ceremony the queen's shoes and stockings were taken off; then her robe was removed and her cloak thrown aside, and, supported by two bishops, one on either side, she was led to the torture. The bishops who led her were weeping and those who were much more afraid than she were encouraging her not to fear. Uncontrollable weeping broke out all over the church and all voices were united in the cry "St. Swithin, O St. Swithin, help her!" If the thunder had pealed forth at this time the people could not have heard it, with such strength, with such a concourse of voices did the shout go up to Heaven that St. Swithin should now or never hasten to her aid. God suffers violence and St. Swithin is dragged by force from Heaven. In a low voice the queen offered this prayer as she undertook the ordeal: "O God, who didst free Susanna from the wicked elders and the three youths from the fiery furnace, from the fire prepared for me deign to preserve me through the merits of St. Swithin."

Behold the miracle! With the bishops directing her feet, in nine steps she walked upon the nine ploughshares, pressing each one of them with the full weight of her whole body; and though she thus passed over them all, she neither saw the iron nor felt the heat. Therefore she said to the bishops: "Am I not to obtain that which I especially sought? Why do you lead me out of the church when I ought to be tried within it?" For she was going out and yet did not realize that she had gone through the ordeal. To which the bishops replied as well as they could through their sobs: "O lady, behold, you have already done it; the deed is now accomplished which you think must yet be done." She gazed and her eyes were opened; then for the first time she looked about and understood the miracle. "Lead me," she said, "to my son, that he may see my feet and know that I have suffered no ill."

6. The Finding of the Holy Lance and the Ordeal of
Fire. Source: Raymond d'Aguiliers, *Historia francorum qui
ceperunt Jerusalem,* c. 18, *Receuil des historiens des Croisades,
Historiens Occidentaux,* Vol. III, p. 283 (Paris, 1866). See
also John H. and Laurita L. Hill, *Raymond d'Aguiliers: Historia francorum qui ceperunt Jerusalem* (Philadelphia, 1968).
The finding of the Holy Lance (the spear allegedly used by
Longinus to pierce Christ's side) in Antioch in June of 1098
played an important role in the crusaders' defense of Antioch
and was the subject of widely diverse opinions. Raymond here
describes the ordeal to which Peter Bartholomew, the finder of
the Lance was subjected. Other versions in Edward Peters,
ed., *The First Crusade* (Philadelphia, 1971), with suggestions
for further reading.

    . . . All these things were pleasing to us, and having
enjoined on him [*i. e.,* Peter Bartholomew,] a fast, we
declared that a fire should be prepared upon the day on which
the Lord was beaten with stripes and put upon the cross for
our salvation. And the fourth day thereafter was the day
before the Sabbath. So when the appointed day came round a
fire was prepared after the noon hour. The leaders and the
people to the number of 60,000 came together; the priests were
there also with bare feet, clothed in ecclesiastical garments.
The fire was made of dry olive branches, covering a space
thirteen feet long; and there were two piles with a space about
a foot wide between them. The height of these piles was four
feet. Now when the fire had been kindled so that it burned
fiercely, I, Raimond, in presence of the whole multitude, spoke:
"If Omnipotent God has spoken to this man face to face, and
the blessed Andrew has shown him our Lord's lance while he
was keeping his vigil, let him go through the fire unharmed.
But if it is false let him be burned together with the lance
which he is to carry in his hand." And all responded on bended
knees, "Amen." The fire was growing so hot that the flames
shot up thirty cubits high into the air and scarcely any one
dared approach it. Then Peter Bartholomew clothed only in his
tunic and kneeling before the bishop of Albar called to God to
witness "that he had seen Him face to face on the cross, and

that he had heard from Him those things above written. . . ."
Then when the bishop had placed the lance in his hand, he
knelt and made the sign of the cross and entered the fire with
the lance, firm and unterrified. For an instant's time he paused
in the midst of the flames, and then by the grace of God passed
through. . . . But when Peter emerged from the fire so that neither his tunic was burned nor even the thin cloth with which
the lance was wrapped up had shown any sign of damage, the
whole people received him after that he had made over them
the sign of the cross with the lance in his hand and had cried,
"God aid us!" All the people, I say, threw themselves upon
him and dragged him to the ground and trampled on him, each
one wishing to touch him or to get a piece of his garment, and
each thinking him near some one else. And so he received
three or four wounds in the legs where the flesh was torn
away, his back was injured and his sides bruised. Peter had
died on the spot, as we believe, had not Raimond Pelet, a brave
and noble soldier, broken through the wild crowd with a band
of friends and rescued him at the peril of their lives. . . . After
this Peter died in peace at the hour appointed to him by God,
and journeyed to the Lord; and he was buried in the place
where he had carried the lance of the Lord through the fire.

7. THE ORDEAL OF THE CROSS. Sources: (A) E. Baluze, *Cap-
itularia Regum Francorum* (Venice, 1772-1773), Vol. I, col.
309, from a capitulary of Charlemagne, early ninth century;
(B) *Monumenta Germaniae Historica, Legum, Sectio* II. Cap-
itularia Regum Francorum, Vol. I, p. 279. A capitulary of
Louis the Pious, ca. 818-819.

A.

[In the ordeal of the cross the two litigants were placed standing before a crucifix with their arms outstretched. The one
who was able to maintain this position the longer won his case.
This is the only form of ordeal in which both parties to the litigation were subjected to the same test. Consequently it par-
takes more of the nature of a duel, and does not leave so wide
a discretion to the court.]

If a dispute, contention, or controversy shall arise between parties regarding the boundaries or limits of their kingdoms of such a nature that it cannot be settled or terminated by human evidence, then we desire that for the decision of the matter the will of God and the truth of the dispute may be sought by means of the judgment of the cross, nor shall any sort of battle or duel ever be adjudged for the decision of any such question.

B.

It is enacted that hereafter no one shall presume to undertake any sort of ordeal of the cross; lest that which was glorified by the passion of Christ should be brought into contempt through any one's temerity.

8. HENRY II's DISTRUST OF ORDEALS. Source: *Gesta Henrici II,* ed., W. Stubbs, 2 vols. (London, 1867), p. 153, Vol. II. The Assize of Clarendon, c. 14.

Also the lord king wishes that those who shall make their law and shall be acquitted by the law, if they be of very bad repute and evilly defamed by the testimony of many legal men, shall abjure the realm, so that within eight days they shall cross the sea unless the wind shall detain them; and with the first wind they shall have thereafter they shall cross the sea; and moreover they shall not return to England except by the grace of the king; and there let them be outlawed. And if they return let them be seized as outlaws.

9. THE ABOLITION OF ORDEALS. Sources: (A) *Corpus Iuris Canonici,* ed. E. Friedberg, Vol. II (Leipzig, 1881), cols. 659-660; Pope Gregory IX, *Liber Extra* III. 50. c. 9 *Sententiam sanguinis* (from the Fourth Lateran Council, c. 18), the prohibition of 1215 against ordeals; (B) Thomas Rhymer, *Foedera,* Vol. I (The Hague, 1739), p. 288, the instructions of King Henry III of England to his judges in 1219, four years after the abolition of ordeals by the Fourth Lateran Council (above, 9. A); (C) *Corpus Iuris Canonici,* ed., E. Friedberg

(Leipzig, 1881), Vol. II, col. 878; Pope Honorius III's decretal of 1222 forbidding the imposition of the ordeal in Livonia, *Liber Extra,* V. 35. 3 *Dilecti filii;* (D) Frederick II, *Constitutiones Sicularum,* Lib. II, Tit. 31, in E. Huillard-Bréholles, *Historia Diplomatica Frederici Secundi,* Vol. IV (Paris, 1852), Part I, p. 102.

A.

Also let no ecclesiastic be placed in command of low soldiery, or bowmen, or men of blood of that sort, nor let any subdeacon, deacon, or priest practice any office of surgery which requires burning or cutting. Nor let any one pronounce over the ordeal of hot or cold water or glowing iron any benediction or rite of consecration, regard being also paid to the prohibitions formerly promulgated respecting the single combat or duel.

B.

The king to his beloved and faithful Philip de Ulletot and his fellow judges traveling in the counties of Cumberland, Westmoreland, and Lancaster, greeting: Since it was doubtful and undetermined at the beginning of your eyre by what sort of judgment they ought to be brought to trial who were accused of theft, murder, incendiarism, and similar crimes, inasmuch as the Roman Church has prohibited the judgment of fire and water, it is enacted by our council that in this your eyre the matter be thus conducted for the present in regard to those accused of such excesses. To wit, that those accused of the aforesaid major crimes, who may be strongly suspected of being guilty and regarding whom the suspicion might still be entertained that they would do harm should they be allowed to abjure the realm; that such persons should be retained in our prison and guarded carefully that they may incur no danger of life or limb by occasion of our prison. But those who may be accused of moderate crimes, in whose cases the ordeal of fire or water would have been applicable had it not been prohibited, and who are not suspected of being liable to do harm afterwards if they should abjure our realm, let them abjure the realm. As to those, however, who may be accused of minor crimes, and who are not held in suspicion, let them give sure and sufficient pledge of fidelity and intention to keep the peace and so let them be dismissed.

Since, therefore, our council has provided nothing more definite in this matter, we leave to your discretion to observe the aforesaid regulation, so that you who are better able to recognize the persons of the men, the form of the crime and the truth of the matter itself may proceed in this according to your conscience and discretion.

C.

Our beloved sons recently baptized in Livonia have addressed a serious complaint to us that the Teutonic Knights of Livonia and certain other advocates and judges who exercise temporal power in the country, if ever the inhabitants are accused of any sort of crime, compel them to undergo the judgment of red-hot iron; and if they suffer any burns from this, they inflict civil penalties on them much to the scandal and terror of the converts and of those about to be converted. Since, therefore, this sort of judgment has been utterly forbidden by legitimate and canonical decrees, inasmuch as God appears thereby to be tempted, we command thee that, setting aside any appeal, and warning them by ecclesiastical censure, thou shouldst compel the said brothers and others to desist from all similar oppression of the converts.

D.

The laws which are called by certain ingenuous persons *paribiles,* which neither regard nature nor give heed to the truth, We, who investigate the true science of laws and reject their errors, abolish from our tribunals; forbidding by the edict published under sanction of our name all the judges of our kingdom ever to impose on any of our faithful subjects these *paribiles* laws, which ought rather to be called laws that conceal the truth; but let them be content with ordinary proofs such as are prescribed in the ancient laws and in our constitutions. Indeed, we consider that they deserve ridicule rather than instruction who have so little understanding as to believe that the natural heat of red-hot iron grows mild, nay (what is more foolish), even turns to coldness without the working of an adequate cause; or who assert that on account of a troubled conscience alone a criminal does not sink into the cold water, when rather it is the holding in of sufficient air that does not allow of his being submerged.

Pennsylvania Paperbacks

Pennsylvania Paperbacks continued